AGRICULTURAL CREDIT AND RURAL DEVELOPMENT IN DROUGHT REGIONS

AGRICULTURAL CREDIT AND RURAL DEVELOPMENT IN DROUGHT REGIONS

A Study of Cooperative Banks of A.P.

C.S. RAYUDU

CONCEPT PUBLISHING COMPANY, NEW DELHI-110059

The Indian Council of Social Science Research gave the financial support towards the publication of this work. However, the responsibility for the contents of the book-facts, opinions, conclusions etc. — are entirely that of the author and not to ICSSR.

ICSSR Consultant : Dr. S Athar Raza Bilgrami

ISBN 81-7022-385-7

First Published 1992

Published and Printed by
Ashok Kumar Mittal
Concept Publishing Company
A/15-16, Commercial Block, Mohan Garden
NEW DELHI-110059

Lasertypeset by
Microtech Advance Printing Systems (Pvt.) Ltd.
H-13, Bali Nagar
NEW DELHI-110015

Dedicated
to
My
Parents

PREFACE

It is the policy of the Government to channel rural credit both of short-term and long-term through the co-operative organisations. The efforts towards co-operative rural credit have been officially commenced in India from 1904. The first Co-operative Societies Act, 1904 has been enacted with the primary objects of relieving the farmers from the clutches of village money-lenders and to facilitate an institutional arrangement of beneficiaries to promote their economic interest by themselves voluntarily. Though, slow and steady the co-operative credit movement has grown in size and coverage. In the multi-credit co-operative credit structure, long-term credit institutions play an important role in the development of agriculture.

Long-term credit has special significance in relation to chronically drought affected areas. The present study is with reference to chronically drought-affected Rayalaseema region located in the State of Andhra Pradesh. The concepts of drought, drought prone, chronically drought affected are closely associated and applied to this region. As against 44 taluks in this region, as many as 38 taluks have been identified as chronically drought affected areas. Of them some areas have been classified as hardcore. The agricultural problems of this region have been well considered from time to time by many Commissions such as Famine Commission (1878 and 1898), Indian Irrigation Commission, (1903), the Ceded Districts Irrigation Commission (1939) and Famine Code Revision Committee (1938). The Rayalaseema region has been often described as "Famine zone of South India", "Stalking Ground of Famines", "Chronically Drought Affected".

The general problem in respect of farmers in this region is that of long-term investment on durable and productive activities or assets. The short-term co-operative credit institutions extend credit facilities to only seasonal agricultural operations in the nature of short-term and medium-term credit. Long-term credit in a required quantity is of crucial importance among the three types of credit needs of the farmers. In this way co-operative agricultural development banks can play an effective role.

The problems of drought areas have been receiving increasing attention at the hands of both the Governments. To this effect a number of special rural development programmes like Drought Prone Area Programme, Command Area Development Programme etc., have been formulated and implemented. In their efforts the role of co-operative institutions can not be over emphasised. It is equally essential to support integrated rural development with necessary additional initiative efforts from the co-operative sector. The basic problem in these areas today is the heavy under-employment and unemployment in rural areas due to lack of employment in agricultural and allied activities.

The present work is a modest attempt to evaluate the role and working of Co-operative Agricultural Development Banks in Rayalaseema region of Andhra Pradesh. It emphasises the progress made by these banks in enroling members, mobilisation of resources, extent of beneficiaries, credit disbursement, outstanding, recovery, overdue problem etc.

The chapter scheme of the work has been considered broadly under seven chapter heads. Chapter 1 gives sketch of the research design to investigate the problem. Chapter 2 is relating to the profile of drought and economics of Rayalaseema region. Chapter 3 describes in brief the growth and development of co-operative movement in the State of Andhra Pradesh. Chapter 4 deals with mobilisation of resources by the primary co-operative agricultural development banks. The operations of credit disbursement and overdue management are discussed in Chapter 5. Chapter 6 emphasises on the role of Central Co-operative Agricultural Development Bank. The assessment of the study alongwith finding and conclusions are presented in Chapter 7.

I have borrowed liberally from various standard publications and the reports of the Government, RBI and other institutions. I take this opportunity of expressing my indebtedness to all the sources. I am equally indebted to all the banks and the apex bank for supply of required information.

I would like to place on record my thanks to the Indian Council of Social Science Research, New Delhi for sanctioning this research project.

I am also thankful to the Sri Krishnadevaraya University,

Anantapur, A.P., for all its co-operation and for providing necessary facilities throughout.

I am also grateful to Prof. T. Subbi Reddy, Dean Faculty of Commerce and Dr. D.P. Sharma, Professor of Commerce, Sri Krishnadevaraya University. My thanks are also due to Dr. L. Venugopal Reddy, Head Department of Commerce, Sri Krishnadevaraya University, Anantapur. I am thankful to Dr. C.R. Reddy, Reader in Commerce, Sri Krishnadevaraya University.

I would be failing my duties if I do not record my gratitude at personal level to my paternal uncles Choudem Balaiah and Choudem Subbaiah who supported me in various ways and brought me up to the present academic position.

Anantapur

C.S. RAYUDU

CONTENTS

LIST OF TABLES

LIST OF FIGURES

ABBREVIATIONS

ACB	:	Agricultural Credit Board
ACCMB	:	Andhra Co-operative Central Mortgage Bank
ACD	:	Agricultural Credit Department
ACLMB	:	Andhra Central Land Mortgage Bank
ADB	:	Agricultural Development Bank/Agricultural Development Branch
ADBI	:	Agricultural Development Bank of India
AFC	:	Agricultural Finance Corporation
AIRCSC	:	All India Rural Credit Survey Committee
APCCADB	:	Andhra Pradesh Co-operative Central Agricultural Development Bank
APCCLMB	:	Andhra Pradesh Co-operative Central Land Mortgage Bank
APCOB	:	Andhra Pradesh State Co-operative Bank
APSCRIC	:	Andhra Pradesh State Co-operative Rural Irrigation Corporation
APSEB	:	Andhra Pradesh State Electricity Board
APSIDC	:	Andhra Pradesh State Irrigation Development Corporation
APSM & PDC	:	Andhra Pradesh State Meat and Poultry Development Corporation
ARDC	:	Agricultural Refinance and Development Corporation
CAD	:	Command Area Development
CADB	:	Co-operative Agricultural Development Bank
CBEC	:	Central Banking Enquiry Committee
CBS	:	Commercial Banks
CCADB	:	Central Co-operative Agricultural Development Bank
CCB	:	Central Co-operative Bank
CD	:	Co-efficient of Determination

CDEDB	:	Ceded Districts Economic Development Board
CFI	:	Central Financial Institutions
CGR	:	Compound Growth Rate
CLDB	:	Central Land Development Bank
CLMB	:	Central Land Mortgage Bank/Co-operative Land Mortgage Bank
CMCLMB	:	Composite Madras Co-operative Land Mortgage Bank
CSS	:	Centrally Sponsored Scheme
CV	:	Co-efficient of Variation
CVV	:	Co-operative Vikas Volunteer Vahini
DCCBs	:	District Central Co-operative Banks
D/E Ratio	:	Debt-Equity Ratio
FSSs	:	Farmers Service Societies
GOAP	:	Government of Andhra Pradesh
GOI	:	Government of India
GPSC	:	Government Paid-up Share Capital
HACA	:	Hyderabad Agricultural Co-operative Association
HCAB	:	Hyderabad Co-operative Apex Bank
HCCLMB	:	Hyderabad Co-operative Central Land Mortgage Bank
HCLMB	:	Hyderabad Central Land Mortgage Bank
ICBEC	:	Indian Central Banking Enquiry Committee
IDA	:	International Development Association
LGR	:	Linear Growth Rate
LICI	:	Life Insurance of India
LT	:	Long-term
MCLMB	:	Madras Central Land Mortgage Bank
MPSC	:	Members Paid-up Share Capital
NABARD	:	National Bank for Agricultural Rural Development
NAC (LTO) FUND	:	National Agricultural Credit (Long-term Operations) Fund
NAC (Stabilisation) Fund	:	National Agricultural Credit (Stabilisation) Fund
NCDC	:	National Co-operative Development Corporation
NLP	:	Normal Loaning Programme

NRC (LTO) Fund	:	National Rural Credit (Long Term Operations) Funds.
NRC (Stabilisation) Fund	:	National Rural Credit (Stabilisation) Fund
OR	:	Outstanding Ratio
PACS	:	Primary Agricultural Co-operative Society
PCADB	:	Primary Co-operative Agricultural Development Bank
PCB	:	Provincial Co-operative Bank
RBEC	:	Rural Banking Enquiry Committee
RBI	:	Reserve Bank of India
RCA	:	Rayal Commission on Agriculture
RCEC	:	Rayalaseema Co-operative Enquiry Committee

1

THE RESEARCH DESIGN

What in me is dark
Illumine, What is low Raise and Support

— John Milton

India is a land of villages with nearly 5.68 lakh villages. This reflects that real India lies in Rural India. Rural economy is the back bone of Indian economy. Our country lives in its villages. It has been rightly remarked long back that Indian Peasant is born in debt, lives in debt, dies in debt and bequeaths debt. The aim of rural development is essentially one which involves agricultural development from all sides which in turn promotes various agro-based industries and other employment generating occupations. The variables of rural development are creation of farm assets, technological break through, exploration of underground water, soil conservation, dryland farming, use of drought resistance seeds etc.

It involves adequate credit for investment in farm sector, to boost agricultural production. In other words it means in the words of Belshaw, "the conversion of static into dynamic credit".[1] Hough, E.M.,[2] Gadgil, D.R.,[3] Saraiya, R.G.,[4] Gorwala, A.D.,[5] Darling, M.,[6] Nijlingappa, S.,[7] Mehta, V.L.,[8] Misra, S.D.,[9] and Venkatappaiah, B.,[10] etc. studied the rural credit.

Statement of the Problem

A Judicious and an integrated flow of credit is indispensable for balanced regional development. Today there is no universal assent against regional development. One of the important approaches to regional front is imbalance in the endowment of natural resources in the development process of a region. In so far as agriculture is concerned the crucial factor is water resources. It is a perennial problem in this region under study, which is declared as chronically drought affected. Thus, there is a close relationship, which exits between water endowment and regional economic growth. The requirement is, therefore, one, of credit break through. The economic growth of a region is directly related in the relatively advantage of agriculture development. The region which is geographically, economically unbalanced and that there is a need for the emergence of some strong credit agency in which agriculture can benefit. The land development bank is one which has been endeavouring ever since to uplift the conditions. The technique of regional analysis has made practical and operational significance.

The regional balance in the credit policy and distribution of credit by co-operative sector is desirable. The very identification of problem region, which require special attention particular and peculiar to the region warrants special outlays. In view of diversified economic activities, and concentration in well developed areas the proportion of credit ratios and actual disbursements have not been systematically done on requirement basis in view of the magnitude of the need in backward region.

The Rayalaseema region is in the hierarchy of economic regions for planning in India and is the major economic area in Southern Region. "The Rayalaseema plateau is also treated as a separate agriculture region with in the dry peninsular plateau as Meso region and is rated very high in terms of agricultural efficiency. The Rayalaseema plateau is also treated as physiographic region. Certain problem regions have been demarcated and Rayalaseema areas finds a place in the list of problem regions with the level of socio-economic development being rated low and the capacity at diverting rural population to industrial and urban nuclei rated low both in the immediate and district future".

Andhra Pradesh State has three economic regions namely Coastal Andhra, Rayalaseema and Telangana. Of these three regions Rayalaseema region is a typically, chronically drought prone area situated in an unfavourable zone and has been declared as famine zone of "South India". The region consists four districts and occupy 27.4 per cent of the total state area. The drought conditions and famines have cyclical trend for the last ten decades. The problem is one of the financial aid for dry farming, digging wells, development of wells, pumpsets, horticulture, sericulture and other diversified purposes like dairy, sheep rearing, poultry, pisciculture etc.

The short-term co-operative credit structure consisting of primary societies, central banks and State Co-operative Banks which provide only short-term credit. The Co-operative Agricultural Development

Banks have been started in this region to extend long term credit. The problem to be investigated covers the role of these banks, in geographical coverage in this area, members, mobilisation of resources, utilisation of funds for this region, regional disparities, the problem of recoveries, overdules, financial results, etc., and how best these banks have been promoting the economic interest of the farmers. The operational problems are many and they can be identified when a deliberate attempt is made to study on regional basis. The value of the study is to be viewed in the light of problems and the role of these banks.

The case study of Rayalaseema in the context of co-operative rural credit is thus proposed to be presented in this volume. To highlight briefly the problem of the area, to redress the regional imbalance, and to frame policy implications etc., promoted the author to select the problem "Co--operative Agricultural Development Banks in Rural Finance — with Reference to Rayalaseema Drought Prone Areas in Andhra Pradesh".

Over view of Literature

A careful perusal of the existing literature available on the subject reveals that:

The Deccan Commission on Agriculture (1875)[11] which made an earliest study on the problem of rural credit. The Committee strongly advocated an easy supply of credit.

Sir William Weddersburn and Justice Ranade (1882)[12] who after thorough grasp of the need of credit to the ryots prepared a scheme for starting agricultural Banks. Deccan Agriculturists, Relief Act, 1879, Land Improvement Loans Act, 1883 and the Agriculturists' loans Act 1884 provided provisions under which the agriculturists were supplied money by the Government for productive purposes. These enactments were passed as a remedial measure to the serious problem of ryots' credit.[13]

Nicholson, F.D. (1892)[14] in his study after touring extensively the European countries as to various methods they adopted to rural credit strongly suggested for introduction of Co-operative Credit Societies. In his exhaustive report submitted in 1895 favoured in starting of Rural Banks on the model of Raiffeisen Societies. In his study he suggested that "small locally worked institutions on the lines of European village institutions were ideal agencies for the supply of rural credit....".

The Famine Commission (1901)[15] felt that it was essential that credit should be made available to the farmers to improve agriculture.

The study of Maclagan (1914)[16] was really a break through on co-operative movement which examines co-operative credit from grass roots. In order to make rural credit societies truely co-operative he made a number of points and identified glaring defects on the way to co-operative movement. He submitted his report in 1915. Which was considered as a historical document in the annals of co-operative movement and a number of recommendations to remedy them. A part of the report pointed out that "It was found in many parts of India as in most European countries that inspite of the rapid growth of commerce and improvement in communications, the economic condition of the peasants had not been progressing as it should have done, that indebtedness instead of decreasing had tended to increase, that usury was still rampant, that agricultural methods had not improved and that the old unsatisfactory features of a backward rural economy destinated persistently to remain."

The Royal Commission on Agriculture (1928)[17] emphasised the lack of the requisite education and adequate supervision and guidance. The Commission rightly remarked that "the Indian peasant is born in debt, dies in debt and bequeaths debt.

The Central Banking Enquiry Committee (1930)[18] made searching enquiries. The Committee offered valuable suggestions for making the co-operative credit a success. It recommended for de-officialisation of the movement. It hinted that the movement deserves every possible assistance from every quarter.

The Reserve Bank of India (1936)[19] soon after its establishment studied the existing set up of co-operative organisation.The Reserve Bank of India in its report in 1936 made certain recommendations in respect of co-operative movement. It favoured conversion of credit societies into multipurpose societies, loans once in a year etc.

The Vijayaraghavacharya Committee on Co-operation (1940)[20] appointed by the Government of Madras State examined the depression effects on co-operative movement. While making suggestions for their re-construction the committee recommended the expansion of rural credit movement, to form larger size societies etc.

The Sahakari Samaj (1962)[21] reported that the co-operative movement was hit hardly by the depression and suffered severely. It observed that "This Great Depression gave a tremendous set-back to co-operative activity. Not only did it stall the progress of the movement, but created grave difficulties for the existing institutions.."

Pantulu, R. (1942)[22] characterised the growth of co-operative as the "the period of unplanned expansion". He came to a right conclusion because the passing of the Government of India Act 1919, by which made the co-operation subject a provincial, consequently gave stimulus to the movement. The period 1919-1929 witnessed a rapid expansion of the movement and several types of co-operative societies came into existence.

The Reserve Bank of India in its report of the Review of Co-operative movement in India (1941)[23] reviewed the co-operative movement and found that the movement in India was passing through a phase of rectification and consolidation.

The review brought to light that "the war period broadened the functional range of the co-operative movement and it brought about a shift, in the lopsided emphasis from credit aspect to the productive and distributive functions or to its multipurpose potentialities, a long felt need for imparting that richness and balance which is necessary for proper development of the movement."

Anwar Iqbal Quereshi in his work on co-operative movement in Hyderabad State (1947)[24] traced the origin and growth of co-operative movement in Hyderabad, which was the princely state then, formed part of Andhra Pradesh. He had expressed the causes for slow progress on the way to co-operative movement and difficulties for their success. Since the co-operative credit societies Act, 1904 nor the Co-operative Societies Act, 1912 were applicable to the princely jurisdiction of Telangana region of Andhra Pradesh.

The 24th Standing Advisory Committee of the Reserve bank of India, (1964)[25] had opined its deep feeling that instances of misuse of loans came to its notice.

The Food and Agricultural Organisation (1966)[26] on its agricultural studies particularly on co-operative credit in India is a worth study. It is more appropriate to quote here the observations of its study: "The farmer who needs long term credit is very often also in need of short and medium term credit. Since his repaying capacity is one, all institutions providing loans to him must depend on his one and only repayment capacity".

Rao, L.R.,[27] in his Rural Co-operatives — A study with reference to Andhra Pradesh probed and ascertained at increase in percentage of overdues. He found in his field studies the need for second long term loans. he expressed that it would be desirable to permit society's members to drawn loan amounts under the fixed loan limits in proportion to the increased cost of land in instalments according to their needs.

The Rayalaseema Co-operative Enquiry Committee (1945-46)[28] after enquiring into rural credit problem in Rayalaseema region expressed its favour for supplying finance to agriculturists by the Apex Co-operative institutions directly by abolishing the intermediary co-operative credit institutions like district central co-operative banks and Primary Land Mortgage Banks. However, this suggestion, among other were not implemented.

Gadgil, D.R., the Chairman of the Agricultural Finance Sub-Committee (1944)[29] reported about his studies in 1945 reported that, the co-operative developments were not uniform in different provinces and suggested the establishment of Agricultural Credit Corporation (ACC) for each province. He further expressed that the liquidation of old outstanding by scaling down the debts and making payments through land mortgage banks or ACC was an essential factor in the reorganisation of rural credit. He said the spread of co-operation would provide the best and the more lasting solution for most problems or rural economy in general and for the problem of agricultural credit in particular.

The Report of the Co-operative Planning Committee (1946)[30] under the Chairmanship of R.G. Saraiya found many lacunas in the supply of rural credit. The report pointed out that the "main causes of the limited progress of the movement was the fact that it did not, especially in its initial stages, take the life of the individual as a whole". He recommended that the primary credit societies should be so reformed and re-organised so as to serve as centres for the general economic development of their members.

All India Rural Credit Survey Committee (1954)[31] emphasised the problem of competition to co-operatives from private individuals and other institutions. It remarked that "the co-operation form of organisation has to face not merely the competition but also in large degree to the positive opposition of a powerful array of non-co-operative private individuals and institutions".

The problem of overdues was well studied by study team. The Report of the Study Team on overdues in Co-operative Credit Institutions under the Chairmanship of Datey (1974)[32] examined the problem of overdues in co-operative banks and remarked that: "About three-fourth of overdue arose due to willful default besides internal reasons". It suggested that the stern action on recalcitrants should be taken up.

On the aspect, whether the organisational pattern should be unitary or federal, the Committee on Takkavi loans and co-operative credit (1962)[33] preferred a federal structure.

All India Rural credit Review Committee (1969)[34] recommended that efforts should be made to encourage the evolution of a structural pattern for co-operative long-term agricultural credit under which independent units will function at the primary level, managed by qualified trained and efficient staff drawn from a cadre to be constituted by the Central Land Development Bank in each State".

The Report of the Committee on Co-operative Land Development Banks (1975)[35] had emphatically remarked that "the problem of overdues in LDBs is common in all states whether they are co-operatively well developed or less developed. Overdues are high even in areas where the banks are undertaking intensive lending operations under ARDC — refinanced schemes".

Poor recovery is a main task of rural credit management. The Report of the working Group on Agricultural Credit Schemes of Commercial Banks (1978)[36] had examined the reasons for the poor recovery of agricultural term loans. It stated that "the causes for the poor recovery are due to over-optimistic assumptions made in the formulation of schemes for term loans about: (a) the incremental income and (b) the gestation period required to generate this income. The assumptions are not born out and hence, considerably poor recovery performance of the term loans."

The CRAFICARD (1979)[37] while studying efforts towards other improvements in long-term co-operative credit structure stated that the duration of grace period should be sufficiently long to facilities repayment out of incremental income generated.

Obul Reddy, D., (1986)[38] studied about the co-operative agricultural development banks with reference to Andhra Pradesh. He examined the various financial operations of the banks working in the state such as loans, borrowings, recoveries, overdues and outstandings etc.

Bhorali, R., (1987)[39] discussed the role of co-operative banking in economic development. He analysed the recent trends in co-operative credit and its future importance.

Reis Jung Committee (1925)[40] examined the incidence of overdue, interest and bad and doubtful debts. The Committee recommended

Government's grants to the central co-operative banks with a view to enable them to pay the Dominion Bank overdue interest and instalments of principle.

The Technical and Research Cell of the National Co-operative Land Development Banks Federation (1979)[41] had undertaken a study on impact of the Discipline Governing Regulations of Advances in the State of Maharashtra. It mainly deals with the link between the loans of minor irrigation and mounting over dues.

Report of the committee on Integration of Co-operative Credit Institutions (1976)[42] had greatly emphasised the close relationship between the supply of long term credit and short-term credit. The committee remarked that "giving long term loans to a farmer and not ensuring him short-term credit would defeat the very purpose of institutional credit. Further, it reported the delay on the part of land development banks in sanctioning loans is mainly related to the procedure of collecting several certificates from various officers. This leads to a major cause for the delay and shows a seed of corruption demanding for seed money. To remove this hurdle, a radical reform special mention".

The Report of the Expert Committee (1979)[43] stated "dues from farmers should be recoverable as arrears of land revenue and the provincial Government should share the responsibility of recovering agricultural loans".

Reddy,C.R., conducted survey on co-operative agricultural Finance (1988)[44] and in his analysis of data revealed that 27.50 per cent of farmers got inadequate credit due to credit limits for crops, escalation of inputs, (cost of cultivation) unscientific approach towards the problem of unsystematised agricultural cultivation.

Kutumba Rao, (1985)[45] M, had made a study on Management of Central Co-operative Banks in which he attempted the compatibility of democratic set up with co-operative efficiency.

Agricultural Development Finance with reference to small farmers, was a study conducted by Mohanan, N., (1981).[46] The study emphasises the necessity of effective participation of all farmers for agricultural development.

Rayudu, C.S., (1988)[47] conducted a detailed study on the entire structure of co-operative organisation including short-term long-term and the role of apex bodies. Though the work is with reference to Andhra Pradesh, simultaneously he covered and traced the role of co-operative credit from the earliest time.

Rayudu, C.S., (1989)[48] in his Management of Rural Development study dealt at length the role of rural financial agencies. The agencies covered includes, besides other rural institutions, the co-operative institutions also.

Kadam, (1968)[49] in his study of A Study of Well Finance highlighted that about 35 per cent of borrowed long term credit had misutilised.

Mita Barman (1985)[50] conducted a survey in Burdwan district, west Bengal on sociological appraisal of agricultural co-operative societies. It was a comparative study of four agricultural co-operatives covered aspects like co-efficient of membership by ethnic category, place of residence, socio-economic category, ethnic category, educational role etc.

Khan, A.R., (1987)[51] in his survey made operational comparative evaluation of the performance or rural banking system in India and Bangladesh. It covered aspects like relative share of agencies, extension of rural credit, change in relative share, etc.

Sambasiva Rao, B., and Dharma Rao, G., (1983)[52] in their survey of case study concluded that the "landlords are benefiting more from the banks' assistance. They are dominating the whole co-operative structure by virtues of their socio-economic and political power. Nearly 90 per cent of the Bank management dominated by rich land-lords. So it is natural that the loaning operations are mobilised in favour of the rich. Another defect is the delay in disbursement of the loan amount. It takes nearly 7 to 8 months to obtain the loan.":

Rayudu, C.S., (1986)[53] made study on NABARD's Rural Credit and Co-operatives examined the role of the NABARD in rural credit with reference to co-operatives. He analysed the progress in its refinance activities during its short period of working. The areas covered for analysis were, functions, re-finance to co-operatives, schematic assistance to co-operatives, disbursements, purposewise distribution, loans to state Governments for contribution to share capital of co-operative institutions, medium short-term loans to SCBs.

Narasimha Reddy, P. (1984)[54] conducted a survey on functional analysis of land reforms and examined the functioning of land reforms and impact of distribution of land to landless poor. He studied land reforms and the co-operative farming with reference to a district selected purposefully.

Gupta, G.P. (1982)[55] analysed the structure of agencies providing credit in rural areas. He concluded in his study that "In the matter of structuring the agencies for rural credit. One must not only take full account of the spectacular increase in the tempo of agricultural activity; it must also be based on various other important implication of the new situation, which are emerging with the change in the outlook, occupational structure and socio-economic aspirations of the rural sector.

Rayudu, C.S., (1984)[56] surveys with reference to Andhra Pradesh about participation of co-operatives in small farmers development. He highlighted the active participation of co-operative banks in the successful implementation of agricultural development strategy, scheme of small farmers development agencies. He greatly tressed that the co-operatives were giving more credit both short-term and long-term, whereas the commercial banks were giving more medium term credit.

Jan, H.C., and Sarawgi, A.K., (1982),[57] they conducted a study of tribal areas of Madhya Pradesh. They investigated and analysed the effects of farm loans provided by the banks of the structural and operational aspects of farm business of selected tribal borrowers. Their analysis revealed that there was a tremendous increase in the net income of all categories of tribal farmers in the post loan period. On the whole the relative importance of Central Co-operative bank to tribal, small and medium farmers was more in raising their income as compared to the State Bank of India.

Besides there are many other surveys and studies specifically undertaken which discussed and reviewed the working, performance, management of co-operative agricultural development banks. To mention they are Choubey (1953),[58] Naidu, V.T., (1968),[59], Ghosal, S.N., (1968),[60], Mathur, B.S., (1982),[61] Mamoria, C.B., (1983)[62], Samiuddin and Mahfoozfur Rahman, (1983),[63] Reddy, C.R., (1987),[64] Goel, S.L., and Goel, B.B.,[65] Gupta, K.K., (1983),[66], Gupta, K.K., (1987),[67] Lal Sahab Singh, (1983),[68] Munshi, M.A., and Pandya, D.N., (1985),[69] Choudhary, C.M., (1985).[70]

To sum up : Thus the studies on rural credit and in particular with reference to co-operative credit have greatly increased in recent years. The above review of literature is not an exhaustive one but inclusive. The overview of literature on the subject detailed above summarises the current status of the work and research on the subject. The above studies contained a mine of valuable information and findings on co-operative agricultural development banks which formed the ground for the present work. As a result of the study and examination of the above literature in rural finance, a much insight into the working and the role of these banks in rural credit is gained.

The review of pertinent literature clearly demonstrates some short coming and limitations, in the sense that there is a lack of a detailed investigation on the working of these banks in drought prone areas at micro level. Some of the studies generally covered. The present study is, therefore, a quite different from earlier studies. It contributes partly to methodology and partly to the theory, and fills the gap in the existing knowledge of co-operative agricultural development banks in rural finance in drought areas. The findings of this study would enable to divert our attention on deviations revealed in the study so that corrective measures can be taken up on time. It examines the most crucial areas of financial operations of the bank like limited share capital of the members, overdues, loss, foreclose, outstanding, recoveries etc., which recently gained so much importance for discussion. This study in turn helps for further research and studies on some other areas of regions.

Coverage

In the light of the objectives to be achieved and hypothesis to be tested a specified coverage of the problem is necessary. The universe of the present study is thus covers co-operative agricultural development banks in Rayalaseema region of Andhra Pradesh, having four districts with 42 co-operative agricultural development banks endeavouring for promotion of economic interest of the farmers in drought affected tracts. The banks have been providing long-term finance for productive and for creating durable farm assets. For the purpose of the study each co-operative bank has been taken as unit. The number of units taken for observation are 12 divided and selected 3 units from each district. Thus the sample size is nearly 25 per cent. The units are selected on the basis of date of their establishment i.e., earliest date of their registration with the Registrar of co-operative societies, Government of Andhra Pradesh.

Objectives

The principal object of the research project is to collect relevant statistical data and other information about the working of the co-operative agricultural development banks in Rayalaseema region in respect of their financial operations. However, broadly the objects of the project cover :

1. To examine the nature and the extent of drought magnitude in the region.
2. To study the need for long-term credit.
3. To observe briefly the growth of co-operative credit including long-term.
4. To examine the extent of state aid and support to these institutions.
5. To investigate the financial results of the banks.
6. To analyse the problem of recoveries, overdues, and foreclosed loans.
7. To identify the problems and offer suggestions on all matters incidental and ancillary to the above.

Hypothesis

While making this study and keeping in view the objectives to be achieved, the following hypotheses have been formulated and the validity of which are tested in appropriate chapters:

1. That there is an increasing trend of overdues.
2. The relationship between the overdues and the agronomic factors is positive.
3. That the number of cases and the amount under fore-closed are more.
4. That most of the banks are running on losses.

Methodology

The methodology to be adopted for a particular research project would depend upon the purpose and objectives to be achieved. A bank level sample based on age of the banks has been used and accordingly units have been identified and selected. The selection of co-operative banks is presented in the following statement. Both primary and secondary methods of data are adopted.

Selection of Units

District		Name of the Bank		Year of Establishment
I	Chittoor	A.	Chittoor	1936
		B.	Chandragiri	1938
		C.	Madanapalli	1938
II	Cuddapah	A.	Rajampet	1935
		B.	Cuddapah	1936
		C.	Proddatur	1939
III	Kurnool	A.	Banaganapalli	1958
		B.	Kurnool	1965
		C.	Nandyal	1965
IV	Anantapur	A.	Dharmavaram	1935
		B.	Hindupur	1938
		C.	Tadpatri	1950
	4		12	12

Data Source and Collection

Based on the objective and the hypothesis to be tested, the required data has been gathered from both primary source and secondary source. The collection of all relevant data and other basic information relating to the financial operations of the banks working in this region have been collected from unit banks and apex bank. Records of the co-operative banks and Apex bank, circulars, action plans, policy letters and the, audit report are the main sources of data. Personal interviews, observations and discussion with the co-operators and the personnel of the co-operative agricultural development banks form part of the data and information gathering.

Techniques for Data Analysis

Introduction of statistical techniques for analysis of data is necessary to draw meaningful conclusions. The objectively collected data has been suitably classified and arranged in tables in appropriate chapters. The following are the techniques adopted for analysis of data.

Co-efficient of variation (C.V.)

The co-efficient of variation is the most commonly used technique particularly in studies like this. With this it is possible to compare the variability of two or more than two series of their relative variation. It is called as Karl Pearson's Co-efficient of variation. It is more suitable in our study in order to compare the variability of two or more than two series. The series for which the co-efficient of variation is greater is said to be more variable or conversely less consistent, less uniform, less stable or less homogenous. Similarly, the group for which co-efficient of variation is less, is said to be less variable or more consistent, more uniform, more stable or more homogeneous. The co-efficient of variation is calculated with the help of the following :

$$\text{Co-efficient variation OR C.V} = \frac{\text{r}}{\bar{\text{x}}} \times 100$$

$$\text{Where, q} = \sqrt{\frac{X^2}{N}}$$

$$x = \frac{\Sigma x}{N}$$

Correlation Analysis

The technique of correlation is used to know whether the relative changes are correlated or not. The degree of relationship between the quantities under observation is measured through the correlation analysis, which reveals the direction and degree of correlation. The most widely used method to measure correlation is the Karl Pearson's method. It is popularly called as Pearsonian Coefficient of Correlation. It is denoted by the symbol *r*. The formula to compute it is as under :

$$r = \frac{\Sigma xy}{\sqrt{x^2 \times y^2}}$$

Where,

$$x = x - \bar{x}$$
$$y = y - \bar{y}$$

The coefficient of variation lies between ± 1.. If $r = +1$, it means there is perfect positive correlation between the variables. If $r = -1$, it means there is perfect negative correlation between the variables.

Growth Rate

Where there is a time series data which is increasing or decreasing over a period of time, it can suitably be fitted in semi-long trend, $y = ab^x$. The equation in logarithmatic form minimises the square deviations of observed values from the logarithmatic trend values. In log linear form, the equation can be written as :

$$Log\ y \quad = \quad log\ a + x\ log\ b$$

where,

log	*y*	=	*value of variables*
log	*a*	=	*Intercept*
	x	=	*time period*
log	*b*	=	*Regression coefficient*

The rate of growth in relatives is derived by solving the equation;

$$(1 + r) = Log\ b,\ or\ r = Anti\ log\ b\text{-}1 \times 100$$

Regression Analysis

It is a basic technique for measuring or estimating the relationship among variables. The variable which is the basic for prediction is called Independent variable and the variable that is to be predicted is known as the Dependent variable. The tool or regression can be used to three or more variables. If more than one independent variable is used to predict the nature of dependent variable, it is known as "Multiple Regression". With the help of this technique it is possible to know magnitude of the collective impact of any number of independent variables upon a dependent variables. The agro-economic factors and overdue of the banks are described as independent and dependent variables respectively.

Overdues with that of agronomic factors is explained by fitting in the regression coefficient model, i.e., $Y = a + b\,x$

The regression coefficient of $X_1,\ X_2,\ X_3, \ldots x_n$ are determined by solving simultaneously the normal equations. The formula of multiple regression analysis is written as :

$$Y \;=\; a + b_1 x_1 + b_2 x_2 + b_3 x_3 \ldots b_n x_n$$

where,

y = Dependent variable (overdue)
$b_1\ b_2\ b_n$ = Regression Coefficients
$x_1\ x_2\ x_n$ = Independent variables
a = Intercept

Others:

The Elasticity of Coefficient and Location Quotient techniques are applied for analysis.

Test:

Test Statistic t is used to know the significance.

Period of study

A period of ten years is selected to study the performance of all the sample units in various financial operation. Thus the investigation covers a period of decade commencing from co-operative year (July, 1 st to 30 June) end, 1977-78 to 1986-87. The ending year of the decade 1986-87, *X* was purposely taken. Because the year 1986-87 was a significant year in the history of long-term co-operative credit structure in the Andhra Pradesh Co-operative movement, in which year was introduced a novel "single window Rural Credit Delivery Scheme". Consequently, the entire co-operative credit structure i.e. Multy-credit structure, comprised of short-term, Medium-term and long-term, was completely reorganised. From 1-4-1987, a single society i.e., single unit has been delivering all credit requirements to the farmers. The primary banks were merged with primary single units. Hence the data for 1986-87 was only provisional. A brief not about Single Window Rural Credit Delivery schemes is appended to this report (Annexure I).

Significance of the Study

The significance of the study of Co-operative Agricultural Development Banks in Rural Finance with Reference to Rayalaseema Drought Prone Area in Andhra Pradesh needs no elucidation and can not be over emphasised in the context of this state whose economy is biased towards agricultural and unfortunately the recurring drought has become a common feature. Nearly 70 per cent of the area selected for the study is reeling under famines. The significance of the study lies in the fact that these banks' long term credit and other services have a profound influence on the economic and agro industrial level of activity in the state. The study also highlights its schematic pattern of assistance of the Government, extent of state aid and support and the role of central financial institutions to the agricultural sector through these banks, removal of regional imbalance etc.

It helps to know co-operative efforts of agriculturists to tackle their problem themselves by collective action and how best land development banks bettering and promoting the economic interest of ryots. The work constitutes the most important piece of findings of supporting role of the Reserve Bank of India, Agricultural Re-finance and Development corporation, National bank for Agriculture and Rural Development and State Level Central Co-operative Agricultural Development Bank. The present members, perspective members financial institutions, Government, planners, co-operators, researchers, academic persons and general public are interested to know the working and performance of long-term co-operative agricultural development banks. It has become necessary to understand how this sector has been acting as a balancing institution among other institutions. The significance of the study to all those who are concerned is that it helps to know how best co-operative efforts delivering the goods to the beneficiaries and to the society in general utilising funds provided by both the Government and financial institutions. Its value lies in its being not so much a theoretical presentation but a model focussing the attention to the problem with adequate and relevant statistical evidence. A summary of suggestions along with the identified problems gives scope for policy implications and for future course of action.

Its Relevance to the Present Day Problems

Rural credit by co-operatives for agriculture development in recent years has become a subject of great relevance for debate. It is because of the fact that their performance has not been satisfactory in terms increasing outstanding, overdues, foreclosed loans and amount, demand for write off, Government participation and interference and their viability etc. Thus the study of this kind, at right time, has a great relevance to the present day problems of co-operative rural credit, to the society, members society and the country in general and to the State Government in particular. The co-operative sector is the most useful tool of the society in reaching the plan benefits to the illiterate and poverty striken agriculturists. Today there is a great need for regional studies. It has a great value of the formulation and implementation of correct future strategies. In the light of fast changing socio-economic conditions and changing role assigned to co-operatives, a revision of their working, financial operations, general performance and identification of problems is necessary because which need a different look.

Contribution to the Existing Knowledge

This moderate piece of research work is, therefore, contributes a lot to the knowledge of co-operative movement in general and in particular with reference to long-term co-operative agricultural development banks in drought areas. It enriches the scanty literature on the subject on regional basis and adds to the existing co-operative knowledge in better understanding the role of co-operative sector in rural credit. Special contribution to the existing knowledge is that it covers different aspects of crucial importance in financial operations in their functioning which has received in sufficient treatment so far. Many of the issues in the study throw up added light in the context of wide co-operative base with federal structure. A study of this nature would provide useful and necessary statistical and analytical frame to be more useful for further similar studies in other regions or a special detailed study on any one or more areas of interest.

NOTES

1. Belshaw, H., *Rural Progress Through Co-operatives*, pp. 6-7.
2. Hough, E.M., *Co-operative Movement in India*, Oxford University, Bombay.
3. Gadgil, D.R., *Report of the Agricultural Finance Sub-Committee*, Bombay, 1945.
4. Saraiya, R.G., *Report of the Co-operative Planning Committee*, R.B. I, Bombay, 1946.
5. Gorwala, A.D., *All India Rural Credit Survey Committee's Report*, R.B.I., Bombay, 1951-54.
6. Darling, M., *Evaluation of the Co-operative Movement* RBI, Bombay, 1957.
7. Nijlingappa, S., *Report of the working Group on Co-operative Farming*, RBI, Bombay, 1959.
8. Mehta, V.L., *Report of the Committee on Co-operative Credit*, RBI, 1960.

9. Misra, S.D., *Report of the Working Group and Panchayats* and Co-operation, New Delhi, 1961.
10. Venkatappaiah, B., *The All India Rural Credit Review Committee*, 1969.
11. *Report of the Deccan Commission on Agriculture*, 1875.
12. Sir, William Weddersburu and Justice Ranade, *Scheme for starting Agricultural Banks*, 1882.
13. Government of India, *Deccan Agriculturists' Relief Act*, 1879, *Land Improvement Loans Act*, 1883, *Agriculturists Loans Act*, 1884.
14. *Government* of Madras, *Nicholson's Report*, 1895.
15. Government of India, *Report of the Famine Commission*.
16. Government of India, *Report of the Maclagan Committee on Co-operation* 1915.
17. Government of India, *Report of the Royal Commission on Agriculture*, 1929.
18. Government of India, *Report of the Indian Central Banking Enquiry Committee*, 1930.
19. Reserve Bank of India, *Report on Co-operation* 1936.
20. Government of Madras, *Report of the Committee on Co-operation*, 1940.
21. Ministry of Community Development and Co-operation, *Sahakari Samaj, A Symposium on the Co-operative Movement in India*, New Delhi, 1962.
22. Pantulu, R., *Yearbooks and Directory of Indian Co-operation*, 1942, p. 1.
23. Reserve Bank of India, *Review of the Co-operative movement*, 1941, p. 4.
24. Anwar Iqbal Quereshi, *Co-operative Movement in Hyderabad State*, 1947.
25. Reserve Bank of India, *Report of the 24th Standing Advisory Committee*, 1964, p. 71.
26. Food and Agricultural Organisation, *Credit through Co-operatives and other Institutions, Agricultural Studies*, No. 68, 1966, p. 129.
27. Rao, L-R., Rural Co-operatives — *A study with reference to Andhra Pradesh*, Sultan Chand and Sons, p. 201.
28. Government of Andhra State, *Report of the Rayalaseema Co-operative Enquiry Committee*, 1945-46.
29. Government of India, *Report of the Agricultural Finance Sub-Committee*, 1945, p. 47.
30. Reserve Bank of India, *Report of the Co-operative Planning Committee*, 1946, pp. 218-227.
31. Reserve Bank of India, *Report of the All India Rural Credit Survey Committee*, Vol. II, 1954.
32. Reserve Bank of India, *Report of the Study Team on Overdues in Co-operative Credit Institutions*, 1974, pp, 25-71.
33. Reserve Bank of India, *Report of the Committee on Takkavi loans and Co-operative Credit*, 1962.
34. Reserve Bank of India, *All India Rural Credit Review Committee Report*, 1969, pp. 748-749.
35. Reserve bank of India, *Report of the Committee on Co-operative Land Development Banks*, 1975.
36. Reserve Bank of India, *Report of the Working Group on Agricultural Credit Schemes of Commercial Banks*, 1978.
37. Reserve Bank of India, *Report of the Committee to Review Arrangements for Institutional Credit for Agriculture and Rural Development*, 1981, p. 394.
38. Obul Reddy, D., *Co-operative Agricultural Development Banks — A Case Study of Andhra Pradesh*, D.K. Publications, 1986.

39. Bhorali, R., *Co-operative Banking and Economic Development, Deep and Deep Publications,* New Delhi, 1987.
40 .Government of Hyderabad State, *Report of the Reis Jung Committee* (1937F).
41. National Co-operative Land Development Banks Federation, *A Study on Overdues and Impact of the Discipline Governing Regulations of Advances in Maharastra,* 1979.
42. Reserve Bank of India, *Report of the CRAFICARD,* 1981.
43. Reserve Bank of India, *Report of the expert Committee on co-operation,* 1979.
44. Reddy, C.R., *Co-operative Agricultural Finance, Chugh Publications,* Allahabad, 1988, p. 141.
45. Kutumba Rao, M., *Management of Central Co-operative Banks,* As high Publishing House, 1985.
46. Mohannan, N., *Agricultural Development Finance,* Rainbow Publication, 1981.
47. Rayudu, C.S., *Rural Credit in India,* Mittal Publications, New Delhi, 1988.
48. Rayudu, C.S., *Management of Rural Development,* Discovery Publishing House, New Delhi, 1989.
49. Kadam, D.B., *A Study of Well Finance* (un published Thesis), Gokhale Institute of Economics and Politics, 1968, p. 65.
50. Mita Barman, (1985), *A Sociological Appraisal of Agricultural Co-operative Societies in Burdwan District, West Bengal, Indian Co-operative* Review National Co-operative union of India, July, 1985.
51. Khan, A.R., (1987), *Evaluation of the Performance of Rural Banking System — A Comparative Study of India and Bangladesh,* Indian Co-operative Review, National Co-operative union of India, New Delhi, January, 1987.
52. Sambasiva Rao, B., and Dharma Rao, G., *Flow of Credit By Co-operative Land Development Banks : A Case Study.* Indian Co-operative Review, National Co-operative Union of India, 1983, p. 162.
53. Rayudu, C.S., *NABARD'S Rural Credit and Co-operatives,* India Co-operative National Co-operative union of India, January, 1986.
54. Narasimha Reddy, P., *Functional Analysis of Land Reforms and Co-operative Farming Societies,* Co-operative perspective, Pune, April — June, 1984.
55. Gupta, G.P., *The Structure of Agencies Providing Credit in Rural Areas,* Co-operative perspective, VMNICM, Pune, Jan — March, 1982, p. 37.
56. Rayudu, C.S., *Participation of Co-operatives in small Farmers Development, — A Case Study, Indian* Co-operative Review, National Co-operative Union of India, 1984, pp. 369-381.
57. Jain, H.C., and Sarawgi, A.K., *A Comparative study into the Impact on farm credit provided by the co-operative and the Commercial banks in Tribal areas of Madhya Pradesh,* Co-operative perspective, Vaikunth Mehta National Institute of Co-operative management, Pune, 1982, p. 68.
58. Choubey, B.N., *Agricultural Banking in India,* National Publishing House, New Delhi, 1953.
59. Naidu, V.T., *Farm Credit and Co-operatives in India,* Vora and Company, 1968.
60. Ghosal, S.N., *Agricultural Finance in India, with reference to Land Mortgage Banks,* Asia Publishing House, 1968.
61. Mathur, B.S., *Co-operation in India,* Sahitya Bhavan, Agro, 1982.
62. Mamoria, C.B., *Rural Credit and Agricultural Co-operation in India,* Kitab Mahal, Agra, 1983.

63. Samiuddin and Mahfoozfur Rahman, *Co-operative Sector in India,* S. Chand and Sons, New Delhi, 1983.
64. Reddy, C.R., *Co-operative long Term Finance — A Regional Study,* Mittal Publications, 1987.
65. Goel, S.L., and Goel, B.B., *Administration of Personnel in Co-operatives,* D.K. Publishers Distributor, New Delhi.
66. Gupta, K.K., *Need of Development Cell in Co-operative Banks,* Co-operative perspective, Vaikunth Mehta National Institute of Co-operative Management, Pune, 1983. (April — June).
67. Gupta, K.K., *Co-operative Credit System in 2001 A.D.,* Sahakarita Samghodhan, Indian Society for Studies in Co-operation, Pune, July — December, 1987.
68. Lal Sahab Singh, *Changing Role of Co-operative Banks in Rural Development and the Role of the Executives,* Co-operative Perspectives, Vaikunth Mehta National Institute of Co-operative Management, Pune, January — March, 1983.
69. Munshi, M.A., and Pandhy, D.N., *Utilisation Pattern of Agricultural Credit by Co-operative Societies,* Indian Co-operative Review, National Co-operative Union of India, New Delhi, 1985.
70. Choudhary, C.M., *Loans Disbursement and their recovery, A Case Study of Rajasthan Land Development Bank,* Co-operative perspective, Vaikunth Mehta National Institute of Co-operative Management, Pune, january — March, 1985.

2

DROUGHT AND ECONOMIC PROFILE

No one theory of Regional Development that commands universal assent

— Friedman

Bifurcation

Andhra State was a part of Andhra Pradesh, in which Rayalaseema region situated both formed part of the then composite Madras State. The Andhra Part of the State was constituted out of the composite Madras State on the 1st October, 1953. This part of the Andhra State comprised of 11 districts, namely Srikakulam, Visakhapatnam, East Godavari, West Godavari, Krishna, Guntur, Kurnool, Anantapur, Cuddapah, Chittoor and Nellore.

Formation

A part of the state known as Telangana region which was a Princely State ruled by Princes for centuries. In the year 1956 an integrated State of Andhra Pradesh was constituted. Before it was constituted, its total land area formed part of the the composite Madras State and a part included under jurisdiction of the erstwhile princely state of Hyderabad. The Telangana region composed of 9 Telugu speaking districts, were existing in a separate Hyderabad State. In accordance with recommendations of the States Reorganisation Commission the states were reorganised. Accordingly the 9 districts of Telangana region were merged with Andhra State for the purpose of carving out an integrated State of Andhra Pradesh. In other words the constitution of the new Andhra Pradesh State was the result of fusion of two regions, namely Telangana and Andhra Regions. As such on 1st November, 1956 the full fledged State of Andhra Pradesh was born with 20 districts. Later Prakasam, Rangareddy and Vizianagaram districts were created. At present the state has 23 districts.

The Prakasam district originally was named as Ongole district, but subsequently the district was named as Prakasam district. It was formed on Second February 1970 with four taluks namely Kandukur, Kanigiri, Podili, and Darsi from Nellore District, two taluks Markapur and Giddalur from Kurnool district, and Ongole taluk; 41 villages from Narsarao pet taluk; 44 villages from Bapatla taluk of the old Guntur district. The villages of Narsaraopet and Bapatla taluks were formed into Addanki and Chirala taluks.

Today the State has three distinct economic regions. They are Coastal Andhra comprising of 9 districts viz., (a) Srikakulam (b) Vizianagaram (c) Visakhapatnam (d) East Godavari (e) West Godavari (f) Krishna (g) Guntur (h) Prakasam (i) Nellore. The second region is Rayalaseema comprising of 4 districts, namely; (a) Chittoor (b) Cuddapah (c) Anantapur (d) Kurnool. The Telangana region is a former princely state of Hyderabad, which comprising of 10 districts, namely; (a) Ranga Reddy (b) Mahabubnagar (c) Hyderabad (d) Medak (e) Nizamabad (f) Adilabad (g) Karimnagar (h) Warangal (i) Khammam (j) Nalgonda.

The Zamindaris covered some areas earlier. Those areas were taken over by the Government in 1949 and 1950 under the Madras State (Abolition and conversion into Ryotwari) Act, 1948 and the Madras Estate Land (Reduction of Rent) Act 1948.

Thus these three economic regions have diverse political, economic and social background. Consequently, therefore, there are regional disparities in peoples life, habits, socio-economic conditions, agricultural practices and in the levels of rural development.

The state has an area of 2.77 lakh square kilometres. It ranks fifth largest state in terms of area and population in the Indian union. The state is located in a tropical region between 13°N to 22°N and 77°E to 85°E. As such it is bounded on the east by the Bay of Bengal, on the North by Maharashtra, on the West by Karnataka and on the South by Tamilnadu. The map shows that by viewing the state as a whole 3 distinct physical zones can be discerned. They are coastal plains, the Eastern Ghats and Western peneplains.

According to 1981 census count it has a population of 53.5 million accounting 7.8 per cent of the country's population. In the state only a smaller percentage of workers engaged in non-agricultural occupations. It means only 30 per cent of workers are engaged in non-agricultural occupations as against 33 per cent for the country as a whole. In neighbouring states like in Kerala which has higher percentage of workers in non-agricultural occupations (59 per cent), Tamilnadu (39 per cent), Maharashtra (38 per cent), and Karnataka (35 per cent). The total crop area was 122.8 lakh hectares forming 7% of the total cropped area in Indian Union. On the basis of average yields during the 5 years period of the Sixth Plan the state ranked 3rd, in regard to yield per hectare of rice and sugarcane and fourth in respect of groundnut and cotton.

It may be mentioned that the state has started developing the state from relatively low levels of development only after the formation of integrated state in 1956. Before that the growth was rather stagnant due to various constraints faced by the State like political and reorganisation etc. The planned efforts have given high priority to the development of State economy and it has made a break through in allround development.

Carving the Region

In drought economics the name of the Rayalaseema region is popularly known. This region covers the tract comprising of ceded or Deccan Districts. Originally this region comprised of Bellary, Anantapur, Cuddapah, Kurnool and Chittoor districts. This part of the state till 1953 formed part of the then composite Madras State. Consequent on the re-organisation of states some parts of the region were transferred to neighbouring states and some parts of neighbouring states were transferred to this region. To mention parts of Bellary and a few villages from Chittoor district were transferred to Mysore and Tamilnadu. Similarly some parts from Tamilnadu were transferred to this region. Today Rayalaseema region consists of 4 districts, namely Anantapur, Cuddapah, Kurnool and Chittoor districts. The two taluks viz., Giddalur and Markapur were originally in Kurnool district. Presently these two taluks are in the newly formed Prakasam district consequent on the carving of new district in February 1970. Historically, Rayalaseema region was once a part of the famous Vijayanagar Empire (1336 to 1649 A.D.).

Rayalaseema — A Retrospect

Rayalaseema region has certain district natural disadvantages for dovetailing for the work of economic planning. This region has the broad characteristic required for being treated on different footing. The basic problem is that of technological break-through for which huge investment has to be made in nonfarm section to utilise the richly endowed natural resources effectively along with a break-through in dry farming. It demands the co-operative agricultural development banks in this region to formulate a scientific long-term plan which would enable to solve various development works.

The region has been considered as cognisable homogeneous economic region. Rayalaseema, a historical part of the state long suffered untold sufferings due frequent famines because of scanty and uncertain rainfall. The total area irrigated to the area cultivated would be nearly one-forth with fuller utilisation of available water. The existing deposits of underground water is also limited. The region lacks adequate rainfall experiences untimely rain, failure and erratic distribution ,etc., are the serious problems. The terrain is mostly undulating and the rain water is easily lost through run-off. Frequent failure of crops and recurring famines are the common features. As such soil conservation, dry farming practices, use of drought resistant varieties of crops should receive priority in the economic development of this region. It is a poor and backward region in all respects comparing with other regions of the state.

The issue of improving and increasing the irrigation facilities in the area have been well considered from time to time, like Famine Commission 1878 and 1898, Indian Irrigation Commission 1903, the Ceded Districts Irrigation Commission 1939 and Famine Code Revision Committee 1938.

The concepts 'Drought', 'Drought Prone', Chronically Drought Prone', and 'Hard Core' are closely associated and applied practically to this region. It may be mentioned that, it is more appropriate to understand the words with standard criteria to demarcate the region as drought affected area.

A minimum annual rainfall is indispensable for sustaining normal crop growth. A rainfall less than minimum means crops failure or low yield. An annual minimum rainfall is 30 inches. With reference to this criterion, areas receiving less than 27 inches of rainfall for a majority of years during the period 1942-62 or receiving only 23 inches and below in at least one out of every three years during the same period have been considered as chronically drought affected areas.[1] On the basis of this twin criteria as out of 44 taluks in Rayalaseema as many as 38 taluks have been identified as chronically drought affected areas. This figure represents substantial nature of drought when compare to

Telengana region, where only 23 taluks out of total 72 taluks and in Coastal Andhra region only 14 out of 73 taluks have been figured under chronically drought affected areas.

According to Andhra Pradesh Irrigation Committee, those taluks among the chronically drought affected areas which received an annual rainfall of less than 22.5 inches, 560mm in more than one out of every three years (i.e. for at least 8 years during 1942 to 1962) have been classified as "hard core" areas. Out of the 75 chronically drought, affected taluks in the state, 34 taluks fall in the "hard core" category. The bulk of the hard core area is in the Rayalaseema region which has 25 taluks under this category as against only 5 in Telangana and 4 in Coastal Andhra.[2]

The expression drought is to be understood in its comprehensive and with reference to agriculture. There are three types of droughts. They are meteorological drought, hydrological drought and agricultural drought. Agricultural drought is a situation of deficit rainfall, high temperature during growing season. Webster has defined the term 'drought' as "dryness for want of rain or water, specially such dryness of weather or climate as affects the earth and prevents the growth of plants."

"The two hydro-meteorologic conditions that cause drought or an absence or large deficiency in rainfall and high temperatures and the degree of their synchronization will determine the severity of drought". This is according to B. Venkatanarayana in his paper presented at the seminar on "Planning and development of Backward regions-A Case Study on Rayalaseema". Thus the term drought has been variously defined depending upon the purpose for which it has come to be applied. In so far as agricultural drought is concerned it is caused by the delay in on set or failure of monsoon and lack of under ground water.

Meteorological drought is a situation where there is significant decrease from climatologically expected and seasonally normal precipitation over a wide area. Meteorological droughts if prolonged, will result in hydrological drought with marked depletion of surface water and consequent drying up of reservoirs, lakes, streams and rivers, cessation of spring flows and fall in ground water levels. This may necessitate curtailment of hydel power generation and affect industry as well as agriculture. Agricultural drought occurs when soil moisture and rainfall are inadequate during the growing season to support healthy crop growth to maturity and causes extreme moisture stress and witting. In the major crops of the area an agricultural drought may exist even when a meteorological drought may not, and vice-versa.[3]

It may be concluded that "Drought is the result of an imbalance between the soil moisture and evapotranspiration needs of an areas over a fairly long period, so as to cause damage to standing crops and a reduction in crops yield". In other words it is a condition of steady rise in temperature and severe deficiency of rainfall fairly over a long period. Several factors like precipitation, temperature, wind velocity, sunshine, soil texture, soil moisture and antecedent rainfall interact to produce this situation.[4]

The case study presented by the Planning and Panchayat Raj Department, Government of Andhra Pradesh includes an analysis of the monthly rainfall over a period of 20 years from 1950 to 1969 relating to the. two monsoon, viz., South-West and North-East benefitting this area and has very clearly brought out the large magnitude of the percentage co-efficient of variation.[5] Sankara Reddy and Satyanarayana Moorthy in 1967 worked out drought occurrence at Anantapur based on 55 years of rainfall data. One of the conclusions is that the probability of occurrence of drought is more from 11th June to 12th August during which the crops are in early growth period.[6] A more scientific method to measure the variation is the standard deviation. Among the Rayalaseema districts, Anantapur district has substantial variation over the period of 20 years (1950-69). The standard deviation of the rainfall in various taluks of Anantapur district varies from 78.6 mm. to 146.1 mms[7] in South-West Monsoon. The dispersion of taluks as per average rainfall and its co-efficient of variation in South-West Monsoon during 1950-69 reveals some interesting features:

1. A large number of taluks in Anantapur district have a mean rainfall which is low followed by Chittoor, Cuddapah and Kurnool in that order.
2. The co-efficient variation in rainfall is quite large in most of the taluks of all the four districts and especially in Anantapur and Chittoor districts.
3. The large co-efficient of variation in the rainfall in the South-West monsoon period coupled with low mean rainfall in Anantapur district followed by Chittoor District makes these two districts extremely vulnerable for drought.[8]

Based on rainfall data a more scientific approach to measure the variation of rainfall received in four districts of Rayalaseema during 1961 to 1986 has been studied through co-efficient of variation. The figures are arranged in Table 2.1.

TABLE 2.1: Rain Fall

Particulars	Anantapur	Chittoor	Cuddapah	Kurnool	Region
Mean rainfall (cms. 1961-86)	48.8	74.1	64.9	64.3	63.0
Co-efficient of variation	21.35	22.81	19.75	19.45	17.86
No. of years with rainfall less than mean	14	13	16	16	14
No. of drought years	24	11	17	18	19
No. of chronically drought years	21	7	11	8	12
No. of hard-core drought years	20	6	9	8	11

Source: Based on Rainfall data of A.P.

In order to formulate special programmes for the economic development of drought prone areas in this region, the chronically drought affected taluks have been identified on the basis of a particular criteria. The criteria is adopted by the state in consultation with the planning commission. Accordingly, drought affected taluks in the state and in the Rayalaseema in particular have been identified, on the basis of minimum average annual rainfall of 30" in each taluk for a period of 21 years between 1942-1962 as detailed below:

1. "All taluks where the annual average deficit rainfall wās short of the minimum of 30" by 3" or more for 10 years or more during the period of 21 years i.e. 1942-62 to be treated as chronically drought affected.
2. All taluks where the annual average deficit rainfall was short of the minimum of 30" by 7" or more for 7 years or more during the period of 21 years i.e., 1942-62 to be treated as chronically drought affected and
3. All taluks where the annual average deficit rainfall was short of the minimum of 30" by 7.5" or more for a period of 8 years or more during the period of 21 years i.e., 1942-62 to be treated as

hard-care of the drought affected areas".[9]

Accordingly, 75 taluks in the state have been delineated as drought affected taluks in the entire state and of which 34 taluks have been considered as 'hard core' of these figures Rayalaseema taluks represent bulk proportion. Out of total 42 taluks in this region 38 taluks are chronically drought affected taluks, 25 taluks fall in the hard core category. The bulk of the hard core area is in the Rayalaseema region which has 25 taluks under the category, while there are only 5 in Telangana area as against 73 taluks and 4 taluks in Coastal Andhra out of 80 taluks.

In Rayalaseema, Anantapur district has the lowest normal annual rainfall of 21.5 inches and all the eleven taluks this district are in the hard core area. Next is the Kurnool district. All the taluks in the district are chronically drought affected and 7 out of 11 taluks fall in the hard core tracts. The Table 2.2 furnishes detail of drought affected taluks in each of the district of the state.

In our sample study of taluks, all the three taluks selected in Anantapur district viz., Anantapur, Tadpatri and Hindupur are delineated as 'hard core'. In Kurnool district, Kurnool and Banaganapalli are under the same above category. While in Chittoor district two taluks are classified as hard core. In Cuddapah district Proddatur and Rajampet taluks are classified as hard core. In these taluks the sample unit banks have been operating. The list of chronically drought affected taluks in Rayalaseema region may be seen in Table 2.3.

The Rayalaseema region was once a very prosperous and agricultural land well irrigated. The gradual reduction in annual rainfall basically, destruction of forests, inadequate soil conservation works etc., have been the responsible attributable factors for drought and recurring famine conditions now obtaining in this region. In this region these two problems have been a cyclical features for the last nearly 100 years.

Abul Razzakar, a persian Ambassador, who visited the kingdom of Vijayanagar in 1443 described this region as extremely large and thickly populated and that it was for the most part well cultivated and very fertile. In that period, the districts of Bellary (Mysore State). Anantapur, Cuddapah, and Kurnool appear to have been very well irrigated.[10]

TABLE 2.2: Drought Prone in Rayalaseema

District	Drought Prone Taluks	Hard core Taluks	Percentage to total Taluks	Drought Prone area (Sq. Kms.)	As percentage to District area	Population covered by Drought prone area	As percentage to the Dist. population
Kumool	11	7	84.6	17.600	99.7	21,33,456	88.7
Anantapur	11	11	64.7	19,130	100.0	18,05,547	69.0
Cuddapah	8	3	66.7	13,805	89.9	13,01,277	67.5
Chittoor	8	4	53.3	14,162	93.5	18,25.044	66.4
	38	25	66.7	64.697	96.2	70,65,324	72.9

Source : Statistical Abstract: A.P., 1981, p. 107.

TABLE 2.3: List of Chronically Drought Affected Taluks in Rayalaseema

Sl. No.	District/Taluk No.	Sl.	District/Taluk No.	Si.	District/Taluk No.	Sl.	District/Taluk
I.	Anantapur	II.	Chittoor	III.	Cuddapah	IV.	Kurnool
1.	Anantapur	11.	Chittoor (including Bangarupalem sub-taluk)	20.	Cuddapah	28.	Kurnool
2.	Tadpatri	12.	Chandragiri	21.	Kamalapuram	29.	Dhone
3.	Dharmavaram	13.	Madanapalli	22.	Rayachoti	30.	Nandikotkur
4.	Kalyandurg	14.	Vayalpad	23.	Rajampet	31.	Adoni
5.	Rayadurg	15.	Punganur	24.	Badvel	32.	Aluru
6.	Penukonda	16.	Palamaner	25.	Jammalamadugu	33.	Pattikonda
7.	Hindupur	17.	Kuppam	26.	Proddatur	34.	Banaganapalli
8.	Kadiri	18.	Putturk	27.	Pulivendla	35.	Koilkuntla
9.	Madakasira	19.	Satyavedu			36.	Arlagadda
10.	Uravakonda					37.	Atmakur
						38.	Nandyal

Source: Sixth Five Year Plan, A.P., 1980-85, Vol. I. p. 283.

At the beginning of the 10th Century Sir Thomas Munro who was appointed to settle the ceded Districts described that in the above four districts, "to attempt the construction of new tanks is perhaps a more hopeless experiment that the repairs of those which have been filled up for there is scarcely any place where a tank can be made to advantage that has not already been applied to this purpose by the inhabitation".[11] According to Gribble who was for some time the Principal Revenue Officer in Cuddapah district towards the end of the 10th Century, there were in an area of 3574 square miles in that district, no less that 4194 tanks of various sizes.[12]

In the year 1938, the then Composite Madras State appointed the Famine Code Revision Committee to investigate and formulate measures to prevent recurrence of famine in Rayalaseema region. It was one of the steps made in this direction for the development of this region which formed part of the Composite Madras State. Famine relief was, for several decades, formulated on the criterion that the duty of the Government stopped with the prevention of death from starvation and that it was no part of its duty to maintain the people at their normal level of comforts to insure them against are sufferings.[13] But the above Committee recommended that the famine code be suitably amended to the effect that "it is also essential for the state to maintain its people in good health and prevent physical deterioration and dispiritedness".[14]

Later, the Ceded Districts Economic Development Board was constituted in 1941 and was in existence till the end of July, 1949. In accordance with the recommendations of the Development Commissions of the Board, it was abolished and constituted in its place the "Rayalaseema Development Board" in 1949.

The Development Commissioner of the Rayalaseema Development Board in its reports in 1954 remarked that: "The problem of Rayalaseema is to eradicate famine and to development the area economically so as to bring it to the level of the rest of the state. The Rayalaseema Development Board has made several recommendations for an integrated development of this area based on the proposals of Sri P.V. Subba Rao and also the suggestions made by the Development Commissioner, Heads of Departments and Non-official members. But most of the recommendations made by the Board have been either deferred or dropped for want of funds. The creation of a block grant was recommended by the Board in 1950 but the Government have not accepted the suggestion and ordered that highest priority would be given for the execution of all Department Schemes relating to Rayalaseema including those in the Five Year Plan. In spite of this preference by the Government there are still many schemes awaiting sanction and the solution to the problem of Rayalaseema ultimately lies in their speedy implementation on a priority basis."[15]

Broad Divisions

Broadly Rayalaseema may be divided into number of regions:

(a) The Tungabhadra Low level Canal area covering the Western portion of Alur, northern portion of Adoni, parts of Yammiganur and a small portion of Kurnool taluk. But this project serves patches of lands in number of villages and, therefore, would not constitute a solution to the area in any substantial way.

(b) The K.C. Canal area flowing from North to South covering parts of Nandikotkur, Atmakur, Allagadda and Koilkuntla, Proddatur, etc., taluks has to be viewed as one zone for purposes of planning.

(c) The Central Rayalaseema region could be broadly divided into the black soil belt and the red soil belt. The black soil belt generally with Groundnut, Cotton, Korra, Jowar mix dependent mostly on dry farming has only a sprinkling of tank irrigation. The concentration of wells is not very substantial except in patches. This belt covers western portion of Kurnool district, parts of Anantapur district and the Western portion of Cuddapah district. There are certain pockets covered by Tungabhadra High Level Canal which is under execution and Pulivendla Project which is under contemplation and, therefore, require a separate treatment. Otherwise the whole zone has to be treated as a dry-farming zone with predominant black soils.

(d) The other zone constitutes again the Central Rayalaseema area with red soils which have a fairly good concentration of wells and quite a few tanks.

(e) Yet another zone could be the eastern zone of Rayalaseema covering Giddalur, Markapur, Badvel, Sidhout, Rajampet, Kalahasti etc. This zone has red soils and heavy concentration of wells and tanks and economy is dependent on rainfall only.

(f) Another zone is the Southern portion of Rayalaseema covering

Madanapalle, Vayalpad, Punganur, Hindupur, etc. Where there is a good concentration of tanks and wells. The soils are red except in patches of Kuppam sub-taluk. It has comparatively cool climate. Therefore, this possibly could have a different strategy.[16]

This in short is the economic, political and geographical features of this region with peculiar farm problems which warrants an innovation in the rural development of Rayalaseema, a "stalking ground of famines" "hard core" "chronically drought affected" and "famine zone of south" of Union of India.

The Setting:

The Rayalaseema region occupies 27.4 per cent of the State area and lies mostly at an altitude of 1000 to 2000 feet above the sea level.[17] The map of this region appended to this part shows the position of Rayalaseema an the administrative boundaries. This region is a land-locked region spreading over an area about 73,494.9 square Kms.[18] In other words Rayalaseema forms nearly one-fourth of the state total area and about one-fifth of the total population of Andhra Pradesh. This region represents southern part of Andhra Pradesh and is founded on the South by the States of Tamil Nadu and North by Telangana region and on the east by three coastal districts of the state viz., Guntur, Nellore and Prakasam districts. For administrative purposes the area is sub-divided into taluks. This region has been often declared as famine zone of South India. It is typically dry tract of Andhra Pradesh and naturally located in an unfavourable zone. The region lies between the North latitude 12° 30′ and 16° 20′ and East latitude 70° 30′ and 80°.

Physiography

A brief description of physiographic particulars of this region is more useful in general which gives the impression of drought character of the terrain. "No high mountain ranges, no thick forests, the paucity of perennial rivers, a low rainfall, an enervating climate– these are part of what nature has given to this land and no wonder its material progress is hampered".[19] The region is in continuation of Mysore plateau from the South, the Telangana plateau from the North and the Eastern ghats in East. The altitude of the southern portion of the region covering the taluks of Madakasira, Penukonda, Hindupur, Madanapalle, Palamaner, Punganur and Kuppam taluks which is a continuation of the Mysore plateau is 600 metres above M.S.L. Similarly, some of the areas covered by Eastern-ghats in the taluks of Markapur and Giddalur are at the above altitude. The altitude of this region of the West, south west and south varies from 300 to 600 metres M.S.L. The whole region slopes down from north and east first and then towards south-east. Actually a through is formed towards the east of the region known as Kundu Valley with an altitude of 150 to 300 metres above M.S.L. The area with an altitude of less than 75 metres are only a few parts in Sri Kalahasti and Satyavedu bordering Nellore districts i.e., towards the Coast of Bay of Bengal.[20] The only prominent mountains in Rayalaseema are Nallamalais noted for their beautiful scenery. They are in Kurnool District running about 70 miles long, 25 miles broad, and reaching occasionally a height of 3,000 feet. In Cuddapah District there are Seshachalam and Palakonda mountains. Anantapur District has no hill range of any significance except for a few rocky elevations here and there. Chittoor District abounds in small groups of hills among which are Horsley hills, Avulapalli hills and Tirupati hills deserve mention.[21]

Geology

The region possessed variety of geological formations. Throughout the Rayalaseema tract and possessed rich minerals and other natural resources. The oldest rocks in the district of Cuddapah are Dharwars. It is a formation made up partly of basic igneous rocks and partly altered sedementory beds. The next is the peninsular gneisses. The geological formations met in the district are superficial deposits (Alluvium, gravels, soils etc.) Kurnool group (quartzites, shales and lime stones), Cuddapah group (Quartzites, dolomites, shales on slades and traps), and Crystallines (gneisses, granites, traps etc.) Dharwars – schists, quartzites. In Kurnool district also the oldest rocks are called as Dharwars and the next is peninsular gneisses. The geological formations met within the Kurnool district are Nandyal shales (limestones), Paniam quartzites, owk shales, Narji limestones, Banaganapalli sand stones and quartzites etc.

In Chittoor district rock type consists of precambrian rocks, mostly archaean formations. These formations include biotite gneiss, pink quartz felspathic granitic gneiss, amphibolites, biolite schists hornblendeschists, haematite and magnetite quartzites and talk-schist. The recent and subrecent are alluvium and soil with occasional artefacts and laterites. The upper gondwanas consists conglomerates and sand stones. The entire Anantapur district is occupied by rocks belonging to the Archaean and Dharwar formations. The Tadpatri taluk and the Eastern Fringes of Gooty and Anantapur taluks do not possess these rocks. The various rock types found under various systems are basic gneiss rocks Tadpatri slates, Pulivendla quartzites, Vempalle dolomitic limestones, Gulcheru quartzites, Dolerite, quartz veins, Pegmatites and gneissic granites, ultrabasic rocks (talc schist, actionoloite schist). Basic orthoschists (Hornblende schist, hornblends granulite, metagrabbro), Meta-sediments (Biotites-Chist, quartz schist banded magnetite quartzites).[22]

Soils

The soils of Rayalaseema region in particular and of the state in general can be broadly divided into six types. They are Black clay, Black sandy, Red Clay, Red Loams, Red sandy, Black loams. The major part of the region is covered red variety of soils may be of Red loam, Red sandy, Red clay. Thus red soils predominate the Rayalaseema region. But still in Kurnool and Cuddapah districts Black soils are also found in wide area. The Red soils are generally efficient in organic matters and the moisture holding capacity of Red soils is poor. The Black soil is the next largest proportion. This soil is more suitable for cotton cultivation. Other dry crops like Bajra, Jowar are grown in this region on black soils. In Kurnool district all taluks except Pattikonda the black clay soil is distributed. The percentage distribution of area under black clay cultivable land is 85 per cent in Aluru taluk and similar percentage in Kurnool. In Aluru taluk 5 per cent is under black loam and 10 per cent under red loams. In Chittoor district the bulk percentage distribution of area under red loams and red sandy takes bulk proportion. In Anantapur district black loam and red loam soils predominate the district. To support in this districts the percentage distribution of red loam cultivable land constitutes 90 percent and the rest of percentage is equally distributed between black loam and red sandy. The percentage of red loam soil in Madakasira is 88 per cent, Penukonda 85 per cent and Hindupur 80 per cent. In Cuddapah district no taluk has all varieties of land. This is evident from appendix II. It gives talukwise picture of percentage distribution of areas under different types of soils, cultivable land.

River Systems

In general the state is popularly referred to as a "River State". There are about 34[23] major as well as minor rivers that flow through the state. On state level pattern of river system the Rayalaseema region also traversed by various major, medium and minor rivers. Of this river system in this region the major river is Krishna which constitutes the Northern border of the region. It has a length of 1400 Kms. of which 620 km fall within the State.[24] Tungabhadra is its main tributory. This river courses through a plateau of 338 km length covering Kurnool and Nalgonda districts. Besides there are number of medium and minor rivers. To name they are Pennar, Tungabhadra, Hajari, Hundri, Papagni, Kundere, Chitravathi, Gundlakamma, Paler, Araniar, Kushestathli, Swarnamukhi etc.

Land Utilisation

Land is a valuable natural resource and hence it is a productive asset. The proper utilisation is more crucial to solve many of the economic problems. The availability of land is limited for productive activities but there is a greater scope for intensive cultivation and extensive within the availability of land. The existing land should be fully utilised to our best advantage possible. The study of land utilisation is more appropriate with reference to our research work. The role of these banks in land development is studied in detail in the forthcoming chapters. The total geographical land is divided into 9 categories. They are Forests, Barren and un-culturable land, Land put to non-agricultural uses, culturable waste, Land under miscellaneous tree crops and groves not included in the net area sown, permanent pastures and other grazing lands, current follows, Fallow lands other than current follows, Net area sown. Land can be used for different purposes. According to use, the available land will be classified into two types viz., Agricultural use and non-agricultural use.

The distinct feature is that the percentage of forest land to total geographical area was the highest in Rayalaseema region in 1967-68 when compared to other two regions of the State and represents 24.6 per cent which was higher than the state average of 22.3[25] per cent. The most distressing feature of this region is that the permanent pastures and other grazing land is only about 2 per cent of the total geographical area. The categorywise land utilisation analysis reveals that the forest land constitutes 22.14 per cent by the end of the Sixth Plan. The culturable waste land was brought-down to 4.56 per cent from 6.9 per cent in 1967-68. While the forest land which was 24.6 per cent of the total geographical area in 1967-68 marginally fell down to 22.14 cent. The current fallows accounted 6.96 per cent. The net area sown was 39.18 per cent of the total area. But in Kurnool district the percentage of net area sown was 52.39 per cent and it was least in Cuddapah district which was only 26.20 per cent. The Table 2.4 gives comparative picture of land utilisation districtwise in Rayalaseema region. As a whole the net area sown in this region does not show any appreciable trend.

TABLE 2.4: Land Utilisation

(in lakh hectares)

Particulars	Anantapur	Chittoor	Cuddapah	Kurnool	Total
Geographical area	19.13	14.99	15.38	17.60	67.10
	(100)	(100)	(100)	(100)	(100)
Forests	2.13	4.29	4.98	3.45	14.85
	(11.13)	(28.62)	(32.38)	(19.60)	(22.14)
Barren and	1.90	1.69	2.26	0.99	6.84
uncultivable land	(9.93)	(11.27)	(14.69)	(5.62)	(10.19)
Land put to non	1.58	1.39	1.53	0.97	5.47
agricultural use	(8.26)	(9.27)	(9.95)	(5.51)	(8.15)
Cultivable waste	0.86	0.53	0.70	0.97	3.06
	(4.50)	(3.54)	(4.55)	(5.51)	(4.56)
Permanent pastures	0.23	0.46	0.23	0.04	0.96
	(1.20)	(3.07)	(1.50)	(0.23)	(1.43)
Area under trees &	0.21	0.29	0.28	0.02	0.80
grooves	(1.10)	(1.93)	(1.82)	(0.12)	(1.19)
Other follows	1.23	0.70	1.07	1.16	4.16
	(6.43)	(4.67)	(6.96)	(6.59)	(6.20)
Current follows	2.14	1.45	0.30	0.78	4.67
	(11.19)	(9.67)	(1.95)	(4.43)	(6.96)
Net area sown	8.85	4.19	4.03	9.22	26.29
	(46.25)	(27.95)	(26.20)	(52.39)	(39.18)
Area sown more than once	0.30	0.40	0.08	0.44	1.22
Gross area sown	9.15	4.59	4.11	9.66	27.51
Intensity of land (Use in %)	3.39	9.55	1.98	4.77	4.64

Source: Andhra Pradesh Year Book, 1986, pp. 324-325.

Rainfall

Timely and adequate rain-fall is essential for substantial normal crop growth. Monsoon is crucial to this region whose economy is agriculturally biased. This region today is mainly depending mostly on vicissitudes of the monsoon. Failure of rain, inadequate rain-fall, irregular rain-fall have become common features of this region. The observation of rain fall figures for about 45 years shows the region received only less than required rain-fall and in many years below required inches of rainfall in atleast one out of every two-three years an average. This is the reason why this region is declared as "Chronically affected tract". Similarly it is because of the lowest average annual rain-fall the Rayalaseema region has been long called as "Stalking Ground of Famines". Among the four districts the rain fall is the lowest in Anantapur district. It is a hard core district.

The region receives the rain-fall both from South West Monsoon as well as North East Monsoon. The South West Monsoon is generally distributed between June and September. The North East Monsoon occurs and spreads itself from October to December. But generally most of the rain-fall occurs in the months of August and September and occurs by intervals in the months of October and November. This region is a zone of precarious rain fall because the average annual rain fall is being less comparing to other two regions of the State. The normal South West Monsoon rain fall is 368 milli metres in this region, while its occurrence in 1985-86 was only 316 milli metres. The same in Coastal Andhra was 531 milli metres, and 585 milli metres in Telangana region. The Table 2.5 furnishes detail of rain-fall in comparison with other two regions.

Temperature

For the purpose of climatological observation the state has three seasons. They are summer, rainy and winter. The Rayalaseema region experiences and may be generally described as having a hot summer and present and mild winter. The climate is hot for major portion of the year and in certain parts of the districts in this region is quite severe. The climate is dry almost the entire year. Maximum temperature varies from 30°C to 42°C while the minimum temperature varies from 15°C to 28°C. The region has a hot summer period which extends from March to June and mild winter from November to February. The peak

TABLE 2.5: Comparative Rainfall Region and Season-wise

(Rain fall in Milli metres)

Monsoon	Costal Andhra	Rayalaseema	Telangana	Andhra Pradesh
South-West Monsoon (June-Sep):				
Normal	570	368	726	602
1981-82	672	498	904	743
1982-83	499	305	700	553
1983-84	810	598	1,114	906
1984-85	523	332	570	510
1985-86	531	216	585	517
North-West Monsoon (Oct-Dec.):				
Normal	317	213	95	203
1981-82	190	180	71	136
1982-83	288	225	123	205
1983-84	277	170	207	227
1984-85	218	171	99	157
1985-86	337	218	117	221
Winter Hot Weather Period (Jan-May):				
Normal	113	91	72	91
1981-82	68	56	68	66
1982-83	81	68	40	61
1983-84	87	105	30	65
1984-85	90	59	46	66
1985-86	167	90	107	127
Total				
Normal	1000	672	893	896
1981-82	930	734	1,043	945
1982-83	868	598	863	819
1983-84	1174	873	1,351	1,198
1984-85	831	562	715	734
1985-86	1035	624	809	865

Source: Handbooks of statistics, A.P., various Issues.

of summer is reached in May when temperature goes up to 42°C. But the nights are generally fairly cool under the influence of clear skies and low humidity. The figures relating to temperature minimum and maximum in selected parts of the Rayalaseema region are arranged in Table 2.6.

TABLE 2.6: Temperature At Selected Centres

(in centigrade)

Centre	1981		1982		1983		1984		1985	
	Maximum	Minimum	Maximum	Minimum	Maximum	Minimum	Maximum	Minimum	Maximum	Minimum
Anantapur	41.7	11.2	38.3	17.6	40.1	16.2	40.9	18.3	39.9	18.8
Cuddapah	43.5	13.6	40.6	19.1	41.6	18.4	42.2	18.2	41.6	19.6
Kurnool	43.2	9.8	39.6	16.7	41.1	17.1	42.1	17.9	40.3	18.4
Nandyal	44.1	16.9*	40.5	12.1	40.7	16.7	42.1	18.0	42.2	18.2
Tirupati	40.0*	15.0*	38.2	16.0	39.6	14.3	41.3	19.0	41.3	16.3

Source: Hand books of Statistics, Govt. of A.P. various issues.

* Relate to 1980

Occupational Structure

The economy of Rayalaseema region is basically and pre-dominantly agriculture oriented. This naturally typified the existence of problems of rural un-employment and under-employment. The occupational distribution of population and its analysis discloses the fact that the proportion of agricultural labour is very high in Rayalaseema region as compared to other parts of the state and to the All India figures. The total work force may be divided into workers engaged in agricultural sector and workers engaged in non-agricultural sector. Worker as defined at the 1971 census, as a person whose main activity was participation in any economically productive work by his physical or mental activity. Total main workers in this region were 41.22 lakhs. A large number of workers engaged as cultivators or agricultural labourers. As such there were 30.38 lakhs workers, of them 14.84 lakhs engaged as cultivators and 15.54 lakhs as agricultural labourers. The average percentage of cultivators relating to agriculture was 48.32 per cent, and the percentage of agricultural labourers over agricultural workers was 51.68 per cent. In this region the percentage of cultivators over total main workers was 36.00 per cent. This was highest in Chittoor district accounted for 43.12 per cent and next Anantapur where the percentage of cultivators over total main workers was 40.87 per cent. In the region as a whole the percentage of agricultural labourers over total main workers was 37.70 per cent. Thus, the proportion of agricultural labourers is very high. The percentage at non-workers over the total population of the region was 57.75. Workers engaged in non-agricultural sector includes household industry, non-workers, marginal workers and other workers. The mean percentage of household industry over total main workers was 4.82 per cent and other workers over total main workers was 21.75. The district-wise distribution of workers as cultivators and as agricultural labourers particulars are depicted in Table 2.7. The similar particulars relating to workers engaged in non-agricultural sectors are arranged in Table 2.8.

There is a high positive correlation between the proportion of workers in non-agricultural occupations and the degree of urbanisation. The state as a whole has a small percentage of workers engaged in non-agricultural occupations compared to the All India average. Only 30 per cent of the workers in the state are engaged in non-agricultural occupations as against 33 per cent of the country as a whole.

TABLE 2.7: Agricultural Workers

(Workers in lakhs)

District	As Cultivators	As Agricultural labours	Total	% of cultivators to total	% of Agricultural labourres to total	Total main workers	% of cultivators over T.M.W.	% of A.L. over T.M.W.
1. Kurnool	2.80 (18.87)	5.01 (32.24)	7.81 (25.71)	35.87	64.13	10.73 (26.03)	26.10	46.69
2. Anantapur	4.52 (30.45)	3.82 (24.58)	8.34 (27.45)	54.14	45.86	11.06 (26.83)	40.87	34.54
3. Cuddapah	2.57 (17.32)	3.03 (19.50)	5.60 (18.43)	45.93	54.07	7.95 (19.29)	32.33	38.11
4. Chittoor	4.95 (33.36)	3.68 (23.68)	8.63 (28.41)	57.34	42.66	11.48 (27.85)	43.12	32.06
5. Rayalaseema	14.84 (100.00)	15.54 (100.00)	30.38 (100.00)	93.28 (48.32)*	206.72 (51.68)*	41.22 (100.00)	144.00 (36.00)*	150.8 (37.70)*

TMW : Total Main Workers; AL : Agricultural Labourers
Figures in bracket indicate percentage to total of that category
* mean (x)
Source: Based on Census of India 1981, Series 2 of A.P.

TABLE 2.8: Workers Engaged in Non-Agricultural Sector

(Workers in Lakhs)

District	Household industry*	Other workers	Non-** workers	Total main workers	% of house hold industry over TMW	% of other workers over TMW	% of non-workers over total population
Kurnool	0.47 (24.23)	2.44 (27.38)	13.31 (23.88)	10.73 (26.03)	4.38	22.74	55.36
Anantapur	0.51 (26.29)	2.22 (24.92)	15.12 (27.13)	11.06 (26.83)	4.61	20.07	57.75
Cuddapah	0.50 (25.77)	1.86 (20.88)	11.32 (20.31)	7.95 (19.29)	6.29	23.40	58.71
Chittoor	0.46 (23.76)	2.39 (26.82)	15.99 (28.68)	11.48 (27.85)	4.01	20.82	58.21
Rayalaseema	1.94 (100.00)	8.91 (100.00)	55.74 (100.00)	41.22 (100.00)	19.29 (7.82)+	87.03 (21.75)+	230.03 (57.75)+

TMW = Total Main Workers
* Including Manufacturing, Processing, Servicing and Repairs.
** Includes Marginal Workers
\+ Mean (X)
Note: Figures in bracket indicate percentage to total.
Source: Based on Census of India 1981 (Series 2 of Andhra Pradesh)

Ethnological Analysis

The total population of scheduled castes in Rayalaseema region was 14.55 lakhs of which rural scheduled castes population accounted 12.75 lakhs as per census 1981 representing 87.63 per cent. The district-wise particulars are as follows:

District	Rural (lakhs)	Total (lakhs)	% of Rural to total
Kurnool	3.06 (24.00)	3.76 (25.84)	81.38
Anantapur	3.01 (23.61)	3.49 (23.99)	86.25
Cuddapah	2.25 (17.65)	2.51 (17.25)	89.64
Chittoor	4.43 (34.77)	4.79 (32.92)	92.48
Rayalaseema	12.75 (100.00)	14.55 (100.00)	87.63
Coastal Andhra	27.29	32.14	84.91
Telangana	27.48	32.93	83.45

Source: Based on Census figures 1981.

The total population of scheduled tribes in the Rayalaseema region accounted 2.39 lakhs, of which rural concentration was 2.14 lakhs constituting 89.54 per cent of rural population to total scheduled tribes population. The following statement shows the number of scheduled tribes population in each of the 4 districts of the Rayalaseema.

District	Rural	Total	% of Rural to total
Kurnool	0.34 (15.89)	0.40 (16.74)	85.0
Anantapur	0.75 (35.05)	0.82 (34.31)	91.46
Cuddapah	0.34 (15.89)	0.38 (15.90)	89.47
Chittoor	0.71 (100.0)	0.79 (33.05)	89.87
Rayalaseema	2.14	2.39 (100.0)	89.54
Coastal Andhra	11.78	12.85	91.67
Telangana	15.86	16.53	95.95

Source: Ibid.

There are about 33 tribal groups in the state. Their traditional occupations are fishing, begging, washing, religious mendicants, pig rearing, watchman at burial grounds, agricultural labourers, carriers and labourers, bamboo workers, bird catchers, snake-charmers, game snarers, drum beaters, basket making, mat making from data leafs toddy tapping and earth work, small farmers, marginal farmers etc. Their main problem is of getting required credit facilities, inputs and other services. If these are provided they would no longer lag behind in raising their economic position. The land development banks have programmes for their development.

TABLE 2.9: Percentage Distribution of S.Cs., S.Ts working population — by occupational categories

(Percentage)

District	Culti-vators	Agricul-tural labourers	Household Industry manufac-turing processing servicing and repairs	Other workers	Total main workers	Marginal workers
Kurnool	19.65 (8.94)	26.27 (13.97)	40.51 (36.37)	36.89 (22.52)	26.39 (16.63)	17.83 (12.09)
Anantapur	30.42 (55.89)	22.74 (27.70)	18.91 (24.76)	20.54 (25.99)	23.76 (33.55)	21.13 (32.35)
Cuddapah	9.33 (7.58)	18.49 (14.68)	17.09 (26.75)	16.56 (17.78)	16.74 (14.90)	19.70 (20.52)
Chittoor	40.60 (27.59)	32.50 (43.65)	23.49 (12.12)	26.01 (33.71)	33.11 (34.92)	41.34 (35.04)
Total SC Population (% to State total)	1,23,172 (17.65)	5,30,146 (19.38)	8,350 (14.80)	73,593 (14.19)	7,35,221 (18.35)	48,914 (15.67)
Total ST Population (% to State Total)	26,468 (3.90)	59,658 (8.70)	13,456 (22.54)	16,338 (11.24)	1,15,920 (7.39)	8,708 (6.00)

Figures in Brackets indicates S.T. Percentages.
Source: Based on Census of India, 1981

The figures shown in Table 2.9 indicate S.Cs and S.Ts percentage distribution of working population by occupational categories. S.Cs and S.Ts are engaged as cultivators, agricultural labourers, household industry manufacturing processing etc., marginal workers and other workers. Total main workers in this region were 7.35 lakhs which accounts 18.35 per cent to state total. The percentage of S.Ts to state total was 7.39 per cent in the case of total main workers. Similarly, the percentage distribution of SCs. and STs. working as cultivators in Chittoor district was 40.60 and in Anantapur 30.42 per cent and 27.59 per cent, 50.89 per cent respectively of STs. The percentage distribution of SCs. engaged as agricultural labourers in Kurnool district was 26.27; Anantapur district 22.74; Cuddapah 18.49; and Chittoor 32.50. While in the case of STs. respectively 13.97 per cent, 27.70 per cent, 14.68 per cent and 43.65 per cent.

Size of Holdings

One of the main agricultural problems is that of size of operational holding and utilisation. An optimum size of land holding is necessary for the effective farm activities. The success and profitability of farm operations are depending on the size of land holding. According to the agricultural statistics available the average size of operational holding is very less. The number of operational holdings and area operated in this region below 0.5 hectares were 2.26 lakhs and the area only 0.61 lakhs hectares. The examination of holding size between 5.00 - 7.50 hectares reveals the number of holdings were 0.71 lakhs while area was more, accounted 4.65 lakhs hectares. In this range though the number is less comparing to the range of below 0.5 hectares the area operated was more by 7.6 times. The statistical analysis of percentage distribution of number of holdings and area operated in this region in the size class of holdings below 1.0 hectares it was 36.2% in this region, in Chittoor 49.7%, in Cuddapah 42.3% and in Kurnool and Anantapur districts respectively 25.0%, 24.9%. The percentage of area operated in the entire region in this size class was only 5.9 per cent average. The percentage of area operated in Chittoor district accounted 13.2 per cent and in Cuddapah 8.2 per cent. The size class holdings 10 and above, the percentage distribution of number of holdings was nearly 7 times less compared to sizes class below 1.0 hectare.

TABLE 2.10: Percentage Distribution of Number of Holdings and Area Operated According to Different Size Classes of Holdings

District	Size Class of Holdings (in Hectares) Below 1.01		1.0 - 2.0		2.0 - 4.0		4.0 - 10.0		10 & above		Total	
	H	A.O	H	A.O	H	A.O	H	A.O	H	A.O	H	A.O
Kurnool	25.0	3.3	21.3	8.1	23.5	16.6	21.5	33.6	8.7	38.4	100	100
Anantapur	24.9	3.1	21.9	8.4	24.7	16.5	20.3	32.5	8.2	39.5	100	100
Cuddapah	42.3	8.3	22.4	13.8	19.1	22.3	12.8	32.8	3.4	22.8	100	100
Chittoor	49.7	13.2	24.0	19.9	16.9	26.4	7.9	26.4	1.5	14.1	100	100
Rayalaseema	36.2	5.9	22.5	11.3	20.9	19.3	15.2	31.7	5.2	31.8	100	100
Coastal Andhra	56.2	15.3	20.1	17.5	14.2	24.0	7.9	28.2	1.6	15.0	100	100
Telangana	40.5	5.9	19.5	10.3	19.5	19.4	15.8	35.4	4.7	28.0	100	100
Andhra Pradesh	46.6	9.3	20.4	12.8	17.4	20.8	12.2	32.3	3.4	24.8	100	100

H = Holdings; A.O : Area Operated

Source: World Agricultural Census Report, Statistical Abstract, A.P., 1981.

NOTES

1. Government of Andhra Pradesh, *Report of Irrigation Commission*, A.P., 1973, p. 21.
2. *Ibid.*, p. 22.
3. Government of Andhra Pradesh, Finance and Planning (Plg. Wing) Department, *Seventh Five Year Plan A.P.*, 1985-90, Vol. II, p. 161.
4. *Ibid.*
5. Government of Andhra Pradesh, *Planning and Development of Backward of Backward Regions — A case study of Rayalaseema*, 1970, Vol. I, p. 309.
6. *Ibid*, p. 234.
7. *Ibid.*
8. *Ibid.*, p. 152.
9. Government of Andhra Pradesh Finance and Planning (Plg. Wing) Department, *Sixth Five Year Plan, A.P.*, 1980-85, Vol. I, p. 268.
10. Government of Andhra Pradesh Planning and Co-operation Department, *Planning and Development of Backward Regions — A case study of Rayalaseema*, 1970. p. 3.
11. *Ibid.*
12. *Ibid.*
13. *Ibid.*
14. *Ibid.*
15. *Ibid.*, p. 5.
16. *Ibid.*, p. LXX.
17. *Ibid.*, p. 3.
18. *Ibid.*, p. xcix.
19. *Ibid.*, p. 113.
20. *Ibid.*, p. xcix.
21. *Ibid.*, p. 113.
22. *Ibid.*, p. 114-115.
23. Government of Andhra Pradesh, Finance and Planning Department, *Seventh Five Year Plan, A.P.*, 1985-90, Vol. I, p. 2.
24. *Ibid.*, p. 3.
25. Government of Andhra Pradesh, Planning and Co-operation Department, *Planning and Development of Backward Regions — A case study of Rayalaseema*, 1970, p. 121.

3

RURAL CREDIT — A RETROSPECT

The movement did not take long to outgrow the dreams of its founders

— Maclagan Committee

Introduction

In this chapter an attempt is made to discuss in brief the network of rural credit arrangement in the supply of both short-term and long-term to the farmers in Andhra Pradesh with reference to co-operative credit movement in the state, as also touching other institutions in the rural credit field before to study the operations of long-term agricultural co-operative development banks in the region under study. A number of institutions both of organised and unorganised have been working to extend necessary financial and other services to the farmers. The primary agencies which have been operating in the field of agricultural credit are the indigenous un-organised private money-lenders, the co-operatives, the commercial banks and the recent entry of regional rural banks. Besides these, federations, apex banks, State Government and the National Bank for Agriculture and Rural Development are worth mentioning. For obvious reasons the importance of unorganised sector of private money lenders has been declining from day-to-day because of wide coverage of farmers by various institutions and under economic and welfare schemes of the Government.

Multi-Agency System

The peasantry today obtaining credit for agriculture and in turn rural development, from various sources. Thus the rural credit structure today is essentially a multi-agency system. The development and adoption of multi-agency approach to rural financing has given an opportunity to the ryots to borrow required type of credit from appropriate agency identifiably available under the roof of multi-agency rural credit structure. As a matter of fact, the institutional effort of rural credit was originally started, with the organisation of co-operative credit societies in 1900s. The All India rural credit review committee reported in 1969 that "At the same time, effort in the sphere of rural credit should not be solely concentrated in the co-operative sector. Co-operatives should be strengthened, but they would be all the better-and the farmer better served if other institutions co-existed with them in healthy competition".[1]

This approach popularly came to be known as the multi-agency approach which put together providing funds for annual disbursements to the rural sector. In order to look after small farmers, marginal farmers, agricultural labourers regional rural banks came to be organised from 1975. Presently rural institutional credit structure comprises of the following institutions:

(1) Primary Agricultural Co-operative Societies (PACS).
(2) District Central Co-operative Banks (DCCBs). Along with their number of branch offices.
(3) State Co-operative Bank (SCB) or Apex Bank.
(4) Primary Co-operative Agricultural Development Banks (PCADBs).
(5) State Central Co-operative Agricultural Development Banks (SCCADB) or Land Mortgage Bank along with their regional offices.
(6) Commercial Banks (CBs) including State Bank of India (SBI).
(7) Regional Rural Banks (RRBs).
(8) Farmers Service Societies (FSS).
(9) Specialized Bank Branches Rural oriented.

Besides these organisations working at primary level or at grass root level there are other supporting and refinancing institutions operating at National level. They are:

(1) Agricultural Re-finance and Development Corporation (ARDC).
(2) Agricultural Finance Corporation (AFC).
(3) Reserve Bank of India (RBI).
(4) National Bank for Agricultural and Rural Development (NABARD).
(5) National Co-operative Development Corporation (NCDC).

The primary rural credit institutions have been receiving adequate and liberal financing support from the apex institutions. In addition the State Government the Central Government under Centrally Sponsored Schemes (CSS) or under Central Sector Schemes Channelising funds to provide credit under various schemes and strengthening financial structure of the agencies under this multi-agency system. It is our experience that the promotion of economic interest of the farmers is always commensurate with the adequate credit at right time and place.

It is not an appropriate place and purpose to study the working and performance of various agencies working in the field of rural credit. Here we are, therefore, primarily concerned about co-operative sector. Similarly it is also out of place to cover and to trace the role of co-operative credit movement in the country as a whole. Accordingly, in the following paragraphs are covered a brief outline of the growth and development of short-term credit by co-operatives and the need for long-term credit movement and present position. The study, in short, of the co-operative movement in the state would enable us to understand the need of this sector in rural credit in order to achieve the objectives and purpose of the study.

Genesis

Chit fund was the earlier credit arrangement, under which the people of the same village having mutual knowledge of one another join together to organise credit. Similarly Nidhi was a type of mutual loan association. Under this the amount so collected was utilised for granting loans to members in rural areas on personal securities. The Nidhis were developed in this region when it was in Madras State and also in mofussil towns. They did not succeed because of some inherent defects. In India the idea of co-operation developed around 1870s. Then the Deccan ryots faced many credit problems from money lenders. In the year 1875 the Deccan Commission on Agriculture strongly recommended for easy supply of credit to the farmers.

As early as 1882, Sir William Weddersburn and Justice Ranade prepared a scheme for the establishment of agricultural banks to provide loans to ryots. In order to check the role of the money lenders and to provide credit facilities the Government had taken steps in various ways. Those measures were by way of enacting Acts for providing credit facilities to the farmers. The Deccan Agriculturists' Relief Act 1879, the Land Improvement Loans Act, 1883, and the

Agriculturists Loans Act were enacted in order to provide relief to the farmers. Under these Acts the agriculturists could borrow money from the Government for production purpose.

There were a number of defects in the working of these Acts. In the year 1892, the then Madras Government appointed, Fredrick Nicholson with the task of investigating and to report on the advisability of starting agricultural banks and land banks in the then Madras presidency. He submitted his report in two parts in 1895 and 1899 after touring European countries. He strongly recommended for the introduction of rural banks on co-operative lines on "Find Raffeisen". Later, in 1901 the Famine Commission too favoured the starting of Mutual Credit Associations. Again in the same year the Government of India appointed a committee to consider the question of starting co-operative societies in India. Consequently, thereafter in accordance with the recommendations of the committee, Government of India decided to establish co-operative societies in the country. A draft bill was, however, introduced in the Legislative Council. The Bill took the shape of India's First Co-operative Credit Societies Act 1904. It was based on the English Friendly Societies Act.

During the various stages of implementation of the Act it was brought to light many deficiencies and limitations in its working. In order to rectify the short-comings the said Act was drastically amended and passed a comprehensive New Act in 1912 known as the co-operative societies Act 1912.

We have discussed in the preceding paragraphs the origin of co-operative movement in India. This movement in the State of Andhra Pradesh had originated under varying set of circumstances. Because a part of the state was in the then Composite Madras state and a part under the Princely Jurisdiction of Hyderabad state of Telangana region. Thus the state obtained the movement partly from Madras state and partly from princely state.

On the other hand the co-operative movement in the neighbouring states is calculated to have its impact on the progress of credit movement in Rayalaseema region in particular and in the state in general. Thus the movement developed in the state under the peculiar social, economic and political set-up. The movement witnessed distinct features of their own in different parts of the state. In Telangana region the credit co-operative movement progressed under princely and feudal impact and in Rayalaseema region under the British Rule.

The Rayalaseema region which was a part of the Andhra state

included in Madras state did not possess unique in having had the original impetus and separate pattern of movement as was prevailing in the country. Since the Madras state had not enacted its own provincial co-operative legislation and hence the Central credit societies Act, 1904 and 1912 were applicable to this state and to this region. Thus the co-operative movement in Andhra state too went on similar lines as that of Madras state under the Central Act only.

During the period 1904, 1912 the rural societies have been divided into rural and urban, and the Act 1904 provided only for the registration and organisation of credit societies. In the year 1908-09, in Andhra area there were 44 societies, of which 35 were rural and 9 were urban. Thus representing 79.5 per cent of rural and urban only 20.5 per cent. In 1911-12 the number of rural societies increased to 266 constituting 98.15 per cent of total 271 societies. Regarding number of members there were 605 in 1908-09 which went up to 5013. The amended act 1912 provided a new mile stone because the Act provided for the registration of both credit and non-credit societies. The societies have been divided into agricultural and non-agricultural societies.[2]

The credit movement in Andhra area during the period 1912-18 witnessed a significant period of rapid progress with hurried expansion of societies. There were 322 agricultural societies in Andhra area, with number of members 17,400 and working capital 9.28 lakhs. Their position respectively gone up to 36,000 and Rs. 26.04 lakhs in 1917-18. In case of non-agricultural societies in 1912-13 in Andhra area, there were 12 societies, 2200 members, Rs. 1.67 lakhs working capital. By the end of the period 1917-18 their position respectively recorded 12100 and Rs. 6.15 lakhs.[3]

In the year 1914 the Government of India appointed a Committee under the Chairmanship of Sir. Edward Maclagan with the task of examining whether the movement was on soundlines and to suggest measures for the improvement. The Committee made a searching investigation and submitted its report in 1915 which was considered a valuable contribution for the future progress of the movement. It identified a number of glaring defects and offered a number of recommendations.

In 1919 the Government of India Act 1919 was passed, popularly known as the Montague-Chelmsford Act. Under this Act Co-operation became a provincial subject and transferred to the provincial Governments. This marked another important land-mark in the co-operative movement. Accordingly the composite provincial Madras state passed its own co-operative societies act in 1932. The Act of 1932 was applicable to the 11 telugu speaking districts of Andhra area, which includes Rayalaseema region, in Madras state.

The period 1918-19 to 1930-31 recorded a phase of unplanned expansion and credit movement made a rapid progress in Andhra districts in particular. By the end of 1930-31, number of societies increased manifold. As such there were 5,217 agricultural societies with 3,105 hundreds of members, reserve fund Rs. 19.29 lakhs and working capital accounted for Rs. 295.22 lakhs. The Act of 1919 gave a further stimulus to the co-operative movement in this region. As far as non-agricultural societies are concerned there were 602 societies with number of members 709 hundreds, reserve fund Rs. 4.85 lakhs and working capital Rs. 80.22 lakhs.[4]

The Indian Central Banking Enquiry Committee's report suggested for de-officialisation of the co-operative movement. The Madras Government appointed the Town Send Committee in 1927 to examine the progress made by the co-operatives in the Madras Province. The committee recommended for a suitable legislation. The Government of India also appointed a Royal Commission on agriculture in 1928 to review the progress in rural areas. Because of all these developments, ultimately, the Madras Co-operative Societies Act, 1932 was enacted by the Madras Legislative Council in 1932.

The period 1932-41 recorded a set back to co-operative movement due to great economic depression. This led to falling prices of agricultural commodities, accumulation of heavy overdues etc., caused a serious problem to the expansion of the co-operative movement. The most significant event that took place in the economic history of this country, during this period, was the establishment of the Reserve Bank of India (RBI) in 1935 and the creation of Agricultural Credit Department in the RBI. Soon after, the RBI in its report 1936 made several recommendations in respect of co-operative movement viz., conversion of credit societies into multipurpose societies, loans once in a year etc. In the year 1940 the Government of Madras appointed a Committee, known as the Vijaya Raghavacharya Committee on co-operation 1940 to examine the depression effects on co-operative movement and to make suggestions for reconstruction.

The analysis of statistical figures relating to credit societies reveals an impressive progress of credit co-operatives in Andhra area. A decade of progress of 1931-32 — 1940-41 is taken to study the trend of progress. There were 3,880 credit co-operatives in 1931-32 with

2,32,400 members, working capital Rs. 207.20 lakhs, the amount of loan disbursed was Rs. 34.84 lakhs with loan outstanding of Rs. 165.70 lakhs. At the end of the decade there were 14,213, 2,41,300, Rs. 193.27 lakhs Rs. 72.94 lakhs and Rs. 139.59 lakhs respectively.[5]

The State Government appointed the Rayalaseema Co-operative Enquiry Committee (RCEC) 1945-46 to make suggestions for supply finance to agriculturist directly by the apex co-operative society by abolishing Land Mortgage Banks and District Co-operative Central Banks. In 1944 Government of India appointed the Agricultural Finance sub-committee under the Chairmanship of prof. D.R. Gadgil to report on the indebtedness of agriculturists and suggest measures to reduce the same. At the same time the Government of India appointed the Co-operative Planning Committee, 1945 under the Chairmanship of Sri R.G. Saraiya with the task of preparing a plan for the future development of co-operative movement. It submitted its report in the year 1946 and made several recommendations.

The Revenue Department of Madras state used to grant loans under the provisions of Land Improvement Loans and Agriculturists' Act and the Land Improvement Loans and Agriculturists' Loans (Madras Amendment) Act, 1935. The Madras Debt conciliation Act XI of 1936 was passed to facilitate the quick settlement of debts. The Statistical Atlas of the Andhra State 1360 Fasli (1950-51) reported that the Co-operative societies continue to render appreciable help to the agriculturists and others in all the directions during the decade 1941-42 to 1950-51.

The pre-plan decade 1941-42 to 1950-51 reveals some interesting features of co-operative movement. There were 3961 co-operatives in Andhra area, with 2.39 lakh members, Rs. 194.45 lakhs working capital, Rs. 85.85 lakhs as the amount of loan disbursed and amount of loans outstanding Rs. 127.48 lakhs. Respectively their progress at the end of the decade year 1950-51 was: 6,330, 4.81 lakh, Rs. 484.21 lakhs, 362.13 lakhs and 350.66 lakhs.[6]

This is in short a brief tracing of growth and development of co-operative movement in Andhra area. A brief outline of similar observations of the movement in Telangana region would reveal some economic and political events in the movement in the state. We have already discussed Telangana region in retrospect. As a princely state less importance had been given for co-operative and rural development. The fact is that the co-operative societies Act 1912 did not have jurisdiction over this region because it was a part of the princely state of Hyderabad. The movement in this region took inception in March 1913. Mr. John Kenny the then Director of Agriculture incharge of the co-operative Affairs submitted a proposal for necessary legislation. Accordingly, the First Co-operative Societies, Act, 1913 was passed and a separate department of co-operation was established. By the end of 1919-20 there were 1,312 societies in existence, while there were only 24 societies in 1914-15. In 1915 the First Central Co-operative Banks (CCB) was organised for Hyderabad district for assisting agricultural societies. The operations of this bank was confined to the cultivators residing in villages adjoining Hyderabad city. Later the CCBs were established in other districts. Later the area of Hyderabad Central Co-operative Bank was confined to the Hyderabad district only. In 1925 it was, however, converted into provincial Co-operative Bank (PCB). Later the Government of Hyderabad State appointed the "Reis Jung Committee" to enquire into the incidence of overdue, interest and bad and doubtful debts.

In 1929-30, in apex bank there were 451 members, working capital Rs. 37.62 lakhs, advances made Rs. 8.90 lakhs. While in Central Banks there were 3446 members, working capital Rs. 12.70 lakhs, advances made Rs. 6.30 lakhs. The total membership in agricultural credit societies was 37,672 and in other societies 14,996.[7]

The first grain bank was registered in Nizamabad district of Hyderabad state in 1943. The Hyderabad Agricultural Co-operative Association (HACA) was an apex level body, Taluk Agricultural Co-operative Associations (TACAs) were in existence as base level societies. The HACA was liquidated in 1967. The Hyderabad Central Land Mortgage bank (HCLMB) was organised in 1953. Thus by the end of 1944-45 there was one apex bank, 46 co-operative central banks, 5,448 agricultural credit societies. Their position respectively in 1940-41 was 1,41, and 3,482.[8] Finally the pace of progress of co-operative movement in this region was arrested due to political unrest which finally led to be "Razakar Movement" in 1946-47 followed by the police action by the central Government in 1948.

Five Year Plans

The next stage in co-operative movement was the planning period. In Five Year plans due importance has been given to co-operative sector. As a matter of fact a separate head of development has been provided in the successive Five Year Plans. Accordingly, therefore, the

Government of Andhra Pradesh accorded priority to co-operation through plan schemes with progressively increasing budgetory allocations. During the First Plan, in October 1953 the Andhra part of the state was separated from the composite Madras State, exactly when the plan scheme implementation was half way through the plan. The First Plan of the Madras State was split-up and tentative break-up of the composite plan was worked out on the basis of co-operative schemes belonging to Andhra segment. In the last year of the First Plan the Telangana region was merged with Andhra state.

As at the end of 30th June 1956 in Andhra area there were 6,679 societies with 6.45 lakh members, Rs. 111.11 lakhs paid-up share capital, deposits from members Rs. 17.44 lakhs, working capital Rs. 742.90 lakhs, total amount of loans issued Rs. 580.30 lakhs while loans outstanding amounted to Rs. 628.48 lakhs. The position in Telangana region on 30th June, 1957 was 3,074 societies, 1.56 lakh members, Rs. 23.06 lakhs paid up share capital, Rs. 0.90 lakhs deposits from members, Rs. 112.62 lakhs working capital, total amount of loans issued Rs. 61.47 lakhs and the amount of loans outstanding was Rs. 90.38 lakhs.[9]

Thus the credit co-operative movement continued to play a significant role during the successive Five Year plans. At the end of the Sixth Five Year Plan there were about 7,002 primary Agricultural Co-operative Societies in the state. They had 71.84 members with paid-up share capital of Rs. 4030.43 lakhs, working capital Rs. 38336.31 lakhs. They issued loans to the extent of Rs. 22093.34 lakhs. The amount of loans outstanding was Rs. 26423. 89 lakhs.

Single Window Rural Credit (SWRC)

During the Seventh Plan period the Government of Andhra Pradesh reorganised the co-operative credit structure to introduce changes in the institutional set-up, namely "Single Window Credit Delivery Scheme", which aims to extend multicredit i.e., short-term. medium-term and long-term through a single unit under this system. A brief note on single window rural credit is appended to the report. (Appendix I).

District Central Co-operative Banks (DCCBs)

These banks occupy intermediary place in the co-operative credit structure in the state. The structure is essentially a federal in character and has three tiers. The intermediary DCCBs constitute key link in the chain of relationship between the apex bank and the primary credit societies. The area of operations and jurisdiction of DCCBs in the state are generally confined to a district. They have opened branches in taluks in different parts of the district.

Mobilisation of savings, supply of credit, to raise funds from RBI and others, to supervise and inspect the primaries, to undertake usual banking operations are the important functions of the DCCBs. By virtue they are concern with short-term and medium-term credit. As at the end of First Five Year Plan there were 15 DCCBs in Andhra area and 10 in Telangana. Their membership respectively was 10,637 and 3,949. They had paid-up share capital of Rs. 91.89 lakhs in Andhra area and Rs. 12.07 lakhs in Telangana region. The working capital was Rs. 1201.16 lakhs in Banks in Andhra area and Rs. 99.38 lakhs in Telangana area banks. These figures show the DCCBs in Telangana region did not function on sound lines. Rs. 935.81 lakhs accounted under loans outstanding in Andhra area and Rs. 63.76 lakhs in Telangana region.[10]

By the end of Sixth Plan there were 26 DCCBs in the state with a members of 32,757. They had share capital of Rs. 3844.96 lakhs and reserve fund 498.14 lakhs. It is significant to note that DCCBs opened branches at taluk head quarters and samithis. There has been a considerable increase in the number of branches. There were 221 branches in 1976 which went up to 395 in the last year of the Sixth Five Year Plan.

Apex Bank-short Term Credit

APCOB, as popularly knows, stands for the Andhra Pradesh state co-operative Bank. In the three tier short-term credit structure APCOB. is the apex institution. It is the nucleus around which all the agricultural credit matters of co-operative sector revolve. Earlier the Madras State Co-operative Bank was the only bank having state-wide jurisdiction equally working for Andhra area and Madras. The bank was so organically connected and its division become inevitable. The Madras Government facilitated the division of the state co-operative Bank by promulgating an ordinance in 1953 known as the Madras State Co-operative Societies (Re-organisation and Formation) Ordinance 1953.

Consequently, Andhra State Co-operative Bank with its head-quarter at Vijayawada was carved out on the pattern of its parent institution and inaugurated on 6th September 1953. This bank had Rs. 8.70 lakhs paid-up share capital on 5th September, 1953 and Rs. 10.20 on 30th June 1954. The working capital was respectively, Rs. 352.88 lakhs and Rs. 357.35 lakhs.[11]

As pointed out already in Telangana region there was a Hyderabad Central Co-operative Bank which was later converted into a provincial Co-operative Bank Limited, Vijayawada working for Andhra area and the Hyderabad Co-operative Apex Banks (HCHB) LTD., Operating in Telangana area. It was proposed to re-constitute the Andhra State Co-operative Bank by merging in it the Hyderabad Co-operative Apex Bank. Consequently a single society known as the Andhra Pradesh State Co-operative Bank was registered and came into existence by amalgamation of the two regional apex banks under Andhra Pradesh State Co-operative Bank Formation Act, 1963.

Thus the short-term co-operative credit structure is a three tier composed of primary Agricultural Co-operative Societies at base level and DCCBs at intermediate level and the Apex bank at the state level.

Need For Long-term Credit

After having a brief discussion about the magnitude of drought and the existing structure of co-operative short-term credit, let us now tress in brief the need for long-term co-operative credit. The general problem in respect of farmers in drought prone areas is that of long-term investment, on farm and productive assets. The fact is that the short-term credit institutions whose main object is to extend short-term finance to meet the expenditure only on short-term operations. They cover only seasonal agricultural operations of the farmers such as purchase of seeds, cost of ploughing, cost of Fertilizers etc.

Medium-term loans (Agriculture), Medium-term loans (conversion), Medium-term loans (Rephasement) and Medium-term (Non-agriculture) are the important activities of the short-term credit institutions. But the importance of long-term credit to the farmers can not be overemphasised. Among the three types of credit the long-term credit which is needed for long period of time say, 5 to 20 years, is indispensable to undertake agricultural development activities. The long term finances are required to the farmers so as to enable them to bring about permanent improvement on land, construction of wells, tanks, repayment of old debts, purchase of land, tractors, installation of irrigation machinery and land reclamation. Naturally the credit needed for those purposes is quite different from short-term credit requirements to meet seasonal agricultural operations, seeds, manures and fertilizers etc., and medium term loans for purchase of bullocks milch cattle, repairs and maintenance and improved implements.

The agricultural operations are mainly dependent upon the monsoons which in this region are unpredictable, uncertain in their occurrence and meagre in absolute terms. As such the importance of short-term credit necessarily is very limited or diminishes gradually. In other words unless structural conditions of the farm infrastructures are improved, like change in cropping pattern, adoption of drought-resistant seeds, provision and extension of irrigation facilities and exploitation of under ground water, the regular seasonal agricultural operations can not be taken up and hence the need for short term credit does not arise increasingly. In an area like Rayalaseema which is known as stalking ground of famines, because which is liable to frequent droughts, what is of crucial significance among three credits is long term rather than short-term credit. In this way co-operative long-term or agricultural development lending agencies can play useful service in Rayalaseema region which is liable to frequent droughts.

A deliberate change in credit policy towards long-term credit in priority than to short-term lending is more desirable. In other words the importance of a sound co-operative long term credit movement for proper development of, particularly tract like this needs no elucidation. The short-term credit structure composed of PACS, DCCBs, APPCOB are thus not suitable because of their activities of seasonal agricultural operations and medium term. Even the commercial banks, to speak truly, are reluctant to advance for long term agricultural operations adequately, and at the same time they are not prepared to block their short term funds for risky long term agricultural purposes. But there is remarkable change visible in recent years in this direction due to the establishment of Regional Rural Banks. Banks are unable to step into the field of big programme of soil conservation in a large measure which is crucial in this region. It is because of the fact large number of farmers and vast land area which involves specialised banks with full time concentration.

It is because of these problems specialised long-term co-operative agricultural development banks are established. These banks originally were called as Land Mortgage Banks and later renamed as Agricultural Development Banks. These banks mainly lend to activities related to the general agricultural development, such as for construction of wells, purchase and installation of pumpsets, reclamation etc.

The Central Banking Enquiry Committee, the Royal Commission on Agriculture (RCA) and the Rural Banking Enquiry Committee consider these banks as most suitable for providing long-term credit.

Objectives

The agricultural development bank means co-operative society registered or deemed to the registered under the Andhra Pradesh Co-operative Societies Act, 1964 and admitted as a member of the Central Agricultural Development Bank. These banks under the provisions of the Co-operative Act extends loans for the following purposes:

1. Land improvement and productive purposes;
2. The erection, rebuilding or repairing of houses for agricultural purposes;
3. The purchase or acquisition of title to agricultural lands by tenants; or
4. The liquidation of debts of agriculturists under the relevant law for the time being in force.

According to explanation under Co-operative Law of the state land improvement or productive purpose means, any work, construction of activity which adds to the productivity of the land and in particular includes the following:

(a) Construction and repairs of wells (including tube wells), tanks and other works for the storage, supply or distribution of water for the purpose of agriculture, or for the use of men and cattle employed in agriculture;
(b) renewal or reconstruction of any of the foregoing works, or alterations therein, or additions thereto;
(c) Preparation of land for irrigation;
(d) Drainage, reclamation from rivers or other waters, or protection from floods or from erosion or other damage by water, of land used for agricultural purposes, or waste land which is

cultivable;

(e) bunding and similar improvements;

(f) reclamation, clearance and enclosure or permanent improvement of land for agricultural purposes;

(g) horticulture;

(h) purchase of oil engines, pumping sets and electric motors for any of the purposes mentioned herein;

(i) purchase of tractors or other agricultural machinery;

(j) increase of the productive capacity of land by addition to it of special variety of soil;

(k) construction of permanent farm houses; cattle-shed, and sheds for processing of agricultural produce at any stage;

(l) purchase of machinery for crushing sugarcane, manufacturing gur or khandsari or sugar;

(m) such other purposes as the Government may specify from time to time, by notification in the Andhra Pradesh Gazette.

Two Tier Structure

The structure of agricultural development banks in the state is essentially a federal one. At the base level there exist Primary Co-operative Agricultural Development Banks (PCADBs) and at the state level there exist an Apex Bank by name Andhra Pradesh Co-operative Central Agricultural Development Bank (APCCADB). The primaries are affiliated to the apex bank which is the only bank extending credit to the primaries to lend in turn to the farmers. In some other states the long-term structure is unitary one. But a federal structure is most suitable in case of agricultural development societies. The rural credit survey committee, the Committee on co-operative credit, the committee on Takkavi loans and co-operative credit and the All India Rural Credit Review Committee etc., favoured the federal structure. But in view of the Hazari Committees recommendations for the integration of multi-credit structure comprising of short-term, medium-term and long-term, the credit structure is substantially re-organised in the state recently. That is single window rural credit delivery scheme introduced during the Seventh Five Year Plan came into operation from First April 1987.

There were 13 Land Mortgage Banks in Andhra region with 3020 members, Loans disbursed Rs. 4.81 lakhs and loans outstanding Rs. 13.34 lakhs. By the end of decennium 1940-41 their position respectively was 50; 26,290, Rs. 19.93 and Rs. 119.71. The observation of trend of progress of land mortgage banks in Andhra area during the decade 1941-42 to 1950-51 reveals that there was no change in number of societies till 1947-48. The number of societies remained constant (50) till 1946-47. By the end of decade there were 54 societies. They had 56,504 members. They issued loans to the extent of Rs. 36.92 lakhs and amount of loans outstanding was Rs. 179.23 lakhs. They recorded Rs. 189.97 lakhs as working capital.[12]

During the Five Year Plans the long term co-operative movement development considerably. Thus by the end of Sixth Five Year Plan before introduction of Single Window Rural Credit Delivery Scheme there were 218 PCADBs in the state. They had 14.35 lakh members with their own paid-up share capital of Rs. 3488.65 lakhs. The share of Government's paid up share capital was Rs. 265.86 lakhs. The amount of loans outstanding as at the end of the Sixth Plan was Rs. 33158.64 lakhs. The amount of overdue was Rs. 4859.97 lakhs. A comparative position of agricultural development banks in Rayalaseema region and in the entire state is given in Table 3.1.

TABLE 3.1: Progress of Primary Agricultural Development Banks

Year	Rayalaseema Region			Andhra Region			Percentage of Rayalaseema over A.P.		
	No. of Banks	Loans issued	Loans out-standing	No. of Banks	Loans issued	Loans out-standing	No. of Banks	Loans issued	Loans out-standing
1	2	3	4	5	6	7	8	9	10
1961-62	22	80.70	198.67	113	333.89	974.57	19.47	24.17	20.39
1962-63	27	68.83	349.01	122	322.54	1221.81	22.13	21.34	20.38
1963-64	28	85.54	315.11	126	403.15	1526.66	22.22	21.22	20.64
1964-65	37	82.59	377.23	163	445.73	1848.11	22.70	18.53	20.41
1965-66	38	276.34	616.20	173	1122.02	2832.09	21.97	24.63	21.76
1966-67	38	278.76	861.19	178	1018.72	3653.95	21.35	27.36	23.57
1967-68	38	274.22	1091.82	178	1194.82	4589.11	21.35	22.95	23.79
1968-69	40	394.44	1443.97	180	1803.07	6077.25	22.22	21.88	23.76
1969-70	41	344.43	1664.75	181	2068.21	7649.57	22.65	16.65	21.76
1970-71	41	365.25	1887.65	181	1980.08	8983.94	22.65	18.45	21.01
1971-72	41	282.53	2036.62	182	1518.47	9701.16	22.52	18.61	20.99

(Contd.)

TABLE 3.1: *Contd.*

1	2	3	4	5	6	7	8	9	10
1972-73	41	169.30	2011.05	184	684.63	9571.96	22.28	24.73	21.01
1973-74	41	314.46	2086.85	184	1175.15	9622.22	22.28	26.76	21.68
1974-75	39	475.78	2238.99	190	1880.86	10230.59	20.53	25.30	21.89
1975-76	39	744.39	2659.09	202	2970.58	11709.69	19.31	25.06	22.71
1976-77	39	781.99	3111.22	205	3349.76	13267.35	19.24	23.34	23.45
1977-78	39	763.73	3447.95	205	4922.09	16325.60	19.24	15.52	25.69
1978-79	39	851.54	3840.47	205	5930.78	20056.50	19.24	14.36	19.15
1979-80	39	926.59	4121.46	205	5853.49	22847.25	19.24	15.83	18.04
1980-81	40	1044.57	4883.30	206	7114.71	27274.31	19.42	14.68	17.90
1981-82	42	576.01	4883.34	218	4810.67	28371.69	19.27	11.97	17.21
1982-83	42	933.16	5360.71	218	6953.81	31599.51	19.27	13.42	16.96
1983-84	42	629.67	5224.70	218	6298.31	33142.19	19.27	10.00	15.76
1984-85	42	516.11	5778.50	218	5192.19	34841.21	19.27	9.94	16.59
1985-86	42	669.93	5493.03	218	6305.91	36435.07	19.27	10.62	15.08

Source : Based on Annual Reports of APCCADB, various Issues.

NOTES

1. Report of the Rural Credit Review Committee, 1969, p. 411.
2. The administrative Reports of the Co-operative Movement, Madras State, 1904-1912.
3. *Ibid.*
4. *Ibid.*
5. Based on statistical Atlas of Madras Province, 1949.
6. Statistical Atlas of the Andhra State, 1360, Fasli (1950-51), p. 21.
7. Administrative Reports of the Co-operative Department.
8. *Ibid.*
9. Report on the working of Co-operative Societies in Andhra Pradesh, 1957.
10. *Ibid.*
11. *Ibid.*, 1954, p. 24.
12. Based on statistical Atlas of Madras Province, 1949 and Statistical Atlas of Andhra State 1950-51, p.22.

4

RESOURCE MOBILISATION

Small locally worked Institutions were ideal agencies for the supply of rural credit

— Fredrick Nicholson

Membership Coverage

All the persons whose membership has been admitted by the co-operative bank are referred to as the members of the society. The members of a society are the persons, who collectively constitute the society as a corporate entity or a body corporate. The members are the shareholders by purchasing shares in the bank. The word "member" and "shareholder" are used interchangeably. By virtue of subscribing to the share capital of the bank a member is called as shareholder. Any person who is not disqualified by the co-operative legislation or by the bye-laws of the society can become a member of the society. Membership is, however, subjected to the provisions of the Andhra Pradesh Co-operative Societies Act, and the bye-laws of the society. The bye-laws may provide that certain persons cannot become members of a society.

The objects of the society primarily is to raise required long term funds to be lent to its members who voluntarily joined to obtain credit facilities from the society. The members who belong to the same class or pursue the same occupation residing in the same town, village or group of villages, generally constitute the area of operation of the society. The user members are the farmers who are primary members, for the promotion of whose economic interest a society is formed are known as 'A' class members. The state Government is also a member in each society, since it is participating in the share capital of the society as state partnership.

The total membership of PCADBs increased from 58,102 in 1977-78 to 73,049 in 1981-82 and further to 73,427 in 1986-87 registering an increase of 26.38 over 1977-78. The percentage of membership in Chittoor district was 26.40 per cent in 1986-87 over the region; the percentage in Cuddapah district was 27.92; 20.55 per cent in Kurnool district, 25.13 per cent in Anantapur district. The percentage of membership was the highest of 47.47 per cent in the case of Madanapalli PCADB in Chittoor district and the lowest percentage represented by Chandragiri PCADB. In Cuddapah district, the Rajampet PCADB recorded least per cent of membership of 50.71, while the proddatur PCADB 47.90 per cent over the district total membership of 20,501.

The bank-wise trend progress of membership during the period under review may be seen from Table 4.1.

The statistical analysis of membership can be gauged from the following results.

District	Mean	CGR	CV
Chittoor	17337.7	4.60	13.86
Cuddapah	21030.4	0.29	6.68
Kurnool	14632.7	1.06	3.75
Anantapur	16894.7	4.71	16.25
Region	69894.6	2.53	8.94

CGR : Compound growth rate
CV : Coefficient of variation

Elasticity Co-efficient

Though there is considerable increase in the rate of growth of membership the study of effectiveness of membership is also essential. All the farmers who became members, among whom what is the extent of beneficiaries. To find out the average rate of change in membership of the co-operative banks in the district to that of beneficiaries in the district, the elasticity of co-efficient is studied. The elasticity co-efficient explains the rate of change. If the elasticity of co-efficient of membership is greater or lesser, it may be inferred that the marginal increase in membership is greater than the average increase in the beneficiaries.

TABLE 4.1: Membership in Primary Banks

(Nos.)

S.No. Name of the Bank	1977-78	78-79	79-80	80-81	81-82	82-83	83-84	84-85	85-86	86-87
I. CHITTOOR DISTRICT										
(a) Chittoor	4,280	4,188	4,037	4,363	4,418	4,943	5,300	5,483	5,666	5,483
	(33.41)	(28.73)	(26.58)	(25.51)	(25.55)	(26.20)	(27.32)	(28.62)	(28.92)	(28.29)
(b) Chandragiri	3,209	3,376	3,623	4,122	4,145	4,568	4,612	4,693	4,791	4,698
	(25.05)	(23.16)	(23.85)	(24.10)	(23.97)	(24.21)	(23.77)	(24.49)	(24.45)	(24.24)
(c) Madanapalli	5,320	7,014	7,528	8,619	8,727	9,358	9,487	8,985	9,138	9,263
	(41.54)	(48.11)	(49.57)	(50.39)	(50.48)	(49.59)	(48.91)	(46.89)	(46.63)	(47.47)
Total I	12,809	14,578	15,188	17,104	17,290	18,869	19,399	19,161	19,595	19,384
	(100.0)	(100.0)	(100.0)	(100.0)	(100.0)	(100.0)	(100.0)	(100.0)	(100.0)	(100.0)
II. CUDDAPAH DISTRICT										
(a) Rajampet	4,795	5,273	5,869	6,713	6,815	7,034	3,136	3,283	3,244	3,221
	(25.57)	(26.34)	(26.88)	(31.19)	(30.10)	(29.90)	(14.82)	(16.44)	(15.93)	(15.71)
(b) Cuddapah	7,803	8,258	9,206	7,227	7,280	7,471	7,471	7,414	7,498	7,461
	(41.61)	(41.25)	(42.17)	(33.58)	(32.15)	(31.76)	(35.30)	(37.12)	(36.82)	(36.39)
(c) Proddatur	6,154	6,488	6,758	7,581	8,546	9,018	10,560	9,276	9,623	9,819
	(32.82)	(32.41)	(30.95)	(35.23)	(37.75)	(38.34)	(49.88)	(46.44)	(47.25)	(47.90)
Total II	18,752	20,019	21,833	21,521	22,641	23,523	21,167	19,973	20,365	20,501
	(100.0)	(100.0)	(100.0)	(100.0)	(100.0)	(100.0)	(100.0)	(100.0)	(100.0)	(100.0)

Contd...

TABLE 4.1 *Contd.*

S.No. Name of the Bank	1977-78	78-79	79-80	80-81	81-82	82-83	83-84	84-85	85-86	86-87
III KURNOOL DISTRICT										
(a) Banaganapalli	5,217	5,312	4,777	4,479	4,536	5,026	4,380	4,491	4,587	4,486
	(37.89)	(36.70)	(34.07)	(31.50)	(31.82)	(33.02)	(29.26)	(29.37)	(30.54)	(29.72)
(b) Kurnool	2,755	2,791	2,907	2,918	2,954	3,121	3,557	3,686	3,174	3,472
	(20.01)	(19.28)	(20.73)	(20.53)	(20.73)	(20.50)	(23.76)	(24.11)	(21.13)	(23.01)
(c) Nandyal	5,798	6,373	6,336	6,820	6,763	7,074	7,031	7,114	7,258	7,134
	(42.10)	(44.02)	(45.20)	(47.97)	(47.15)	(46.48)	(46.98)	(46.52)	(48.33)	(42.27)
Total III	13,770	14,476	14,020	14,217	14,253	15,221	14,968	15,291	15,019	15,092
	(100.0)	(100.0)	(100.0)	(100.0)	(100.0)	(100.0)	(100.0)	(100.0)	(100.0)	(100.0)
IV ANANTAPUR DISTRICT										
(a) Dharmavaram	5,507	5,512	5,512	7,915	8,727	9,051	7,275	7,383	7,136	7,265
	(43.12)	(41.78)	(41.25)	(47.27)	(46.26)	(44.79)	(38.97)	(40.27)	(38.89)	(39.38)
(b) Hindupur	2,889	3,132	3,255	3,663	3,750	4,206	4,342	3,715	3,893	3,983
	(22.62)	(23.74)	(24.36)	(21.87)	(19.88)	(20.81)	(23.26)	(20.26)	(21.22)	(21.59)
(c) Tadpatri	4,375	4,549	4,597	5,168	6,388	6,951	7,051	7,236	7,319	7,202
	(34.26)	(34.48)	(34.39)	(30.86)	(133.86)	(34.40)	(37.77)	(39.47)	(39.89)	(39.03)
Total IV	12,771	13,193	13,364	16,746	18,865	20,208	18,668	18,334	18,348	18,450
	(100.0)	(100.0)	(100.0)	(100.0)	(100.0)	(100.0)	(100.0)	(100.0)	(100.0)	(100.0)
Total I+II+III+IV	58,102	62,266	64,405	69,588	73,049	77,821	74,202	72,759	73,327	73,427

Note: Figures in Brackets indicate Percentage to District total

Source: Based on Annual Reports of APCCADB, various Issues.

Symbolically, the elasticity co-efficient of membership can be expressed as

$$Me = \frac{\Delta m/M}{\Delta b/B}$$

Where Δ m = change in membership
Δ b = change in beneficiaries
M = Total membership
B = Beneficiaries Total
Me = Elasticity Co-efficient of membership

Similarly the elasticity technique is also applied to the beneficiaries. Accordingly, the elasticity co-efficient of beneficiaries is calculated with help of:

$$Be = \frac{\Delta b/B}{\Delta m/M}$$

Where Be = elasticity co-efficient of beneficiaries.

Where symbols stand for same meaning as above. The elasticity co-efficient of membership and beneficiaries are calculated and given below.

Elasticity Coefficient of Membership and Beneficiaries

District	Elasticity coefficient of			
	Membership	Rank	Beneficiaries	Rank
Chittoor	(-) 0.09	(-) II	(-) 1.16	(-) II
Cuddapah	(-) 0.29	(-) I	(-) 4.22	(-) I
Kurnool	(+) 0.26	(+) I	(+) 4.7	(+) I
Anantapur	(+) 0.19	(+) II	(-) 0.96	(-) III
Region	(-) 0.11		(-) 1.42	

Further it is to be tested with reference to elasticity co-efficient of credit.

Funds

To achieve the object of agricultural development sufficient funds should be kept before the counter so as to cover not only members in general but also the poorer sections of small and marginal farmers. These farmers have far long did not get a fair deal in the matter of credit. Adequate credit at right time is the life-blood of rural economic activities. Without credit, now-a-days of high cost of variety of new inputs, no agricultural operation could be performed. It is undoubtedly true that credit is the foundation of any successful economic activity. If the financial supply to a farmer is adequate and timely he would be able to perform the activities efficiently and effectively and his economic interest could be promoted without any problem.

The financial structure of these banks in this region depended on the feeble capacity of resources mobilisation on the part of the owner members whose capacity is inherently weak. The amount of share capital so collected from them has been very small and inadequate in relation to outstanding, overdues etc. The non-availability of adequate funds internally is a main factor responsible for high dependence on state level apex bank which is in turn mobilising funds by issue of debentures which are again in turn subscribed by the Government, financial institutions, sister co-operative institutions, commercial banks etc.

Sources of Funds

The basic concept of co-operative agricultural development banking is that mobilisation of small means from members for promoting thrift and mutual help for collective development by bringing together people of same occupation. A detailed examination of present agricultural development banks in co-operative sector in the state of Andhra Pradesh particularly in the region under study discloses the fact that there has been considerable progress in respect of credit disbursement. But it has been upon comparatively limited amount of members capital base. During the last two decades, there has been a very marked broadening of the fields of these banks as exemplified by the formulation of many rural development programmes. These banks also assumed equal responsibility as the third and balancing banking sector.

There is a vast difference in the financial structure and conditions of these banks. Members' financial position has been weak and can not adequately strengthen these banks financially by themselves. The illiterate and poor farmers think that it is the responsibility of the society to extend services to them. Thus the societies have been endeavouring to gather adequate funds from outside sources. Besides meagre share capital from the members the PCADBs have been mobilising the resources from various external sources. The PCADBs generally raise funds from the following sources:

1. Share capital.
2. Advances from co-operative societies on such terms and conditions as may be decided by the managing committee.
3. Borrowing from Andhra Pradesh State Co-operative Bank (APCOB), APCCADB, ARDC, NABARD, RBI and other financial institutions.
4. Borrowing from other creditors.
5. Grants or subsidies and other financial assistance from Government and other institutions.
6. Loans and subsidies under the subsidised Industrial Housing Scheme of the Government of India.
7. Donations or gifts received from individuals, public bodies and institutions.
8. State assistance under state partnership in the co-operative movement.
9. Acceptance of public deposits both from members and non-members.
10. Any other source as may be decided upon by the Managing Committee and approved by the Registrar as may be required.

Share Capital

The first and the main source of mobilisation of resources in the object of raising funds to be lent to the members is the share capital. The capital of the bank is divided into certain indivisible units of a specified amount. These units are called shares. The word share means a share in the capital of a bank. The total capital of the bank is divided into shares to be subscribed by the members. Each member has to subscribe at least one share in the bank and generally the bye-laws impose restrictions on the number of shares or the maximum amount beyond which a member is prohibited to take shares. The term share is, however, not defined in the co-operative societies Act. But the term can be understood by referring to section 2 (46) of the Companies Act, 1956 which defines a share "as a share in the share capital of a company, and includes stock except where a distinction between stock and share is expressed or implied".

Share capital represents the interest of the members in the society. A person who is purchasing shares in a co-operative bank is known as shareholder individually and collectively called shareholders who are the real owners of the bank. By virtue of entering their names in a separately maintained Registrar of Members they are termed as members. Hence the two words member and shareholder are used interchangeable. The shares of any member in a co-operative bank are a movable property. They are transferable in the manner provided by the bye-laws of the society. The members enjoy voting right by virtue of holding shares. Share capital is an important component in the total working capital and primary variable in the pool of owned funds. In relation to co-operative bank the word Capital means the share capital which is raised by them through issue of shares.[4] The co-operative Agricultural Development Bank registered under the Andhra Pradesh Co-operative Societies Act, 1964 can raise capital by issue of shares. The face value of share in these banks of rural based, in which poor farmers are the members, is generally a small amount so as to enable the farmers to purchase shares and become owner member of a co-operative agricultural development bank.

The share capital is raised from the members by allotting shares at the time of admission of members when once it is raised the share capital becomes the permanent liability of the bank. The bye-laws of the respective co-operative banks may stipulate whether the value of each share would be payable in lumpsum on allotment or by instalments. Similarly the bye-laws may also classify the types of members. For instance 'A' class members are primary members.

The share of the members in the financial operations is generally limited. This is particularly because, unlike other financial institutions which offer the shares for subscription to the public at large, these rural co-operative banks offer their shares for subscription to a limited number of members of a particular class of farmers for the promotion of whose economic interest a Co-operative bank is formed in a particular locality. The financial capacity of the small and marginal farmers is so poor that they find it difficult to purchase more than one share just required to satisfy the legal and procedural requirements.

Members' Share Capital Position

It has been already mentioned that the share capital is the main base and is a strength for borrowing. The total members' paid up share capital in all the 12 sample units was Rs. 203.78 lakhs in 1986-87 while it was Rs. 134.29 lakhs in 1977-78. The difference in the figures during this period reflect an increase of 1.52 times. The percentage of members' paid up share capital was 27.99 over the total in Chittoor district in 1986-87, 28.54 per cent in Cuddapah district, 12.63 in Kurnool district and 30.84 in Anantapur district.

In 1981-82 the percentage of members' share capital contribution was 25.79 per cent out of the total in Chittoor district; 34.33 per cent in Cuddapah district; 12.10 per cent in Kurnool district and 27.58 per cent in Anantapur district. The banks in Kurnool district accounted least of 12.10 per cent comparing the other three districts. While the Cuddapah district scored highest percentage of 34.33 per cent. In the beginning years of the decade their paid up share capital was 22.61 per cent in Chittoor district; 32.67 per cent in Cuddapah district; 18.14 per cent in Kurnool district; and 26.58 per cent in Anantapur district. These figures clearly show increasing progress in the contribution of paid up share capital by the members. It evidently reveals the increasing enrolment of membership with a view to avail long-term credit facilities from the co-operative banks. In Chittoor district the Madanapalli PCADB mobilised, highest amount of share capital representing 50.37 per cent the highest among others and lowest was recorded by Chandragiri PCADB accounting only 20.02 per cent in 1986-87.

The compound growth rate in respect of members' paid up share capital in Rayalaseema region during the decennial of 1977-78 to 1986-87 was 12.06. The co-efficient of variation was 29.99. The trend resulted a linear growth rate of 6.84, while r = 0.48. The mean of y value was Rs. 179.60.

Analysis

	Y-Values mean	r	CGR	CV
Chittoor	50.51	0.66	6.04	19.50
Cuddapah	59.87	0.08	1.61	13.99
Kurnool	25.05	0.66	0.88	3.30
Anantapur	54.07	0.89	6.62	19.11

The figures relating to progress in members' paid up share capital are arranged in Table 4.2.

Government's Share Capital Contribution

The Government of Andhra Pradesh has been assisting the PCADBs by way of share capital participation as state partnership in co-operative movement. The state Co-operative Societies Act empowers the State Government to extent state aid, to co-operative societies by way of loans or advances, subscribe to the share capital, guarantee the repayment of principal and interest, guarantee the repayment of share capital of the society and dividends thereon, guarantee the repayment of principal and interest on loans and advances, deposits and in any other form including subsidies. Consequent on this state aid the Government has the right under the Act to nominate to the committee certain number of members.

The amount of Government's share capital contribution in these societies was Rs. 4.96 lakhs in 1986-87. This shows number of times increased by 3.23 over the period of ten years. From 1977-78 to 1981-82 the amount of Governments share capital remained constant of Rs. 1.55 lakhs. In 1982-83 its stake went up 3.09 times more, 3.47 times more in 1983-84. There was no change in 1984-85. In 1985-86 it fell down to Rs. 4.13 lakhs in Rayalaseema region. In Chittoor district during the first five years of the period under study the Government's share capital contribution was Rs. 0.35 lakhs. The position is the same in the case of Cuddapah district and Anantapur district. In Kurnool district its share capital was Rs. 0.50 lakhs and the remain unchanged during the decade. During next five years of the period the increasing participation is of the Government in the share capital participation is clearly visible. In Chandragiri PCADB, in Chittoor district, Government's share was 91.94 per cent. It was 71.43 per cent of the total district in Cuddapah district. The significant, feature is that there is no Government's share capital in Rajampet PCADB in Cuddapah district, Nandyal PCADB in Kurnool district, and Dharmavaram PCADB in Anantapur district. The analysis of figures relating to Government's share in these banks in the region reveals:

Co-efficient of variation	=	55.98
Compound growth rate	=	18.79
Linear growth rate	=	15.46
Mean - Y-value	=	3.24

TABLE 4.2: Members' Paid up Share Capital

(Rs. in lakhs)

S.No.	Name of the Bank	1977-78	78-79	79-80	80-81	81-82	82-83	83-84	84-85	85-86	86-87
I.	CHITTOOR DISTRICT										
(a)	Chittoor	10.26	10.37	10.12	11.44	12.08	13.99	16.27	16.32	18.07	16.89
		(33.79)	(26.67)	(22.83)	(22.04)	(22.99)	(23.77)	(27.19)	(27.26)	(35.11)	(29.61)
(b)	Chandragiri	7.09	9.49	12.01	13.98	13.98	15.45	14.86	14.64	4.77	11.42
		(23.35)	(24.40)	(27.10)	(26.94)	(26.61)	(26.25)	(24.83)	(24.46)	(9.27)	(20.02)
(c)	Madanapalli	13.01	19.03	22.19	26.48	26.48	29.41	28.71	28.90	28.62	28.74
		(42.86)	(48.93)	(50.07)	(51.02)	(50.40)	(49.98)	(47.98)	(48.28)	(55.62)	(50.37)
	Total I	30.36	38.89	44.32	51.90	52.54	58.85	59.84	59.86	51.46	57.05
		(100.0)	(100.0)	(100.0)	(100.0)	(100.0)	(100.0)	(100.0)	(100.0)	(100.0)	(100.0)
II.	CUDDAPAH DISTRICT										
(a)	Rajampet	13.55	16.33	20.69	26.08	26.29	27.07	13.22	12.95	12.05	12.74
		(30.89)	(31.35)	(34.24)	(37.33)	(37.88)	(38.48)	(23.11)	(22.26)	(20.40)	(21.91)
(b)	Cuddapah	14.71	17.35	18.76	20.01	19.62	19.53	18.96	19.85	20.68	19.83
		(33.53)	(33.31)	(31.04)	(28.64)	(28.27)	(27.76)	(33.14)	(34.12)	(35.00)	(34.10)
(c)	Proddatur	15.61	18.41	20.98	23.78	23.50	23.75	25.03	25.38	26.35	25.59
		(35.58)	(35.34)	(34.72)	(34.03)	(33.85)	(33.76)	(43.75)	(43.62)	(44.60)	(43.99)
	Total II	43.87	52.09	6.43	69.87	69.41	70.35	57.21	58.18	59.08	58.16
		(100.0)	(100.0)	(100.0)	(100.0)	(100.0)	(100.0)	(100.0)	(100.0)	(100.0)	(100.0)

Contd.

TABLE 4.2 *Contd.*

S.No. Name of the Bank	1977-78	78-79	79-80	80-81	81-82	82-83	83-84	84-85	85-86	86-87
III KURNOOL DISTRICT										
(a) Banaganapalli	8.93	9.28	9.10	8.43	7.87	7.86	8.02	8.24	8.72	8.33
	(36.66)	(36.51)	(37.25)	(34.17)	(37.18)	(31.06)	(32.56)	(32.07)	(32.46)	(32.37)
(b) Kurnool	5.26	4.97	4.75	4.81	5.09	5.31	4.85	5.50	5.59	5.31
	(21.59)	(19.55)	(19.44)	(19.50)	(20.80)	(20.98)	(19.69)	(21.41)	(20.81)	(20.64)
(c) Nandyal	10.17	11.17	10.58	11.43	11.50	12.14	11.76	11.95	12.55	12.09
	(41.75)	(43.94)	(43.31)	(46.33)	(47.02)	(47.96)	(47.75)	(46.52)	(46.73)	(46.99)
Total III	24.36	25.42	24.43	24.67	24.46	25.31	24.63	25.69	26.86	25.73
	(100.0)	(100.0)	(100.0)	(100.0)	(100.0)	(100.0)	(100.0)	(100.0)	(100.0)	(100.0)
IV ANANTAPUR DISTRICT										
(a) Dharmavaram	14.40	15.04	16.28	19.04	18.92	20.83	20.58	21.43	22.32	21.44
	(40.34)	(37.07)	(36.40)	(36.12)	(33.93)	(34.76)	(33.73)	(34.22)	(34.41)	(34.12)
(b) Hindupur	11.08	12.83	13.74	15.17	15.36	15.46	15.65	16.10	16.96	16.24
	(31.04)	(31.62)	(30.73)	(28.78)	(27.55)	(25.80)	(25.65)	(25.71)	(26.14)	(25.84)
(c) Tadpatri	10.22	12.70	14.70	18.50	21.48	23.63	24.78	25.10	25.59	25.16
	(28.62)	(31.31)	(32.87)	(35.10)	(38.52)	(39.44)	(40.62)	(40.07)	(39.45)	(40.04)
Total IV	35.70	40.57	44.72	52.71	55.76	59.92	61.01	62.63	64.87	62.84
	(100.0)	(100.0)	(100.0)	(100.0)	(100.0)	(100.0)	(100.0)	(100.0)	(100.0)	(100.0)
Total I+II+III+IV	134.29	156.97	173.90	199.15	202.17	214.43	202.69	206.36	202.27	203.78

Note: Figures in Bracket indicate percentage to District Total.
Source: Based on Annual Reports of APCCADB, various Issues.

TABLE 4.3: Governments' Share Capital Contribution

(Rs. in lakhs)

S.No.	Name of the Bank	1977-78	78-79	79-80	80-81	81-82	82-83	83-84	84-85	85-86	86-87
I.	CHITTOOR DISTRICT										
(a)	Chittoor	0.10	0.10	0.10	0.10	0.10	0.10	0.15	0.15	0.10	0.13
		(28.57)	(28.57)	(28.57)	(28.57)	(28.57)	(2.72)	(4.02)	(4.02)	(4.03)	(3.93)
(b)	Chandragiri	0.15	0.15	0.15	0.15	0.15	3.48	3.48	3.48	2.28	3.08
		(42.86)	(42.86)	(42.86)	(42.86)	(42.86)	(94.56)	(93.30)	(93.30)	(91.94)	(93.05)
(c)	Madanapalli	0.10	0.10	0.10	0.10	0.10	0.10	0.10	0.10	0.10	0.10
		(28.57)	(28.57)	(28.57)	(28.57)	(28.57)	(2.72)	(2.68)	(2.68)	(4.03)	(3.02)
	Total I	0.35	0.35	0.35	0.35	0.35	3.68	3.73	3.73	2.48	3.31
		(100.0)	(100.0)	(100.0)	(100.0)	(100.0)	(100.0)	(100.0)	(100.0)	(100.0)	(100.0)
II.	CUDDAPAH DISTRICT										
(a)	Rajampet	—	—	—	—	—	—	—	—	—	—
(b)	Cuddapah	0.10	0.10	0.10	0.10	0.10	0.10	0.10	0.10	0.10	0.10
		(28.57)	(28.57)	(28.57)	(28.57)	(28.57)	(28.57)	(28.57)	(28.57)	(28.57)	(28.57)
(c)	Proddatur	0.25	0.25	0.25	0.25	0.25	0.25	0.25	0.25	0.25	0.25
		(71.43)	(71.43)	(71.43)	(71.43)	(71.43)	(71.43)	(71.43)	(71.43)	(71.43)	(71.43)
	Total II	0.35	0.35	0.35	0.35	0.35	0.35	0.35	0.35	0.35	0.35
		(100.0)	(100.0)	(100.0)	(100.0)	(100.0)	(100.0)	(100.0)	(100.0)	(100.0)	(100.0)

Contd.

TABLE 4.3 *Contd.*

S.No. Name of the Bank	1977-78	78-79	79-80	80-81	81-82	82-83	83-84	84-85	85-86	86-87
III KURNOOL DISTRICT										
(a) Banaganapalli	0.25 (50.0)	0.25 (50.0)	0.25 (50.0)	0.25 (50.0)	0.25 (50.0)	0.25 (50.0)	0.25 (50.0)	0.25 (50.0)	0.25 (50.0)	0.25 (50.0)
(b) Kurnool	0.25 (50.0)	0.25 (50.0)	0.25 (50.0)	0.25 (50.0)	0.25 (50.0)	0.25 (50.0)	0.25 (50.0)	0.25 (50.0)	0.25 (50.0)	0.25 (50.0)
(c) Nandyal	—	—	—	—	—	—	—	—	—	—
Total III	0.50 (100.0)	0.50 (100.0)	0.50 (100.0)	0.50 (100.0)	0.50 (100.0)	0.50 (100.0)	0.50 (100.0)	0.50 (100.0)	0.50 (100.0)	0.50 (100.0)
IV ANANTAPUR DISTRICT										
(a) Dharmavaram	—	—	—	—	—	—	—	—	—	—
(b) Hindupur	0.25 (71.43)	0.25 (71.43)	0.25 (71.43)	0.25 (71.43)	0.25 (71.43)	0.25 (71.43)	0.25 (31.25)	0.25 (31.25)	0.25 (31.25)	0.25 (31.25)
(c) Tadpatri	0.10 (28.57)	0.10 (28.57)	0.10 (28.57)	0.10 (28.57)	0.10 (28.57)	0.10 (28.57)	0.55 (68.75)	0.55 (68.75)	0.55 (68.75)	0.55 (68.75)
Total IV	0.35 (100.0)	0.35 (100.0)	0.35 (100.0)	0.35 (100.0)	0.35 (100.0)	0.35 (100.0)	0.80 (100.0)	0.80 (100.0)	0.80 (100.0)	0.80 (100.0)
Total I+II+III+IV	1.55	1.55	1.55	1.55	1.55	4.80	5.38	5.38	4.13	4.96

Note: Figures in Brackets indicate percentage to District Total.
Source: Based on Annual Reports of APCCADB, various Issues.

The bank-wise details regarding the Government's share capital contribution during the last ten years are furnished in Table 4.3.

Thus state participation supplements working capital to carry on loan operations effectively and strengthens the capital structure of the co-operative banks to some extent. But it should not be forgotton the Government's interference in the functioning of this banks when there is its share capital participation or other ways of assistance.

Percentage Distribution

The percentage of Government's paid up share capital figures are depicted in Table 4.4. The mean percentage in 1977-78 in 12 co-operative banks was 1.37. There has been slight fluctuations during 1978-79 — 1981-82. The average percentage was 2.89 in 1982-83; 2.96 in 1983-84; 3.01 in 1984-85; 3.77 in 1985-86; and 2.93 in 1986-87. In general it may be concluded that the percentage of Government's paid-up share capital over total paid-up share capital has been a very small proportion in relation to members' contribution and in relation to magnitude of funds required to meet ever increasing demand for long term credit. The individual co-operative bank-wise and year-wise percentage distribution of Government's paid-up share capital over the total paid-up share capital can be observed from Table 4.4.

Reserves

Internal financing accounts a minor proportion of financing in case of co-operative banks for a number of reasons like the objective of the bank is not to earn profit to build reserves out of it, the bulk of their loaning operations are from the funds provided by the apex bank. The solvency of a co-operative bank equally depends on its own sources. The expression reserve may be used with reference to co-operative banks to denote amounts set aside out of profit. Reserves are undistributed profits. A reserve may be built by generally or for any particular purpose or it is called specific reserve. A general reserve is created to meet any contingent or un-expected expenses. A reserve strengthens the financial position or working capital base of a co-operative bank.

TABLE 4.4: Percentage Distribution of Government's paid up Share Capital over Total paid up Share Capital

(Percentage)

S.No.	Name of the Bank	1977-78	78-79	79-80	80-81	81-82	82-83	83-84	84-85	85-86	86-87	Mean
1.	Chittoor	0.96	0.96	0.98	0.87	0.82	0.71	0.91	0.91	0.55	0.76	0.84
2.	Chandragiri	2.07	1.56	1.23	1.06	1.06	22.52	23.42	23.77	32.34	21.24	2.12
3.	Madanapalli	0.76	0.52	0.45	0.38	0.38	0.34	0.35	0.34	0.35	0.35	0.42
4.	Rajampet	0	0	0	0	0	0	0	0	0	0	0
5.	Cuddapah	0.68	0.57	0.53	0.50	1.03	0.51	0.52	0.50	0.48	0.50	0.58
6.	Proddatur	1.58	1.34	1.18	1.04	1.05	1.04	0.40	1.36	0.94	0.97	1.09
7.	Banaganapalli	2.72	2.62	2.67	2.88	3.08	3.08	3.02	2.94	2.79	2.91	2.87
8.	Kurnool	4.54	4.79	5.00	4.84	4.68	4.50	4.90	4.35	4.28	4.50	4.64
9.	Nandyal	0	0	0	0	0	0	0	0	0	0	0
10.	Dharmavaram	0	0	0	0	0	0	0	0	0	0	0
11.	Hindupur	2.21	1.91	1.79	1.62	1.60	1.59	1.57	1.53	1.45	1.52	1.68
12.	Tadpatri	0.97	0.78	0.56	0.54	0.46	0.42	0.40	0.40	2.10	2.39	0.90
	Mean	1.37	1.25	1.20	1.14	1.18	2.89	2.96	3.01	3.77	2.93	1.26

Source: Table 4.2 and 4.3

Co-operative society may create two types of reserve fund, namely statutory reserve fund (SRF) and other reserve funds. SRF is built up under the statutory requirements of the co-operative legislation. Other fund is created according to the requirements of each society. The co-operative bank may create future planning reserves to facilitate the financing of working capital or to provide for contingency transactions. Depending upon the need a society may create several proprietory reserves like reserve for contingency, sinking fund reserve, reserve for dividend, secret reserves, dividend equalisation reserve etc.

A reserve fund maintained by a society belongs to the society and it is intended to meet unforeseen expenses or losses. Under the bye-laws and under the Co-operative Act no part of the profits of a society is to be distributed among its members without providing provision for reserve. Accordingly, a society should out of its net profits in every co-operative year transfer an amount not less than 25 per cent to the reserve fund.

Accordingly the co-operative banks have created reserve fund by transferring to this fund by debiting to profit and loss account. As appointed out earlier the amount of reserve fund constitutes a very small proportion in the total working capital. The total reserve fund of banks was Rs. 12.59 lakhs in 1986-87, the same in 1977-78 was Rs. 12.39 lakhs, represents only 1.62 per cent growth over a decade. But during the years from 1979-80 to 1982-83 the reserve account showing Rs. 13.00 lakhs to Rs. 13.15 lakhs range respectively. The banks in Chittoor district had reserve fund of Rs. 4.14 lakhs in 1986-87 (Rs. 4.24 lakhs in 1977-78), In Cuddapah district for the same year was Rs. 3.05 lakhs (Rs. 3.02 lakhs in 1977-78), while the position in Anantapur District was Rs. 3.81 lakhs (Rs. 3.67 lakhs) respectively. The banks in Kurnool district recorded only Rs. 1.59 lakhs.

The year-wise and bank-wise reserve fund particulars are given in Table 4.5.

Percentage of Reserve Fund to Share Capital

The percentage of reserve fund to members paid up share capital district-wise reveals some interesting features. The percentage of reserve fund to the total members paidup share capital was only 6.18 per cent in 1986-87, 9.23 per cent in 1977-78, 7.88 per cent in 1978-79, 7.48 per cent in 1979-80, 6.53 per cent in 1980-81, 6.46 per cent in 1981-82, 6.13 per cent 1982-83, 6.20 per cent in 1983-84, 6.16 per cent

TABLE 4.5: Reserve Fund of the Primary Banks

(Rs. in lakhs)

S.No.	Name of the Bank	1977-78	78-79	79-80	80-81	81-82	82-83	83-84	84-85	85-86	86-87
I.	CHITTOOR DISTRICT										
(a)	Chittoor	1.81	1.81	1.81	1.81	1.81	1.81	1.81	1.81	1.81	1.81
		(42.69)	(44.04)	(44.04)	(44.04)	(43.51)	(45.25)	(45.25)	(43.51)	(42.49)	(43.72)
(b)	Chandragiri	1.43	1.24	1.24	1.24	1.29	1.29	1.29	1.29	1.29	1.29
		(33.73)	(30.17)	(30.17)	(30.17)	(31.01)	(32.25)	(32.25)	(31.01)	(30.28)	(31.16)
(c)	Madanapalli	1.00	1.06	1.06	1.06	1.06	0.90	0.90	1.06	1.16	1.04
		(23.58)	(25.79)	(25.79)	(25.79)	(25.48)	(22.50)	(22.50)	(25.48)	(27.23)	(25.12)
	Total I	4.24	4.11	4.11	4.11	4.16	4.00	4.00	4.16	4.26	4.14
		(100.0)	(100.0)	(100.0)	(100.0)	(100.0)	(100.0)	(100.0)	(100.0)	(100.0)	(100.0)
II.	CUDDAPAH DISTRICT										
(a)	Rajampet	0.63	0.64	1.27	1.27	1.28	1.28	0.56	0.56	0.57	0.56
		(20.86)	(20.45)	(33.78)	(33.78)	(33.95)	(33.95)	(18.36)	(18.36)	(18.63)	(18.36)
(b)	Cuddapah	1.23	1.33	1.23	1.23	1.23	1.23	1.23	1.23	1.23	1.23
		(40.73)	(39.30)	(32.71)	(32.71)	(32.63)	(32.63)	(40.33)	(40.33)	(40.20)	(40.33)
(c)	Proddatur	1.16	1.26	1.26	1.26	1.26	1.26	1.26	1.26	1.26	1.26
		(38.41)	(40.25)	(33.51)	(33.51)	(33.42)	(33.42)	(41.31)	(41.31)	(41.17)	(41.31)
	Total II	3.02	3.13	3.76	3.76	3.77	3.77	3.05	3.05	3.06	3.05
		(100.0)	(100.0)	(100.0)	(100.0)	(100.0)	(100.0)	(100.0)	(100.0)	(100.0)	(100.0)

Contd.

TABLE 4.5 *Contd.*

S.No. Name of the Bank	1977-78	78-79	79-80	80-81	81-82	82-83	83-84	84-85	85-86	86-87
III KURNOOL DISTRICT										
(a) Banaganapalli	0.55	0.55	0.55	0.55	0.55	0.55	0.68	0.68	0.68	0.68
	(37.67)	(37.67)	(37.67)	(37.67)	(37.67)	(37.67)	(42.77)	(42.77)	(46.90)	(42.77)
(b) Kurnool	0.40	0.40	0.40	0.40	0.40	0.40	0.40	0.40	0.26	0.40
	(27.40)	(27.40)	(27.40)	(27.40)	(27.40)	(27.40)	(25.16)	(25.16)	(17.93)	(25.16)
(c) Nandyal	0.51	0.51	0.51	0.51	0.51	0.51	0.51	0.51	0.51	0.51
	(34.93)	(34.93)	(34.93)	(34.93)	(34.93)	(34.93)	(32.07)	(32.07)	(35.17)	(32.07)
Total III	1.46	1.46	1.46	1.46	1.46	1.46	1.59	1.59	1.45	1.59
	(100.0)	(100.0)	(100.0)	(100.0)	(100.0)	(100.0)	(100.0)	(100.0)	(100.0)	(100.0)
IV ANANTAPUR DISTRICT										
(a) Dharmavaram	1.49	1.49	1.49	1.49	1.49	1.49	1.49	1.49	1.40	1.46
	(40.60)	(40.60)	(40.60)	(40.71)	(40.60)	(38.01)	(38.01)	(38.01)	(39.11)	(38.32)
(b)Hindupur	0.90	0.90	0.90	0.90	0.90	0.90	0.90	0.90	0.90	0.90
	(24.52)	(24.52)	(24.52)	(24.59)	(24.52)	(22.96)	(22.96)	(22.96)	(25.14)	(23.62)
(c) Tadpatri	1.28	1.28	1.28	1.27	1.28	1.53	1.53	1.53	1.28	1.45
	(34.88)	(34.88)	(34.88)	(34.70)	(34.88)	(39.03)	(39.03)	(39.03)	(35.75)	(38.06)
Total IV	3.67	3.67	3.67	3.66	3.67	3.92	3.92	3.92	3.58	3.81
	(100.0)	(100.0)	(100.0)	(100.0)	(100.0)	(100.0)	(100.0)	(100.0)	(100.0)	(100.0)
Total I+II+III+IV	12.39	12.37	13.00	13.00	13.06	13.15	12.56	12.72	12.35	12.59

Note: Figures in Bracket indicate percentage to District Total.
Source: Based on Annual Reports of APCCADB, various Issues.

in 1984-85 and 6.11 per cent in 1985-86. The Kurnool district in 1985-86 the percentage of reserve fund to members total working capital was 5.40 per cent. All these figures reveal that the proportion of internal funds over the paid-up share capital have been a small amount. The percentage distribution of district total reserve fund to district total members' paid up share capital are given in Table 4.6.

TABLE 4.6: Percentage of Reserve Fund to Members' Paid up Capital

(Percentage)

District	1977-78	79-80	81-82	84-85	85-86	86-87
Chittoor	13.97	9.27	7.92	6.95	8.28	7.26
Cuddapah	6.88	6.22	5.43	5.24	5.18	5.24
Kurnool	5.99	5.98	5.97	6.19	5.40	6.18
Anantapur	10.28	8.20	6.58	6.26	5.52	6.06
Region	9.23	7.48	6.46	6.16	6.11	6.18

Source: Table 4.2 and 4.5.

The importance of building up substantial amount of reserve fund is indispensable with reference to co-operative Agricultural Development Bank which needs more long-term resources. It may be mentioned that ploughing back of profit is the sound way of the growth of co-operative organisation of rural character. The fund enables the banks to meet credit requirements of the farmers without seriously impairing credit operations to extend timely credit without depending on apex bank for its release of funds. The fund also facilitates to undertake many diversified and allied activities. Durable community assets can be financed out of accumulated profits. Development activities peculiar to drought region cannot be carried out unless profits have been retained. Thus this free fund not only creates confidence among the members about the soundness of financial position and strengthens the borrowing capacity of a co-operative bank.

Borrowings

The co-operative agricultural development banks are characterised by acute shortage of capital, special funds are required for long term investment purpose. The poor farmer members alone cannot contribute adequate capital to carry on long term financial operations, without outside sources. Since these banks need funds, generally to be blocked for long term. The commercial banks, short-term co-operative banks cannot extend adequate funds.

The owned funds of these banks are not sufficient to meet its loaning business. Not only share capital base of the members in these banks has been limited but also the deposit mobilisation, has been very negligible. Besides the Government's share capital participation in these banks and other financial assistance do not, however, meet the full requirements. The remarkable feature of the rural credit market in India is the establishment of many special Central and State Financial Institutions exclusively for the development of agriculture and rural development. These institutions have been extending credit to agricultural development banks. The recent one of such institution is the NABARD. It is an apex organisation is respect of all matters relating to policy, planning and operational aspects concerning flow of credit for agriculture and other allied rural development activities. Besides separate funds have been also established both at National level and local level. To mention such funds are National Agricultural Credit (Long-term operations) Fund; National Agricultural Credit (Stabilisation) Fund; National Rural Credit (Long Term Operations) Fund; National Rural Credit (Stabilisation) Fund.

The financial institutions which have been operating in the field of rural finance are Reserve Bank of India, Agricultural Re-finance and Development Corporation, Agricultural Finance Corporation, National Bank for Agriculture and Rural Development (NABARD), Agricultural Credit Board, Agricultural Credit Department, Agricultural Development Branch, Agricultural Development Bank of India.

Besides, other Central Financial Institutions like Life Insuration Corporation, Syster Land Development Banks, Commercial Banks, State Bank of India, State Bank of Hyderabad have been subscribing substantially to the debentures issued by the Central Land Development Bank to raise funds, in turn to finance affiliated banks. Government of India and Government of Andhra Pradesh also have been participating in debenture issue.

The Primary Co-operative Banks have been borrowing funds substantially to meet the credit requirements of the farmer members under their jurisdiction. The borrowing by the primaries is not directly from these institutions. But they refinance and subscribe to the debentures. The only source for the primary banks is to borrow from State apex bank of long term (Lt) Credit i.e., APCCADB. Again this borrowing capacity would depend to a great extent upon its owned funds and repayment turn over. Even the borrowing capacity of the co-operative bank is restricted by the bye-laws of the each society. Every society should raise loans only to such an extent and under such conditions as specified in the bye-laws.

Even the Co-operative Societies Rules provide restrictions on borrowings by societies. Rule 40 of the Andhra Pradesh Co-operative Societies Rules, 1964 states that a society may receive deposits and raise loans from persons or institutions who are not members provided that the amount borrowed from such persons and institutions together with the amount borrowed from members does not exceed the limit fixed from time to time by the Registrar for the society or for the class of societies to which it belongs.

The bye-laws generally provide the borrowing limit to 6 to 8 times the aggregate paid up share capital plus reserve fund or such other proportion as may be prescribed by the Registrar of Co-operative Societies from time to time.

Extent of Borrowing

The Primary Co-operative Banks borrow funds mainly from the apex bank which in turn from various financial institutions and Government. Figure 4.2 relating to borrowing by the primary banks, bank-wise and year-wise during the period under review are given in Table 4.7.

Table 4.7 discloses the borrowing of the Co-operative banks during the years from 1977-78 to 1986-87. The total borrowing of co-operative banks in this region ranges between Rs. 186.99 lakhs and Rs. 435.27 lakhs. The total borrowing was highest in 1980-81 of Rs. 435.27 lakhs, Rs. 365.14 lakhs in 1978-79, Rs. 360.66 lakhs in 1979-80, and Rs. 336.22 lakhs in 1982-83. In the remaining years of the decade the borrowing ranges between Rs. 186.99 lakhs and Rs. 283.96 lakhs. The year 1984-85 recorded lowest amount of borrowing of Rs. 186.99 lakhs. These figures show wide fluctuations in the amount of borrowing. The only scientific way of studying the variations is co-efficient of variation. The co-efficient of variation for the region was 26.27, the compound growth rate was 5.04, while the mean borrowing was Rs. 294.327 lakhs.

TABLE 4.7: Borrowings

(Rs. in lakhs)

S.No.	Name of the Bank	1977-78	78-79	79-80	80-81	81-82	82-83	83-84	84-85	85-86	86-87
I.	CHITTOOR DISTRICT										
(a)	Chittoor	9.56	13.32	10.97	31.56	23.03	41.78	42.65	28.09	41.50	37.41
		(14.25)	(10.38)	(8.58)	(24.47)	(43.89)	(37.35)	(71.13)	(59.96)	(54.48)	(61.34)
(b)	Chandragiri	15.25	27.39	36.68	32.64	15.76	29.50	5.64	7.96	15.91	9.84
		(22.72)	(21.34)	(28.68)	(25.30)	(30.04)	(26.37)	(9.41)	(16.99)	(20.89)	(16.13)
(c)	Madanapalli	42.30	87.67	80.26	64.79	13.68	40.57	11.67	10.80	18.76	13.74
		(63.03)	(68.28)	(62.74)	(50.23)	(26.07)	(36.28)	(19.46)	(23.05)	(24.63)	(22.53)
	Total I	67.11	128.38	127.91	128.99	52.47	111.85	59.96	46.85	76.17	60.99
		(100.0)	(100.0)	(100.0)	(100.0)	(100.0)	(100.0)	(100.0)	(100.0)	(100.0)	(100.0)
II.	CUDDAPAH DISTRICT										
(a)	Rajampet	45.56	46.56	41.78	62.96	18.53	18.72	16.52	0.60	4.08	7.07
		(38.25)	(36.24)	(33.73)	(42.11)	(31.82)	(23.66)	(18.70)	(1.01)	(5.13)	(9.32)
(b)	Cuddapah	30.84	35.23	34.95	32.98	16.60	19.84	23.33	23.87	35.17	27.46
		(25.89)	(27.43)	(28.22)	(22.06)	(28.51)	(25.08)	(26.41)	(40.12)	(44.18)	(36.22)
(c)	Proddatur	42.71	46.67	47.12	53.56	23.10	40.55	48.49	35.03	40.35	41.29
		(35.86)	(36.33)	(38.05)	(35.83)	(39.67)	(51.26)	(54.89)	(58.87)	(50.69)	(54.46)
	Total II	119.11	128.46	123.85	149.50	58.23	79.11	88.34	59.50	79.60	75.82
		(100.0)	(100.0)	(100.0)	(100.0)	(100.0)	(100.0)	(100.0)	(100.0)	(100.0)	(100.0)

Contd.

TABLE 4.7 *Contd.*

S.No. Name of the Bank	1977-78	78-79	79-80	80-81	81-82	82-83	83-84	84-85	85-86	86-87
III KURNOOL DISTRICT										
(a) Banaganapalli	3.32	9.62	9.28	12.18	10.89	19.60	13.36	11.19	15.48	13.35
	(21.77)	(29.04)	(35.92)	(29.70)	(33.03)	(40.99)	(42.13)	(39.29)	(39.25)	(40.17)
(b) Kurnool	1.74	2.62	4.59	5.19	5.50	7.88	5.92	7.52	5.88	6.44
	(11.41)	(7.91)	(17.76)	(12.66)	(16.68)	(16.48)	(18.67)	(26.40)	(14.91)	(19.39)
(c) Nandyal	10.19	20.89	11.97	23.64	16.58	20.34	12.43	9.77	18.08	13.43
	(66.82)	(63.05)	(46.32)	(57.64)	(50.29)	(42.53)	(39.20)	(34.31)	(45.84)	(40.44)
Total III	15.25	33.13	25.84	41.01	32.97	47.82	31.71	28.48	39.44	33.21
	(100.0)	(100.0)	(100.0)	(100.0)	(100.0)	(100.0)	(100.0)	(100.0)	(100.0)	(100.0)
IV ANANTAPUR DISTRICT										
(a) Dharmavaram	23.60	14.18	25.85	36.49	20.97	32.32	20.85	22.15	24.67	22.56
	(28.61)	(18.86)	(31.13)	(31.52)	(25.34)	(33.17)	(30.26)	(42.47)	(34.96)	(35.32)
(b) Hindupur	31.96	23.39	23.41	24.38	11.60	20.37	12.98	12.89	20.70	15.52
	(38.74)	(31.12)	(28.18)	(21.06)	(14.02)	(20.91)	(18.84)	(27.71)	(29.33)	(24.30)
(c) Tadpatri	26.93	37.60	33.80	54.90	50.19	44.75	35.08	17.12	25.20	25.80
	(32.65)	(50.02)	(40.69)	(47.42)	(60.64)	(45.92)	(50.90)	(32.82)	(35.71)	(40.38)
Total IV	82.49	75.17	83.06	115.77	82.76	97.44	68.91	52.16	70.57	63.88
	(100.0)	(100.0)	(100.0)	(100.0)	(100.0)	(100.0)	(100.0)	(100.0)	(100.0)	(100.0)
Total I+II+III+IV	283.96	365.14	360.66	435.27	226.43	336.22	248.92	186.99	265.78	233.90

Note: Figures in BracketS indicate percentage to District Total.
Source: Based on Annual Reports of APCCADB, various Issues.

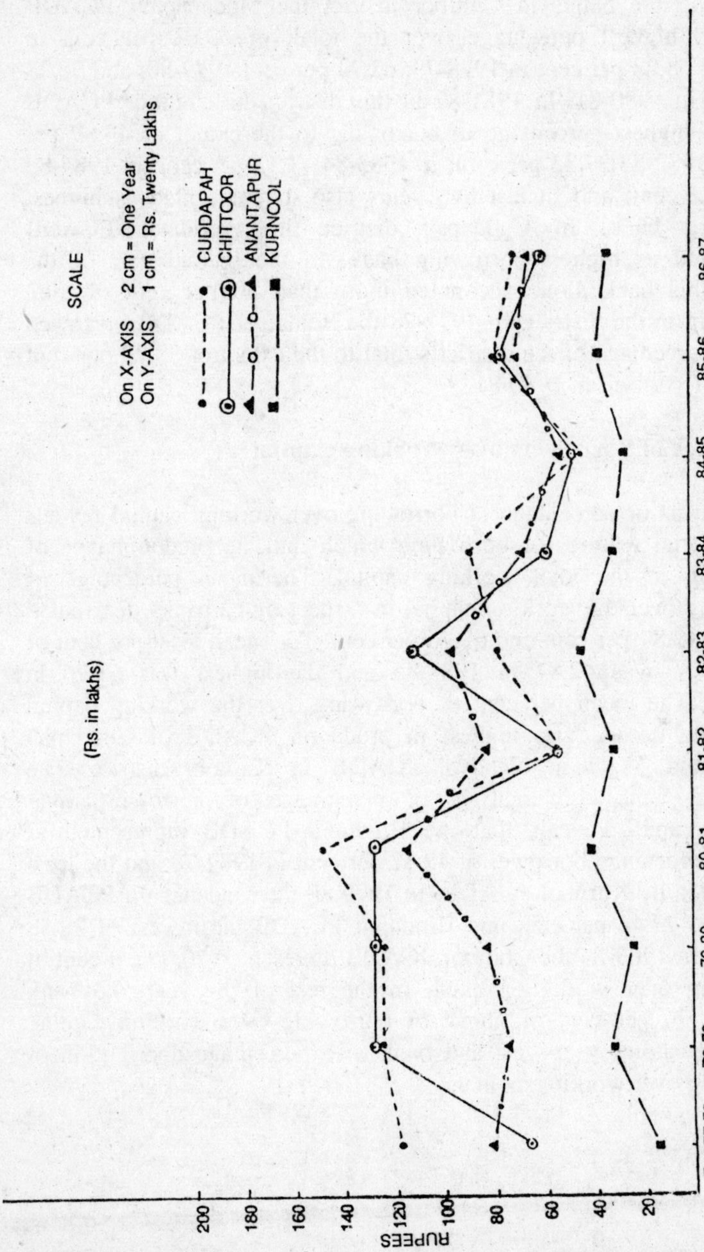

FIG 4.1: Borrowings

Among the banks in Chittoor district the Madanapalli PCADB borrowed highest percentage over the total, of 63.03 per cent in 1977-78; 68.28 per cent in 1978-79; 62.74 per cent 1979-80; and 50.23 per cent in 1980-81. In 1981-82 in this district the Chittoor PCADB recorded highest percentage of borrowing to the extent of 43.89 per cent, in 1982-83 37.35 per cent; in 1983-84 71.13 per cent; in 1984-85 59.96 per cent; and in last two years also it represented as highest borrowing bank. In Cuddapah district the Proddatur PCADB represented as highest borrowing bank. In the second part of the decade this bank alone accounted more than 50 per cent of total borrowing in the district. In 1977-78 the Rajampet PCADB borrowed highest percentage of the district's total to the extent of 38.25 per cent and 42.11 per cent in 1980-81.

Percentage of Borrowing over Working Capital

The analysis of percentage of borrowing over working capital reveals some special features of borrowing which indicate predominance of borrowing in the total working capital. The mean percentage of borrowing over the working capital in respect of 12 banks distributed between 42.87 per cent and 63.76 per cent. The mean least per cent of borrowing was 42.87 in 1984-85 and the highest was 63.76 in 1980-81. The mean per cent of borrowing over the working capital during the decade was highest in proddatur PCADB of Cuddapah district and 57.97 in Nandyal PCADB in Kurnool district. The individual bank-wise analysis of percentage of borrowing over working capital reveals that the Hindupur PCADB represented as highest percentage borrower of 72.32 per cent in 1977-78 and the least represented by Kurnool PCADB. In 1979-80 the Madanapalli PCADB accounted 77.46 per cent and Hindupur PCADB the lowest of 28.58 per cent. In 1983-84 the Chittoor PCADB represented 70.06 per cent of borrowing over working capital. In the rest of the years no bank recorded 70 per cent or above of borrowing over working capital. Table 4.8 shows year-wise and bank-wise percentage distribution of borrowing over working capital.

Analysis of Borrowing

District	Mean Value	CGR	CV
Chittoor	85.47	6.01	40.42
Cuddapah	96.15	7.21	32.89
Kurnool	32.89	5.17	27.08
Anantapur	79.22	3.84	22.55
Region	294.33	5.04	26.27

C.G.R : Compound Growth Rate; *CV :* Co-efficient Variation.

Borrowing Size

In Borrowing size below 25 per cent there were only 2 banks 1977-78, located in Kurnool District, there were two banks in 1981-82 distributed one each in Cuddapah and Anantapur district; in 1983-84 there was only one bank in Chittoor district; in 1984-85 one bank in 1985-86 one bank both in Cuddapah district. In borrowing size between 26 to 60 per cent 75 per cent of banks in 1981-82 fall in this range and 83.34 per cent in 1984-85 and 91.67 per cent in 1986-87 while in borrowing size between 61 per cent and above 66.67 per cent of the total banks come under this in 1980-81. Distribution of banks according to borrowing size is depicted in Table 4.9.

Ratio Analysis

In the preceeding paragraphs, which have been devoted to the discussion of statistical analysis of data. In the previous paragraphs we have highlighted the variations in the growth, variations and calculated other statistical components. In the case of working of co-operative agricultural development banks, a quite distinct type of financial operational information is necessary in modern banking operations. It is intended both for the present members, perspective members, apex bodies, federation, financial institutions, Government and in particular to any co-operator. The farmer member owners who have provided capital to the co-operative bank and others need detailed results of financial analysis. Today a banking industry in co-operative sector, what it is to satisfy is to establish rational relationship between various components and their soundness to be determined on the basis of scientific financial tools to understand how best the co-operative banks are performing. If their financial operations are not on established standards corrective measures can be taken.

TABLE 4.8: Percentage Distribution of Borrowings over working Capital

(Percentage)

S.No.	Name of the Bank	1977-78	78-79	79-80	80-81	81-82	82-83	83-84	84-85	85-86	86-87	Mean
1.	Chittoor	43.99	52.03	47.70	33.29	62.22	72.43	70.06	60.58	67.50	66.52	57.63
2.	Chandragiri	63.75	71.57	73.24	67.99	50.63	59.33	22.32	29.08	65.61	38.39	54.19
3.	Madanapalli	65.00	81.28	77.46	70.10	33.11	57.16	28.20	26.43	38.57	31.49	50.88
4.	Rajampet	55.21	73.29	65.55	69.72	21.20	39.77	54.52	4.25	24.43	34.71	44.27
5.	Cuddapah	65.78	30.00	63.50	60.71	44.21	48.75	53.48	53.09	61.51	56.51	53.75
6.	Proddatur	40.06	70.09	67.69	67.93	48.02	61.62	64.63	56.53	59.16	60.37	59.61
7.	Banaganapalli	25.44	48.83	48.38	56.89	55.67	69.36	59.88	54.96	61.60	59.03	54.00
8.	Kurnool	22.75	9.37	46.36	48.73	48.93	56.94	51.84	55.01	49.08	52.10	44.11
9.	Nandyal	47.59	64.14	51.91	92.42	57.99	61.66	50.32	43.95	58.06	51.61	57.97
10.	Dharmavaram	59.76	46.17	59.26	64.00	50.68	58.51	48.58	49.15	50.98	49.63	53.67
11.	Hindupur	72.32	62.59	28.58	59.90	41.27	54.15	43.59	42.77	53.34	47.16	50.57
12.	Tadpatri	69.83	72.76	67.76	73.43	0.69	62.21	38.25	38.65	47.89	41.03	51.25
	Mean	52.62	56.84	58.12	63.76	42.89	58.49	48.81	42.87	53.14	49.05	52.66

Source: Table 4.7 and 4.18

TABLE 4.9: Distribution of Banks According to Borrowing size

	Below 25%					Between 26% - 60%					61% and above					Total Units
	CHI	CU	KU	AN	T	CHI	CU	KU	AN	T	CHI	CU	KU	AN	T	
1977-78	-	-	2	-	2	1	2	1	1	5	2	1	-	2	5	12
1978-79	-	-	1	-	1	1	1	1	1	4,	2	2	1	2	7	12
1979-80	-	-	-	-	-	1	-	3	2	6	2	3	-	1	6	12
1980-81	-	-	-	-	-	1	-	2	1	4	2	3	1	2	8	12
1981-82	-	1	-	1	2	2	2	3	2	9	1	-	-	-	1	12
1982-83	-	-	-	-	-	2	2	1	2	7	1	1	2	1	5	12
1983-84	1	-	-	-	1	1	2	3	3	9	1	1	-	-	2	12
1984-85	-	1	-	-	1	2	2	3	3	10	1	-	-	-	1	12
1985-86	-	1	-	-	1	1	1	2	3	7	2	1	1	-	4	12
1986-87	-	-	-	-	-	2	3	3	3	11	1	-	-	-	1	12
						Percentage of Borrowing size to total units										
1977-78					16.66%					41.67%					41.67%	100%
1978-79					8.33%					33.33%					58.34%	100%
1979-80					-					50.0%					50.0%	100%
1980-81					-					33.33%					66.67%	100%
1981-82					16.67%					75.00%					8.33%	100%
1982-83					-					58.33%					41.67%	100%
1983-84					8.33%					75.00%					16.67%	100%
1984-85					8.33%					83.34%					8.33%	100%
1985-86					8.33%					58.33%					33.34%	100%
1986-87					—					91.67%					8.33%	100%

CHI :Chittoor; AN : Anantapur; CU : Cuddapah; KU : Kurnool; T : Total

Hence this can be achieved with the help of Ratio Analysis. A ratio is a quotient of two variables or numbers. Ratio analysis is a sound tool of financial analysis even in the case of co-operative banks. According to Webster's, new collegiate Dictionary a ratio is defined as the indicated quotient of two mathematical expressions and as the relationship of two or more things. The ratios measure the relationship between various components which helps the management to take financial decisions.

Leverage

In relation to our study the most appropriate financial tool is leverage or capital structure ratio. This ratio judges the long-term financial position of the banks in co-operative sector. Leverage ratio is calculated with the help of debt and equity figures to determine the proportion of debt in total financing.

Debt – Equity Ratio (D/E Ratio)

The long-term solvency of a co-operative bank is studied with the help of debt-equity ratio. It reflects the relationship between borrowed funds and owners capital or equity. The debt-equity ratio measures the relative claims of outsiders and owners against the co-operative bank's assets. There are different ways to determine the relationship between outside claims and members capital. So there are many variants of debt-equity ratios. One way is to calculate the debt-equity ratio as borrowings divided by the members' equity. Thus

$$\text{Debt-Equity Ratio (D/E Ratio)} = \frac{\text{Long-term Debt}}{\text{Members' equity}}$$

Here debt is considered exclusively the borrowings from the apex bank which are long term borrowings. The members' equity includes the total paid-up share capital of the members.

Hence the debt-equity ratio for the region is arrived at:

$$\text{Debt-equity Ratio} = \frac{233.90}{203.78} = 1.15 \text{ to } 1$$

The ratio of debt to owners equity is 1.15 : 1. This ratio implies that for every one rupee of equity, the co-operative banks in this region raised Rs. 1.15 long-term debt. The relationship can also be expressed by of percentage multiplying by hundred i.e., 115 per cent.

Accordingly, that the long term debt is 115 per cent of equity. In other words it may be inferred that the stake of out side funds are more than the owners' equity.

The debt to equity ratios for each district's total borrowing and members' equity are calculated and results are as follows:

I CHITTOOR DISTRICT

1977-78 $\frac{67.11}{30.36}$ = 2.210:1 or 221.0 per cent

1979-80 $\frac{127.91}{44.32}$ = 2.886:1 or 288.6 per cent

1981-82 $\frac{52.47}{52.54}$ = 0.999:1 or 99.9 per cent

1983-84 $\frac{59.96}{59.84}$ = 1.022:1 or 100.2 per cent

1986-87 $\frac{60.99}{57.05}$ = 1.069:1 or 106.9 per cent

II CUDDAPAH DISTRICT

1977-78 $\frac{119.11}{43.87}$ = 2.715:1 or 271.5 per cent

1979-80 $\frac{123.85}{60.43}$ = 2.049:1 or 204.9 per cent

1981-82 $\frac{58.23}{69.41}$ = 0.839:1 or 83.9 per cent

1983-84 $\frac{88.34}{57.21}$ = 1.544:1 or 154.4 per cent

1986-87 $\frac{75.82}{58.16}$ = 1.304:1 or 130.4 per cent

III KURNOOL DISTRICT

1977-78 $\frac{15.25}{24.36}$ = 0.626:1 or 62.6 per cent

1979-80 $\frac{25.84}{24.43}$ = 1.058:1 or 105.8 per cent

1981-82 $\frac{32.97}{24.46}$ = 1.348:1 or 134.8 per cent

1983-84 $\frac{31.71}{24.63}$ = 1.287:1 or 128.7 per cent

1986-87 $\frac{33.21}{25.73}$ = 1.291:1 or 129.1 per cent

IV ANANTAPUR DISTRICT

1977-78 $\frac{82.49}{35.70}$ = 2.311:1 or 231.1 per cent

1979-80 $\frac{83.06}{44.72}$ = 1.857:1 or 185.7 per cent

1981-82 $\frac{82.76}{55.76}$ = 1.484:1 or 148.4 per cent

1983-84 $\frac{68.91}{61.01}$ = 1.129:1 or 112.9 per cent

1986-87 $\frac{63.88}{62.84}$ = 1.016:1 or 101.6 per cent

V REGION
Total

1977-78	$\frac{283.96}{134.29}$	= 2.115:1	or	211.5 per cent
1979-80	$\frac{360.66}{173.90}$	= 2.074:1	or	207.4 per cent
1981-82	$\frac{226.43}{202.17}$	= 1.120:1	or	112.0 per cent
1983-84	$\frac{248.92}{202.69}$	= 1.228:1	or	122.8 per cent
1986-87	$\frac{233.90}{203.78}$	= 1.148.1	or	114.8 per cent

Interpretation of Ratios

The debt-equity in relation to co-operative banks is a very useful instrument of financial analysis to see the financial structure of banks. Its utility cannot be overemphasised from the view point of illiterate members, apex boxy, financial institutions, depositors, and others interested persons. The above ratios reflect the relative contribution of creditors and owners of a co-operative bank in its financing pattern. A higher ratio reveals a large share of funds provided by the outsiders or apex bank relatively to the owner members. This proportion indicates larger claim against the assets of the bank. Contrary to it a low ratio states smaller stake of funds by way of debt. The D/E ratio implies the margin of safety to the lender. For instance if the D/E ratio is 1:2, it means that for every one rupee of funded debt, the bank has two rupees of members' equity. To say in other sense that debt is half or fifty per cent of equity.

In a co-operative bank where members' equity base is poor the practice is to use more debt as possible. A D/E ratio of 1:3 regard a rare instance. A ratio of 1:1 is appeared marginally in a few co-operative banks. It is usual to find co-operative banks 2:1 or in case of many banks even 3:1. The only reason for such heavy stake of debt is that because of poor capital base of the member owners, the banks have necessarily to depend by and large on the financial institutions which provide bulk of the funds to the primary banks in turn to be lent to the members. This primarily caused the capital structure or leverage of co-operative banks weak and unsound. This is not a sound and prudent financial practice. On the other hand borrowers are finding it difficult to repay instalment loan due to crop failure, drought etc. this leads to overdues.

In the region in 1977-78 the percentage of long term debt to equity was 211.5 per cent. In 1979-80 the debt was 207.4 per cent of equity. In Chittoor district the banks contracted long-term debt to the extent of 221 per cent in 1977-78 and 288.6 per cent in 1979-80. In Cuddapah district in 1977-78 the long-term debt was 271.5 per cent and in 1979-80 204.9 per cent. In Kurnool district debt equity position is better comparing Chittoor and Cuddapah district. But still they recorded 100 and above 100 per cent debt. The banks in Anantapur district in 1977-78 involved 231.1 per cent debt capital.

The individual bank-wise analysis reveals that the banks which have debt equity ratio 3:1 or even above slightly. To support in 1977-78 the percentage of debt equity ratio in Madanapalli PCADB, Chittoor district accounted 325 per cent. In the same year the Rajampet PCADB recorded 336 per cent. In 1978-79 the long-term debt was 461 per cent of equity in the case of Madanapalli PCADB. In 1979-80 the Chandragiri and Madanapalli PCADBs represented debt of 305 per cent and 362 per cent of equity respectively from 1980-81 to 1984-85 no bank contracted a debt of 300 per cent and above. In 1985-86 the Chandragiri PCADB's debt was 334 per cent of equity. In 1986-87 there was no bank whose debt constituting 300 and above per cent. Year-wise analysis reveals that there are many banks in each year having debt per cent 200 and above in case of many banks. The bank-wise and year-wise debt-equity ratios are shown in Table 4.10.

The banks having long-terms debt 200 per cent and above to equity are identified and distributed year-wise in Table 4.11.

The table reveals that there were 7 co-operative banks availed debt 200 per cent and above in 1977-78 and similar number of banks in 1980-81. The significant feature is that there was no bank having debt of 200 and above per cent of equity in the year 1984-85. There was only one such bank in 1986-87, 1983-84 and 1981-82.

Debt to Total Equity

Another approach to the calculation of the debt-equity ratio is to relate total equity to total long-term debt. This ratio considers both members' equity and also paidup share capital contributed by the State Government. Since the Government is participating in the paid up

TABLE 4.10: Bank-wise and year-wise Debt to Equity Ratios

(To Rupee one)

S.No.	Name of the Bank	1977-78	78-79	79-80	80-81	81-82	82-83	83-84	84-85	85-86	86-87
1.	Chittoor	0.93	1.28	1.08	2.76	1.91	2.99	2.62	1.72	2.30	2.21
2.	Chandragiri	2.15	2.89	3.05	2.33	1.13	1.91	0.38	0.54	3.34	0.86
3.	Madanapalli	3.25	4.61	3.62	2.45	0.52	1.38	0.41	0.37	0.66	0.48
4.	Rajampet	3.36	2.85	2.02	2.41	0.70	0.69	1.25	0.05	0.34	0.55
5.	Cuddapah	2.10	2.03	1.86	1.65	0.85	1.02	1.23	1.20	1.70	1.38
6.	Proddatur	2.74	2.54	2.25	2.25	0.98	1.71	1.94	1.38	1.53	1.91
7.	Banaganapalli	0.37	1.37	1.02	1.44	1.38	2.49	1.67	1.36	1.78	1.60
8.	Kurnool	0.33	0.53	0.97	1.08	1.08	1.48	1.22	1.36	1.05	1.21
9.	Nandyal	1.00	1.87	1.13	2.07	1.44	1.68	1.06	0.82	1.44	1.11
10.	Dharmavaram	1.64	0.94	1.59	1.92	1.11	1.55	1.01	1.03	1.11	1.05
11.	Hindupur	2.88	1.56	1.70	1.61	0.76	1.32	0.83	0.80	1.22	0.96
12.	Tadpatri	2.63	2.96	2.30	2.97	2.34	1.89	1.42	0.68	0.98	1.01
	Mean (x)	1.95	2.12	1.88	2.00	1.18	1.68	1.25	0.94	1.45	1.19
Percentage		195%	212%	188%	200%	188%	168%	125%	94%	145%	119%

Source: Table 4.2 and 4.7

TABLE 4.11: Banks with Debt 200 Per cent and Above of Equity

(Percentage)

S.No.	Name of the Bank	1977-78	78-79	79-80	80-81	81-82	82-83	83-84	84-85	85-86	86-87
1.	Chittoor	-	-	-	276	-	299	262	-	230	221
2.	Chandragiri	215	289	305	233	-	-	-	-	334	-
3.	Madanapalli	325	461	362	245	-	-	-	-	-	-
4.	Rajampet	336	285	202	241	-	-	-	-	-	-
5.	Cuddapah	210	203	-	-	-	-	-	-	-	-
6.	Proddatur	274	254	225	225	-	-	-	-	-	-
7.	Banaganapalli	-	-	-	-	-	249	-	-	-	-
8.	Kurnool	-	-	-	-	-	-	-	-	-	-
9.	Nandyal	-	-	-	207	-	-	-	-	-	-
10.	Dharmavaram	-	-	-	-	-	-	-	-	-	-
11.	Hindupur	288	-	-	-	-	-	-	-	-	-
12.	Tadpatri	263	296	230	297	234	-	-	-	-	-
	No. of Banks	7	6	5	7	1	2	1	-	2	1

Source: Calculated Based on Earlier Tables.

share capital, this part of the paid up share capital is also treated as equity. Thus total equity is equivalent to members' paid up share capital (MPSC) plus Government's share of paid up share capital (GPSC). Under this variant approach of debt equity ratio it is arrived by dividing long-term debt by total equity. This ratio has some implication from the view point of the debtor and the creditor. In other words the ratio reflects a relatively higher contribution of owners comparing to earlier debt equity ratio. The difference between this approach and the first approach is basically in respect of treatment of composition of owners equity. The former approach excludes Government's portion of paid up capital, this approach includes it in the denominator (members' equity).

The question is whether the equity of the Government should be included in owners debt or not for the purpose of calculation of debt equity ratio. How should this equity be treated? should it be included in the equity? To include or not will depend upon object for which leverage ratio is being computed. In order to examine the financial solvency of a co-operative bank in terms of its capacity the Governments equity should also be included in the members' equity. For other purposes it may be excluded keeping in view the object for which a ratio is being calculated:

Thus,

$$\text{Debt Equity Ratio} \quad \frac{\text{Long Term Debt}}{\text{Total Equity.}}$$

According to this the ratio for the region in 1986-87 is calculated with the help of:

$$\text{Debt Equity Ratio} = \frac{233.90}{208.74} = 1.120:1$$

or = 1.120 or 112 per cent

The 1.120 to 1 debt equity ratio implies that for every one rupee of equity the banks in this region have raised Rs. 1.12 long-term debt or that the long-term debt was 112 per cent of equity.

This approach reveals that difference in relative contribution and capital structure ratios. In the case of first approach the debt equity ratio was 1.15:1 while in this approach it was 1.120:1 or alternatively 115 and 112 per cent.

Under this approach the debt equity ratios for each district's total borrowing and total equity are calculated and presented as follows in uniform way which facilitates to make comparison as to difference between these two approaches.

I CHITTOOR DISTRICT

1977-78	$\frac{67.11}{30.71}$	= 2.185:1	or	218.5 per cent
1979-80	$\frac{127.91}{44.67}$	= 2.863:1	or	286.3 per cent
1981-82	$\frac{52.47}{52.89}$	= 0.992:1	or	99.2 per cent
1983-84	$\frac{59.96}{63.57}$	= 0.943:1	or	94.3 per cent
1986-87	$\frac{60.99}{60.36}$	= 1.010:1	or	101.0 per cent

II CUDDAPAH DISTRICT

1977-78	$\frac{119.11}{44.22}$	= 2.694:1	or	269.4 per cent
1979-80	$\frac{123.85}{60.78}$	= 2.038:1	or	203.8 per cent
1981-82	$\frac{58.23}{69.76}$	= 0.835:1	or	83.5 per cent
1983-84	$\frac{88.34}{57.56}$	= 1.535:1	or	153.5 per cent
1986-87	$\frac{75.82}{58.51}$	= 1.296:1	or	129.6 per cent

III KURNOOL DISTRICT

1977-78	$\frac{15.25}{24.86}$	= 0.613:1	or	61.3	per cent
1979-80	$\frac{25.84}{24.93}$	= 1.036:1	or	103.6	per cent
1981-82	$\frac{32.97}{24.96}$	= 1.321:1	or	132.1	per cent
1983-84	$\frac{31.71}{25.13}$	= 1.261:1	or	126.1	per cent
1986-87	$\frac{33.21}{26.23}$	= 1.266:1	or	126.6	per cent

IV ANANTAPUR DISTRICT

1977-78	$\frac{82.49}{36.05}$	= 2.288:1	or	288.8	per cent
1979-80	$\frac{83.06}{45.07}$	= 1.843:1	or	184.3	per cent
1981-82	$\frac{82.76}{56.11}$	= 1.475:1	or	147.5	per cent
1983-84	$\frac{68.91}{61.81}$	= 1.115:1	or	111.5	per cent
1986-87	$\frac{63.88}{63.64}$	= 1.004:1	or	100.4	per cent

V REGION

Total 1977-78	$\frac{283.96}{135.84}$	= 2.090:1	or	209.0	per cent
1979-80	$\frac{360.66}{175.45}$	= 2.056:1	or	205.6	per cent

1981-82 $\frac{226.43}{203.72}$ = 1.111:1 or 111.1 per cent

1983-84 $\frac{248.92}{208.07}$ = 1.196:1 or 119.6 per cent

1986-87 $\frac{233.90}{208.74}$ = 1.116.1 or 111.6 per cent

Inferences

This ratio is giving the relationship between long-term debt and total members' equity. According to this approach the capital structure ratio is a variant of the debt equity ratio first approached. But this ratio also gives results similar but virtually with variation. For instance the debt equity ratio under this method in term of percentage was 211.5 per cent in 1977-78 while under the second method it was 209.0 per cent for the entire Rayalaseema region. Thus there is a difference of 2.5 per cent between these two approaches. It implies that the debt in relation to equity is reduced by 2.5 per cent. The difference in the percentage of debt equity ratios and debt total equity ratios and the mean for the region covering all 12 banks is presented in the following term for easy comparison.

TABLE 4.12: Analysis of Ratios

Year	Debt-Equity Ratio		Debt to Total Equity Ratios	
	Mean Ratio	%	Mean Ratio	%
1977-78	1.95	195	1.93	193
1978-79	2.12	212	2.09	209
1979-80	1.88	188	1.86	186
1980-81	2.00	200	1.98	198
1981-82	1.18	118	1.17	117
1982-83	1.68	168	1.63	163
1983-84	1.25	125	1.23	123
1984-85	0.94	94	0.92	92
1985-86	1.45	145	1.35	135
1986-87	1.19	119	1.15	115

Debt equity Ratios for each Co-operative bank during the period are indicated in Table 4.13.

TABLE 4.13: Debt to Total Equity Ratios

(To Rupees one)

S.No.	Name of the Bank	1977-78	78-79	79-80	80-81	81-82	82-83	83-84	84-85	85-86	86-87
1.	Chittoor	0.92	1.27	1.07	2.73	1.89	2.96	2.60	1.71	2.29	2.20
2.	Chandragiri	2.11	2.84	3.01	2.31	1.12	1.56	0.31	0.44	2.26	0.67
3.	Madanapalli	3.23	4.58	3.60	2.44	0.51	1.37	0.41	0.37	0.65	0.48
4.	Rajampet	3.36	2.85	2.02	2.41	0.70	0.69	1.25	0.05	0.34	0.55
5.	Cuddapah	2.08	2.02	1.85	1.64	0.84	1.01	1.22	1.20	1.69	1.38
6.	Proddatur	2.69	2.50	2.22	2.23	0.97	1.69	1.92	1.37	1.52	1.60
7.	Banaganapalli	0.36	1.01	0.99	1.40	1.34	2.42	1.62	1.32	1.73	1.55
8.	Kurnool	0.32	0.50	0.92	1.02	1.03	1.42	1.16	1.31	1.01	1.16
9.	Nandyal	1.00	1.87	1.13	2.07	1.44	1.68	1.06	0.82	1.44	1.11
10.	Dharmavaram	1.64	0.94	1.59	1.92	1.11	1.55	1.01	1.03	1.11	1.04
11.	Hindupur	2.82	1.79	1.67	1.58	0.74	1.30	0.82	0.79	1.20	1.06
12.	Tadpatri	2.61	2.94	2.28	2.95	2.33	1.89	1.38	0.67	0.96	0.99
	Mean (x)	1.93	2.09	1.86	1.98	1.17	1.63	1.23	0.92	1.35	1.15
	Percentage	193%	209%	186%	198%	117%	163%	123%	92%	135%	115%

Source: Based on Table 4.2, 4.3, 4.7.

TABLE 4.14: Ratios of Borrowings to owned Funds

S.No.	Name of the Bank	1977-78	78-79	79-80	80-81	81-82	82-83	83-84	84-85	85-86	86-87
1.	Chittoor	0.79	1.08	0.91	2.36	16.46	2.63	2.34	1.54	2.08	1.99
2.	Chandragiri	1.76	2.52	2.74	2.12	1.02	1.46	0.29	0.41	1.91	0.62
3.	Madanapalli	1.86	4.34	3.43	2.34	0.49	1.33	0.39	0.36	0.63	0.46
4.	Rajampet	1.23	2.74	1.90	2.30	0.67	0.66	1.20	0.04	0.32	0.53
5.	Cuddapah	1.92	1.89	1.74	1.55	0.79	0.95	1.15	1.13	1.60	1.30
6.	Proddatur	2.51	2.34	2.06	2.12	0.92	1.61	1.83	1.30	1.45	1.52
7.	Banaganapalli	0.34	0.95	0.94	1.32	1.26	2.26	1.49	1.22	1.60	1.44
8.	Kurnool	0.29	0.47	0.85	0.95	0.96	1.32	1.08	1.22	0.96	1.09
9.	Nandyal	0.91	1.79	1.08	1.98	1.38	1.61	1.01	0.78	1.38	1.07
10.	Dharmavaram	1.49	0.85	1.45	1.78	1.03	1.45	0.94	0.97	1.04	0.99
11.	Hindupur	2.61	1.67	1.57	1.49	0.70	1.23	0.77	0.75	1.14	0.09
12.	Tadpatri	2.32	2.67	2.10	2.76	2.20	1.77	1.31	0.63	0.92	0.05
	Mean (x)	1.50	1.94	1.73	1.92	2.32	1.52	1.15	0.86	1.25	0.93
	Region	1.58	2.14	1.92	2.04	1.04	1.73	1.13	0.83	1.21	1.06

Source: Based on Table 4.15, and 4.7.

Ratio of Borrowing to Owned Funds

Table 4.14 discloses the ratios of borrowings to owned funds during the years from 1977-78 to 1986-87. The ratio of borrowing of co-operative banks in Rayalaseema region ranges between 0.93 and 2.32 respectively in 1986-87 and 1981-82. The mean ratio of borrowing to owned funds was 1.50:1 in 1977-78; 1.94:1 in 1978-79; 1.73:1 in 1979-80; 1.92:1 in 1980-81; 2.32:1 in 1981-82; 1.52:1 in 1982-83: 1.15:1 in 1983-84; 0.86:1 1984-85; 1.25:1 in 1985-86 and 0.93:1 in 1986-87. The ratio of borrowing was highest in 1977-78 of 2.61:1 in Hindupur PCADB, 2.51:1 in the case of Proddatur PCADB and 2.32:1 in the case of Tadpatri PCADB. The proportion of borrowings to owned funds had been, however, low in respect of many co-operative banks in 1986-87 comparing earlier years. The co-operative bank-wise and year-wise ratios of borrowings to owned funds can be observed from the Table 4.14.

Owned Funds

Really speaking the owned funds should be the only source of working capital available to be lent to the members according to the co-operative principles to be self-reliant. But actually it is not so, because of twin causes of poor financial base of the members and on the other hand requirement of more funds to be invested in long-term production activities. And hence the primary co-operative banks have necessarily to depend more on other than owned funds to achieve its objects. Though owned funds are less than borrowings but constitute the real source for improving and strengthening the financial position of these banks. The extent of availability of owned funds determine the extent of borrowing capacity from financial institutions. The external investors or lenders will judge the financial soundness of these banks in terms of owned funds. Thus the owned funds serve as a cushion to external borrowings. A high percentage progress of building owned funds is a yard stick to measure financial performance and efficiency of management of co-operative banks.

The term owned funds comprise of as follows:

Total members' paid up share capital
Total Government's paid up share capital

Reserve funds
Other retained profits
Deposits
Miscellaneous

Broadly, owned funds consist of above components there may be small proportion of other sources like gifts, donations, subsidy, rehabilitation and other allowances. Share Capital is an important component in the owned funds of co-operative bank on which no servicing cost is payable like interest, except dividend when declared when sufficient amount of profits are available. The Reserve Bank of India or NABARD have been making available funds through State Government. Ploughing back of profits is yet another internal source of owned funds. The reserve fund is created by transferring a fixed percentage of profits from the profit and loss account. Reserve fund is thus an effective source of working capital. The collection of admission fees from the members constitutes a part of owned funds but very small amount.

Table 4.15 indicates the progress of owned funds of the co-operative banks in 12 banks of 4 districts of Rayalaseema region. The total owned funds of the co-operative banks in this region were Rs. 180.22 lakhs in 1977-78 which increased to Rs. 221.28 lakhs in 1986-87, thus shown an increase of Rs. 33.06 lakhs only, over a period of decade. In case of co-operative banks in Chittoor districts, the owned funds were Rs. 64.50 lakhs in 1986-87 which increased from Rs. 43.62 lakhs in 1977-78 representing an increase of Rs. 20.88 lakhs. Thus in this district the percentage of owned funds over the total of the region accounted 29.15 per cent. The Madanapalli PCADB was the only bank which had 52.22 per cent of total owned funds of the district in 1977-78 and 51.34 per cent in 1985-86. All other co-operative banks in this district mobilised owned funds less than 50 per cent.

In Cuddapah district the banks' owned fund in 1986-87 were Rs. 61.56 lakhs representing 27.82 per cent of the total owned funds in the region. The significant feature is that during 4 years the owned funds of the banks were higher when comparing the owned funds during the rest of six years. In other words the total owned funds in this district were Rs. 70.20 lakhs in 1977-78; Rs. 73.98 lakhs in 1980-81; Rs. 73.53 lakhs in 1981-82; and Rs. 74.47 lakhs in 1982-83. The year 1978-79 recorded lowest amount of owned funds of Rs. 55.57 lakhs. In remaining four years the owned fund ranged between Rs. 60.61 lakhs and Rs. 64.54 lakhs.

TABLE 4.15: Owned funds

(Rs. in lakhs)

S.No. Name of the Bank	1977-78	78-79	79-80	80-81	81-82	82-83	83-84	84-85	85-86	86-87
I CHITTOOR DIST										
(a) Chittoor	12.17	12.28	12.03	13.35	13.99	15.90	18.23	18.28	19.98	18.83
	(27.90)	(28.33)	(24.66)	(23.69)	(24.52)	(23.90)	(26.98)	(26.98)	(34.33)	(29.19)
(b) Chandragiri	8.67	10.88	13.40	15.37	15.42	20.22	19.63	19.41	8.34	15.79
	(19.88)	(25.10)	(27.47)	(27.27)	(27.03)	(30.39)	(20.05)	(28.65)	(14.33)	(24.48)
(c) Madanapalli	22.78	20.19	23.35	27.64	27.64	30.41	29.71	30.06	29.88	29.88
	(52.22)	(46.57)	(47.87)	(49.04)	(48.45)	(45.71)	(43.97)	(44.37)	(51.34)	(46.33)
Total I	43.62	43.35	48.78	56.36	57.05	66.53	67.57	67.75	58.20	64.50
	(100.0)	(100.0)	(100.0)	(100.0)	(100.0)	(100.0)	(100.0)	(100.0)	(100.0)	(100.0)
II CUDDAPAH DIST.										
(a) Rajampet	36.96	16.97	21.96	27.35	27.57	28.35	13.78	13.51	12.62	13.30
	(52.78)	(30.54)	(34.03)	(36.97)	(37.49)	(38.07)	(22.74)	(21.94)	(20.20)	(21.60)
(b) Cuddapah	16.04	18.68	20.09	21.34	20.95	20.86	20.29	21.18	22.01	21.16
	(22.91)	(33.62)	(31.13)	(28.85)	(28.49)	(28.01)	(33.48)	(34.39)	(35.22)	(34.37)
(c) Proddatur	17.02	19.92	22.49	25.29	25.01	25.26	26.54	26.89	27.86	27.10
	(24.31)	(35.84)	(34.84)	(34.18)	(34.02)	(33.92)	(43.78)	(43.67)	(44.58)	(44.03)
Total II	70.02	55.57	64.54	73.98	73.53	74.47	60.61	61.58	62.49	61.56
	(100.0)	(100.0)	(100.0)	(100.0)	(100.0)	(100.0)	(100.0)	(100.0)	(100.0)	(100.0)

Contd.

TABLE 4.15 *Contd.*

(*Rs. in lakhs*)

S.No. Name of the Bank	1977-78	78-79	79-80	80-81	81-82	82-83	83-84	84-85	85-86	86-87
III KURNOOL DIST.										
(a) Banaganapalli	9.73	10.08	9.90	9.23	8.67	8.66	8.95	9.17	9.65	9.26
	(36.22)	(36.82)	(37.51)	(34.66)	(32.82)	(31.76)	(33.50)	(33.01)	(33.50)	(33.33)
(b) Kurnool	5.91	5.62	5.40	5.46	5.74	5.96	5.50	6.15	6.10	5.92
	(22.00)	(20.53)	(20.46)	(20.50)	(21.73)	(21.86)	(20.58)	(22.14)	(21.17)	(21.31)
(c) Nandyal	11.22	11.68	11.09	11.94	12.01	12.65	12.27	12.46	13.06	12.60
	(41.78)	(42.65)	(42.03)	(44.84)	(45.45)	(46.38)	(45.92)	(44.85)	(45.34)	(46.36)
Total II	26.86	27.38	26.39	26.63	26.42	27.27	26.72	27.78	28.81	27.78
	(100.0)	(100.0)	(100.0)	(100.0)	(100.0)	(100.0)	(100.0)	(100.0)	(100.0)	(100.0)
IV ANANTAPUR DIST.										
(a) Dharmavaram	15.89	16.53	17.77	20.53	20.41	22.32	22.07	22.92	23.72	22.90
	(40.01)	(37.07)	(36.46)	(36.20)	(34.14)	(34.77)	(33.58)	(34.03)	(34.25)	(33.96)
(b) Hindupur	12.23	13.98	14.89	16.32	16.51	16.51	16.80	17.25	18.11	17.39
	(30.79)	(31.35)	(30.55)	(28.77)	(27.62)	(25.88)	(25.56)	(25.61)	(26.15)	(25.79)
(c) Tadpatri	11.60	14.08	16.08	19.87	22.86	25.26	26.86	27.18	27.42	27.15
	(29.20)	(31.58)	(32.99)	(35.03)	(38.24)	(39.35)	(40.86)	(40.36)	(39.60)	(40.25)
Total IV	39.72	44.59	48.74	56.72	59.78	64.19	65.73	67.35	69.25	67.44
	(100.0)	(100.0)	(100.0)	(100.0)	(100.0)	(100.0)	(100.0)	(100.0)	(100.0)	(100.0)
Total I+II+III+IV	180.22	170.89	188.45	213.69	216.78	194.28	220.63	224.46	218.75	221.28

Note: Figures in bracket indicate percentage to district total.
Source: Based on Annual Reports of APCCADB, various issues.

The banks in Anantapur district had more owned funds than the other three district claiming 30.48 per cent over the total of the region in 1986-87. Over the period of 10 years the owned funds increased by Rs. 27.72 lakhs, from Rs. 39.72 lakhs in 1977-78 to Rs. 67.44 lakhs in 1986-87.

The banks in Kurnool district rank fourth place in respect of owned funds among the other districts in the region. The range of difference during the decade 1977-78 to 1986-87 was only Rs. 1.39 lakhs. In 1977-78 the amount under this head of account was only Rs. 26.86 lakhs which marginally went up to Rs. 27.78 lakhs and the amount was maximum in 1985-86 of Rs. 28.81 lakhs. The owned fund particulars of co-operative banks alongwith percentage share of each bank are furnished in Table 4.15.

Owned Funds to Working Capital

The analysis of percentage share of owned funds to working capital reveals some interesting features the extent of owned funds in the pool of working capital. The figures show smaller proportion of owned funds in the working capital. But, however, the importance of owned funds cannot be overemphasised and needs no special elucidation. The quantitative relationship between owned funds and working capital in general shows nearly 50 per cent share of owned funds in the working capital. In the year 1986-87 in Chittoor district the percentage of owned funds to working capital was 51.39; in Cuddapah district it was 44.82 per cent; 45.56 per cent in Kurnool district, the least of other districts and 47.75 per cent in case of Anantapur district. The percentage of aggregate of owned funds over the aggregate of working capital in the region was 47.58 per cent.

The year-wise and district-wise percentages of owned funds to working capital figures are arranged in Table 4.16.

The above table reveals that the percentage of owned funds to working capital was highest of 63.79 per cent in Kurnool district in 1977-78; 37.23 per cent in Anantapur district in 1978-79; 50.61 per cent in Kurnool district in 1979-80; 39.37 per cent in 1980-81; 52.11 per cent in Chittoor district in 1981-82; 48.49 per cent in Cuddapah district in 1982-83; 52.98 per cent in Chittoor district in 1983-84; 59.12 per cent in 1984-85; 49.53 per cent in Anantapur district in 1985-86 and 51.39 per cent in Chittoor district in 1986-87. In all over a period of ten years the banks in Chittoor district scored more owned funds for four years, in Kurnool district for three years, in Anantapur for two years and in Cuddapah for one year.

TABLE 4.16: Percentage of Owned Funds to Working Capital

(Percentages)

Year	Chittoor	Cuddapah	Kurnool	Anantapur	Region
1977-78	39.39	29.67*	(63.79)	32.50	35.26
1978-79	25.24	22.45*	34.14	(37.23)	27.60
1979-80	27.61*	34.26	(50.61)	27.78	31.80
1980-81	23.96*	33.10	(39.37)	(32.88)	30.58
1981-82	(52.11)	42.48	44.49	41.94*	44.75
1982-83	37.30	(48.49)	36.32*	38.95	33.97
1983-84	(52.98)	40.69	45.73	39.98*	44.19
1984-85	(59.12)	50.90	49.38*	56.36	(54.57)
1985-86	43.31	43.98	42.21*	(49.53)	45.15
1986-87	(51.39)	44.82*	45.56	47.75	47.58

Note: Figures in bracket indicate highest among districts and region.
* Indicate lowest.

The analysis of owned funds gives the following results:

TABLE 4.17: Analysis of Owned Fund

District	Mean	CGR	CV
Chittoor	57.37	4.92	16.51
Cuddapah	65.84	(-)0.70	10.12
Kurnool	27.20	0.58	2.80
Anantapur	57.35	7.39	21.51
Region	204.94	2.73	9.56

CGR : Compound Growth Rate.
CV : Co-efficient of Variation.

Working Capital

In case of co-operative rural credit banks bulk of funds are needed not for investment in permanent fixed assets like capital intensive, productive organisations but funds are needed for loaning operations. And hence the pattern of financial structure is not that of fixed capital but working capital. The working capital is regarded as the life blood of a rural credit banks. An adequate amount of working capital can do much to ensure disbursement of required loan at right time to the farmers to achieve the objects of co-operation. An efficient management of working capital can lead not only to create permanent production assets but also improves economic conditions of the farmers which ultimately contributes to increase agricultural productivity. Much funds have been made available to these banks both by the Government and the financial institutions for long term loaning operations.

The study of working capital potential of these banks is of major importance to members and financing agencies because it has close and direct relationship with the loaning operations. Broadly, working capital comprises of that part of the liquid assets of a bank, particularly the cash. The quantum of working capital is a measure of margin for timely supply of required credit. In other words working capital may be considered as aggregate funds available for disbursement as well as to repay the amount borrowed from the apex bank. Mobilisation of funds from any source that results in an increasing lending operations is a working capital. It reflects inflow of funds.

Raising funds by issue of equity shares play the most significant role in providing working capital finance. In view of poor financial base of the members, the Government has been participating in the share capital of a co-operative bank, which increases working capital. The next source of working capital financing in case of a co-operative bank is to accept deposits both from members and non-members. The issue of tapping of small savings of the members is one of the principles of co-operative banking.

Funds from loaning operations, borrowings from the sister co-operative institutions, issue of additional equity on admission of members, admission fee, gifts, donations, subsidy are the important sources of working capital. Among the various sources of working capital a substantial part of the working capital has been coming from apex bank.

The working capital of the co-operative banks is shown in Table 4.18. The table reveals that the total amount of working capital in the region was Rs. 465.08 lakhs in 1986-87, which shows an increase of Rs. 53.72 lakhs over 1984-85. In the year 1977-78 the amount of working capital was Rs. 511.06 lakhs. These figures show wide fluctuations in the working capital. For instance in 1982-83 it was Rs. 571.84 lakhs and in 1983-84 Rs. 499.33 lakhs, while in 1980-81 it was Rs. 698.84 lakhs. The main reasons for the fluctuation in the

TABLE 4.18: Working Capital

(Rs. in lakhs)

S.No.	Name of the Bank	1977-78	78-79	79-80	80-81	81-82	82-83	83-84	84-85	85-86	86-87
1.	Chittoor	21.73	25.60	23.00	94.79	37.02	57.68	60.88	46.37	61.48	56.24
2.	Chandragiri	23.92	38.27	50.08	48.01	31.13	49.72	25.27	27.37	24.25	25.63
3.	Madanapalli	65.08	107.86	103.61	92.43	41.32	70.98	41.38	40.86	48.64	43.63
	Sub Total	110.73	171.73	176.69	235.23	109.47	178.53	127.53	114.60	134.37	125.50
4.	Rajampet	82.52	63.53	63.74	90.31	87.42	47.07	30.30	14.11	16.70	20.37
5.	Cuddapah	46.88	117.44	55.04	54.32	37.55	40.70	43.62	44.96	57.18	48.59
6.	Proddatur	106.61	66.59	69.61	78.85	48.11	65.81	75.03	61.92	68.21	68.39
	Sub Total	236.01	247.56	188.39	223.48	173.08	153.58	148.95	120.99	142.09	137.35
7.	Banaganapalli	13.05	19.70	19.18	21.41	19.56	28.26	22.31	20.36	25.13	22.60
8.	Kurnool	7.65	27.94	9.90	10.65	11.24	13.84	11.42	13.67	11.98	12.36
9.	Nandyal	21.41	32.57	23.06	35.58	28.59	32.99	24.70	22.23	31.14	26.02
	Sub Total	42.11	80.21	52.14	67.64	59.39	75.09	58.43	56.26	68.25	60.98
10.	Dharmavaram	39.49	30.71	43.62	57.02	41.38	55.24	42.92	45.07	43.39	45.46
11.	Hindupur	44.19	37.37	81.92	40.70	28.11	37.62	29.78	30.14	38.81	32.91
12.	Tadpatri	38.53	51.68	49.88	74.77	73.05	71.93	91.72	14.30	52.62	62.88
	Sub Total	122.21	119.76	175.42	172.49	142.54	164.79	164.42	119.51	139.82	141.25
	Grand Total	511.06	619.26	592.64	698.84	484.48	571.84	499.33	411.36	484.53	465.08

Source: Based on Annual Reports of APCCADB, Various Issues

amount of working capital fund are repayment by the borrowers, disbursement by the apex bank to the primary banks, instalment recoveries etc.

In Chittoor district the amount of working capital was Rs. 125.50 lakhs in 1986-87 constituting 26.98 per cent of the total in the region. The year-wise analysis shows that it was 21.67 per cent in 1977-78; 27.73 per cent in 1978-79; 29.81 per cent in 1979-80; 33.66 per cent in 1980-81; 22.60 per cent in 1981-82; 31.19 per cent in 1982-83, 25.54 per cent in 1983-84; 27.86 per cent in 1984-85; and 27.73 per cent in 1985-86.

The banks in Cuddapah district had working capital constituting respectively from 1977-78 to 1986-87 46.18 per cent; 39.98 per cent; 31.79 per cent; 31.98 per cent; 35.72 per cent; 26.86 per cent; 29.83 per cent; 29.41 per cent; 29.32 per cent; and 29.53 per cent.

The percentage of working capital over total working capital in the region in Kurnool district was 8.24 per cent in 1977-78; 12.95 per cent in 1978-79; 8.80 per cent in 1979-80; 9.68 per cent in 1980-81; 12.26 per cent in 1981-82; 13.13 per cent in 1982-83; 11.70 per cent in 1983-84; 13.68 per cent in 1984-85; 14.09 per cent in 1985-86; and 13.11 per cent in 1986-87.

The proportionate of working capital over the total of the region that the banks in Anantapur district had during the period under review year-wise accounted 23.91 per cent; 19.34 per cent; 29.60 per cent; 24.68 per cent; 29.42 per cent; 28.82 per cent; 32.93 per cent; 29.05 per cent; 28.86 per cent; and 30.37 per cent; respectively from 1977-88 to 1986-87.

Repayments out of Borrowings

Repayments by the primaries to the apex bank as against borrowing represents the capacity of banks to pay back to the apex bank. The central bank extends credit to the primaries so as to enable them to disburse to the members. The repayment capacity of the banks is determined on the basis of instalment loan paid by the members to the primary banks. In turn the farmers repaying capacity would depend upon so many factors like yield of crop, price for commodities, creation and utilisation of production assets created out of loan and incremental income generated.

The primary co-operative banks have not been able to repay every year to the extent of borrowing. Repayment represents as against

TABLE 4.19: Repayments by the Primaries to the Apex Bank

(Rs. in lakhs)

S.No. Name of the Bank	1977-78	78-79	79-80	80-81	81-82	82-83	83-84	84-85	85-86	86-87
I CHITTOOR DIST										
(a) Chittoor	15.51	20.89	16.25	8.99	17.72	7.60	32.05	8.75	34.58	25.13
	(40.51)	(29.91)	(28.95)	(58.84)	(29.99)	(25.54)	(32.20)	(26.52)	(36.68)	(33.24)
(b) Chandragiri	11.14	18.39	13.34	6.04	13.60	12.75	18.41	9.21	21.14	16.25
	(29.09)	(26.33)	(23.77)	(39.53)	(23.02)	(42.84)	(18.50)	(27.91)	(22.42)	(21.49)
(c) Madanapalli	11.64	30.56	26.54	0.25	27.76	9.41	49.06	15.04	38.56	34.22
	(30.40)	(43.76)	(47.28)	(1.63)	(46.99)	(31.62)	(49.30)	(45.57)	(40.90)	(45.27)
Total I	38.29	69.84	56.13	15.28	59.08	29.76	99.52	33.00	94.28	75.60
	(100.0)	(100.0)	(100.0)	(100.0)	(100.0)	(100.0)	(100.0)	(100.0)	(100.0)	(100.0)
II CUDDAPAH DIST.										
(a) Rajampet	14.89	17.41	29.52	21.35	12.76	18.00	27.38	6.77	17.53	17.23
	(24.80)	(21.79)	(33.53)	(58.69)	(14.49)	(23.21)	(28.92)	(13.95)	(31.69)	(26.04)
(b) Cuddapah	21.93	22.13	32.73	6.20	35.19	21.32	23.80	15.59	12.21	17.20
	(36.53)	(27.69)	(37.18)	(17.04)	(39.96)	(27.49)	(25.14)	(32.12)	(22.07)	(25.99)
(c) Proddatur	23.22	40.37	25.78	8.83	40.12	38.24	43.50	26.17	25.58	31.75
	(38.67)	(50.52)	(29.29)	(24.27)	(45.55)	(49.30)	(45.94)	(53.93)	(46.24)	(47.97)
Total II	60.04	79.91	88.03	36.38	88.07	77.56	94.68	48.54	55.32	66.18
	(100.0)	(100.0)	(100.0)	(100.0)	(100.0)	(100.0)	(100.0)	(100.0)	(100.0)	(100.0)

Contd.

TABLE 4.19 *Contd.*

S.No. Name of the Bank	1977-78	78-79	79-80	80-81	81-82	82-83	83-84	84-85	85-86	86-87
III KURNOOL DIST.										
(a) Banaganapalli	11.25	11.60	15.24	6.21	10.50	13.00	13.63	3.25	11.53	9.47
	(38.21)	(38.23)	(44.96)	(28.74)	(38.76)	(51.81)	(40.16)	(47.58)	(36.36)	(39.20)
(b) Kurnool	5.41	7.47	5.26	3.46	2.96	3.39	4.98	1.13	4.83	3.65
	(18.38)	(24.62)	(15.52)	(16.01)	(10.93)	(13.51)	(14.67)	(16.54)	(15.23)	(15.11)
(c) Nandyal	12.78	11.27	13.40	11.94	13.63	8.70	16.33	2.45	15.35	11.04
	(43.41)	(37.15)	(39.52)	(55.25)	(50.31)	(34.68)	(45.17)	(35.88)	(48.41)	(45.69)
Total III	29.44	30.34	33.90	21.61	27.09	25.09	33.94	6.83	31.71	24.16
	(100.0)	(100.0)	(100.0)	(100.0)	(100.0)	(100.0)	(100.0)	(100.0)	(100.0)	(100.0)
IV ANANTAPUR DIST.										
(a) Dharmavaram	19.63	17.59	17.89	4.27	16.50	16.47	23.90	10.95	12.91	15.92
	(46.70)	(38.52)	(37.09)	(17.78)	(32.03)	(30.89)	(34.27)	(31.13)	(30.18)	(32.34)
(b) Hindupur	11.51	15.43	15.71	6.17	11.54	17.40	15.39	5.35	11.30	10.68
	(27.39)	(33.79)	(32.57)	(25.69)	(22.40)	(32.63)	(22.06)	(15.21)	(26.42)	(21.69)
(c) Tadpatri	10.89	12.64	14.64	13.58	23.48	19.45	30.46	18.87	18.56	22.63
	(25.91)	(27.69)	(30.34)	(56.53)	(45.57)	(36.48)	(43.67)	(53.66)	(43.40)	(45.97)
Total IV	42.03	45.66	48.24	24.02	51.52	53.32	69.75	35.17	42.77	49.23
	(100.0)	(100.0)	(100.0)	(100.0)	(100.0)	(100.0)	(100.0)	(100.0)	(100.0)	(100.0)
Total I+II+III+IV	173.80	225.75	226.30	97.25	225.76	185.73	297.88	123.53	224.08	215.17

Note: Figures in bracket indicate percentage to district total.
Source: Based on Annual Reports of APCCADB, various issues.

Analysis

District	Working Capital			Repayment			Borrowing Outstanding		
	Mean	CGR	CV	Mean	CGR	CV	Mean	CGR	CV
Chittoor	148.42	2.46	27.52	56.08	6.07	47.80	478.99	8.05	23.83
Cuddapah	177.15	7.19	25.27	69.47	1.16	27.70	622.31	3.57	12.42
Kurnool	62.05	1.45	17.98	26.41	4.85	30.38	222.95	3.83	12.15
Anantapur	146.22	0.28	14.93	47.17	0.96	21.63	477.17	7.34	21.12
Region	533.84	3.12	16.01	199.53	1.22	28.79	1801.43	5.67	17.14

CGR : Compound Growth Rate; *CV* : Co-efficient of Variation.

outstanding amount at the end of every year. The figures relating to repayment by the primaries to the apex bank are given in Table 4.19. Table 4.7 and Table 4.19 are to be studied to make comparison and relation between borrowing and repayment. In 1980-81 the banks in Chittoor district accounted only 11.85 per cent of repayment to borrowings. In other words the borrowed amount was Rs. 128.99 lakhs while the repayment was only Rs. 15.28 lakhs. In 1980-81 in Cuddapah district the banks could record only 24.33 per cent of repayment to borrowing. In terms of amount repaid it was only Rs. 36.38 lakhs as against borrowed amount of Rs. 149.50 lakhs. In the same year the percentage of repayment to borrowed funds by the banks in Anantapur district was 20.75 per cent, the amount borrowed was Rs. 435.27 lakhs, while the repayment was Rs. 97.29 lakhs. The banks in Kurnool district repaid to the extent of 23.98 per cent to borrowing in 1984-85. There are a very few banks which could repay cent per cent and even more by some banks. It may be mentioned that repayment at the end of the year represents as against total outstanding. The percentage of repayment cent per cent and above to borrowings means that banks have repaid to the full extent of borrowing and outstanding.

In 1981-82 the banks in Chittoor district claimed 112.60 per cent of repayment to borrowing and the banks in Cuddapah district 151.24 per cent. In 1983-84 the percentage of repayment to borrowing was 165.97 in Chittoor district 107.18 per cent in Cuddapah district; 107.03 per cent in Kurnool district and 101.22 per cent in Anantapur district. In 1985-86 and 1986-87 only the banks in Chittoor district represented respectively 123.78 per cent, 123.95 per cent of repayment of borrowing.

The district-wise and year-wise amount repayment by the primaries alongwith percentage of repayment to borrowing particulars are shown in Table 4.20. Table 4.21 gives the amount of borrowing outstanding.

TABLE 4.20: Repayment by Primaries to the Apex

Year	Amount Repaid				Percentage of Repayment to Borrowings			
	CHI	CU	KU	AN	CHI	CU	KU	AN
1977-78	38.29	60.04	29.44	42.03	57.06	50.40	(193.05)	50.95
1978-79	69.84	79.91	30.34	45.66	54.40	62.21	91.58	60.74
1979-80	56.13	88.03	33.90	48.24	43.88	71.08	(131.19)	58.08
1980-81	15.28	36.38	21.61	24.02	11.85	24.33	52.69	20.75
1981-82	59.08	88.07	27.09	51.52	(112.60)	(151.24)	82.17	62.25
1982-83	29.76	77.56	25.09	53.52	26.60	98.04	52.47	54.93
1983-84	99.52	94.68	33.94	69.75	(165.97)	(107.18)	(107.03)	(101.22)
1984-85	33.00	48.53	6.83	35.17	70.44	81.56	23.98	67.43
1985-86	94.28	55.32	31.71	42.77	(123.78)	69.50	80.40	60.61
1986-87	75.60	66.18	24.16	49.23	(123.95)	87.29	72.75	77.07

CHI : Chittoor; CU : Cuddapah; KU : Kurnool; AN : Anantapur.

Note: Figures in bracket indicate the district and year having hundred per cent and above payment.

TABLE 4.21: Borrowing Outstanding

(Rs. in lakhs)

S.No. Name of the Bank	1977-78	78-79	79-80	80-81	81-82	82-83	83-84	84-85	85-86	86-87
I CHITTOOR DIST										
(a) Chittoor	74.37	69.96	64.68	87.25	92.56	126.75	137.35	156.68	163.60	152.25
	(29.81)	(21.38)	(16.21)	(17.02)	(18.29)	(21.55)	(25.03)	(27.85)	(30.05)	(27.60)
(b) Chandragiri	61.08	75.63	98.96	125.55	127.72	144.47	131.71	130.46	125.24	129.14
	(24.48)	(23.11)	(24.80)	(24.49)	(25.24)	(24.56)	(24.01)	(23.19)	(23.00)	(23.41)
(c) Madanapalli	114.05	181.65	235.37	299.92	285.83	317.00	279.61	275.37	255.57	270.18
	(45.71)	(55.51)	(58.99)	(58.49)	(56.47)	(53.89)	(50.96)	(48.96)	(46.95)	(48.99)
Total I	249.50	327.24	399.01	512.72	506.11	588.22	548.67	562.51	544.41	551.57
	(100.0)	(100.0)	(100.0)	(100.0)	(100.0)	(100.0)	(100.0)	(100.0)	(100.0)	(100.0)
II CUDDAPAH DIST.										
(a) Rajampet	139.21	177.32	189.58	231.19	236.96	237.68	226.81	220.65	207.20	218.22
	(30.87)	(33.04)	(33.12)	(33.72)	(36.14)	(36.16)	(34.82)	(33.33)	(30.24)	(32.77)
(b) Cuddapah	150.08	176.72	178.90	205.68	187.09	185.61	185.14	193.42	216.38	198.33
	(33.28)	(32.93)	(31.25)	(30.00)	(28.53)	(28.24)	(28.42)	(29.22)	(31.58)	(29.79)
(c) Proddatur	161.67	182.66	204.00	248.73	231.71	234.02	239.42	247.86	261.59	249.29
	(35.85)	(34.03)	(35.63)	(36.28)	(35.33)	(35.60)	(36.76)	(37.45)	(38.18)	(37.44)
Total II	450.96	536.70	572.48	685.60	655.76	657.31	651.37	661.93	685.17	665.84
	(100.0)	(100.0)	(100.0)	(100.0)	(100.0)	(100.0)	(100.0)	(100.0)	(100.0)	(100.0)

Contd.

TABLE 4.21 *Contd.*

S.No. Name of the Bank	1977-78	78-79	79-80	80-81	81-82	82-83	83-84	84-85	85-86	86-87
III KURNOOL DIST.										
(a) Banaganapalli	74.47	67.66	61.70	67.67	68.06	74.66	74.39	82.22	86.27	80.96
	(37.81)	(34.73)	(33.04)	(32.83)	(32.10)	(31.80)	(31.99)	(32.36)	(32.94)	(32.45)
(b) Kurnool	39.42	34.56	33.89	35.62	38.16	42.65	43.60	49.99	51.04	48.21
	(20.01)	(17.74)	(18.15)	(17.28)	(18.00)	(18.17)	(18.75)	(19.68)	(19.49)	(19.32)
(c) Nandyal	83.09	92.59	91.17	102.86	105.81	117.44	114.54	121.86	124.59	120.33
	(42.18)	(47.53)	(48.81)	(49.89)	(49.90)	(50.03)	(49.26)	(47.96)	(47.57)	(48.23)
Total III	196.98	194.81	186.76	206.15	212.03	234.75	232.53	254.07	261.90	249.50
	(100.0)	(100.0)	(100.0)	(100.0)	(100.0)	(100.0)	(100.0)	(100.0)	(100.0)	(100.0)
IV ANANTAPUR DIST.										
(a) Dharmavaram	108.35	104.93	112.88	145.10	149.57	165.42	162.36	173.55	185.31	173.74
	(34.97)	(30.92)	(30.17)	(31.14)	(30.09)	(30.56)	(30.04)	(31.13)	(31.67)	(30.97)
(b) Hindupur	109.33	117.29	124.99	143.20	143.26	146.22	143.82	151.36	160.77	151.98
	(35.29)	(34.56)	(33.41)	(30.74)	(28.82)	(27.02)	(26.61)	(27.15)	(27.47)	(27.09)
(c) Tadpatri	92.15	117.12	136.28	177.60	204.31	229.61	234.22	232.57	239.11	235.30
	(29.74)	(34.51)	(36.42)	(38.12)	(41.09)	(42.42)	(43.35)	(41.72)	(40.86)	(41.94)
Total IV	309.83	339.34	374.15	465.90	497.14	541.25	540.40	557.48	585.19	561.02
	(100.0)	(100.0)	(100.0)	(100.0)	(100.0)	(100.0)	(100.0)	(100.0)	(100.0)	(100.0)
Total I+II+III+IV	1207.27	1398.09	1532.40	1870.37	1871.04	2021.53	1972.97	2035.99	2076.67	2027.93

Note: Figures in bracket indicate percentage to district total.
Source: Based on Annual Reports of APCCADB, various issues.

5

CREDIT AND OVERDUES

The movement in India . . . was a Government sponsored measure, initiated, if not imposed from above.

– Sahakar Samaj

It is seen from the discussion in the previous chapter, the principal sources of funds available to the co-operative agricultural development banks and the extent of mobilisation to achieve their objectives. We have to consider in this chapter in detail the manner of credit disbursement, overdues foreclosed loans etc. This chapter facilitates statistical reporting and analysis of data to achieve the purpose of the study. We observed in the previous chapter the progress made by the co-operative banks during the last decade which has been remarkable and significant, both from the view point of borrowing from apex bank, share capital etc. The banks have represented a substantial increase, though slow and steady and fluctuating way, in respect of working capital, owned funds. The banks have thus considerably mustered more membership to make available to them the growing need for credit.

To co-operative sector banks play a very important role in the sphere of rural credit. Their contribution cannot be over emphasised particularly in a region where agriculture is a main occupation with the introduction of new technology, need for fertilisers, insecticides and pesticides etc., more and more credit becomes necessary for investment in order to enable the farmers to undertake extensive and intensive activities and increase the production to meet the increasing demand.

The extent of credit disbursement, as a matter of fact, is the ultimate goal of the co-operative banking activities. The increased number of banks for this purpose alone cannot be take as a proper index of the prosperity of the members. The extent of funds mobilisation including Government's participation have a little bearing on the profitability and financial performance. The membership expansion by itself is no index of effective coverage. The success of these banks in long-term credit in the ultimate analysis is to be judged by the manner in which and the extent to which they have been disbursing a credit and recovery. As such the banking capacity of this sector, recovery potential, overdue management are the important aspects in deciding the ultimate success of the co-operative banks in rural credit. The extent of success of the co-operative banks can judged mainly by the credit and recovery turnover which are the ultimate objects of any banking organisation. These are perhaps better yard sticks after coverage of membership and mobilisation of resources to evaluate the financial performance of co-operative banks. Further these components are an integral part of the financial statements of the co-operative banks and a measurement of them is essential from many points of view.

Beneficiaries

The analysis of data relating to beneficiaries does not, however, disclose increasing progress in the number of beneficiaries. It is primarily because of the fact that, since the type of loan is for long-term investment for a period ranging from 3 to 15 years. Unless once borrowed farmer repays he may not get fresh loan. In other words he is a debtor in the books of accounts of co-operative banks till he totally repays the principal amount along with interest. This shows a wide fluctuations in the number of beneficiaries year after year. In one year there may be substantially more borrowers and in another year there may be less number of borrowers.

The figures shown in Table 5.1 indicate bank-wise and year-wise beneficiaries of the co-operative banks.

The table discloses decreasing trend in number of beneficiaries. The number of beneficiaries ranged between 2,299 and 10,116 during the decade under study, respectively in 1984-85 and 1980-81. In general in the first five years of the period the number of beneficiaries were not only more comparing to the later part of the period but also show an increasing trend except in 1981-82. The only scientific way to measuring dispersion is co-efficient of variation. The co-efficient of variation was 47.01 while the mean beneficiary figure was 5112.4, with a compound growth rate of (-) 9.87.

TABLE 5.1: Beneficiaries

Sl. No. Name of the Bank	1977-78	78-79	79-80	80-81	81-82	82-83	83-84	84-85	85-86	86-87
I *Chittoor Dist*										
(a) Chittoor	244	293	311	664	416	493	365	313	394	357
	(14.34)	(10.71)	(11.86)	(20.99)	(51.11)	(23.57)	(62.39)	(53.23)	(44.22)	(51.89)
(b) Chandragiri	272	299	798	843	239	693	68	137	170	125
	(15.98)	(10.93)	(30.44)	(26.64)	(29.36)	(33.13)	(11.62)	(23.30)	(19.08)	(18.17)
(c) Madanapalli	1186	2144	1513	1657	159	906	152	138	327	206
	(69.68)	(78.36)	(57.70)	(52.37)	(19.53)	(43.30)	(25.99)	(23.47)	(36.70)	(29.94)
Total I	1702	2736	2622	3164	814	2092	585	588	891	688
	(100.0)	(100.0)	(100.0)	(100.0)	(100.0)	(100.0)	(100.0)	(100.0)	(100.0)	(100.0)
II *Cuddapah Dist.*										
(a) Rajampet	663	673	894	2015	311	350	349	7	11	122
	(35.44)	(35.55)	(35.13)	(50.77)	(31.16)	(22.52)	(18.20)	(1.08)	(1.17)	(10.44)
(b) Cuddapah	660	640	732	673	285	393	290	338	394	341
	(35.28)	(33.81)	(28.76)	(16.96)	(28.56)	(25.29)	(15.12)	(52.32)	(41.78)	(29.17)
(c) Proddatur	548	580	919	1281	402	811	1279	301	538	706
	(29.28)	(30.64)	(36.11)	(32.27)	(40.28)	(52.19)	(66.68)	(46.60)	(57.05)	(60.39)
Total II	1871	1893	2545	3969	998	1554	1918	646	943	1169
	(100.0)	(100.0)	(100.0)	(100.0)	(100.0)	(100.0)	(100.0)	(100.0)	(100.0)	(100.0)

Contd.

TABLE 5.1 *Contd.*

Sl. No.	Name of the Bank	1977-78	78-79	79-80	80-81	81-82	82-83	83-84	84-85	85-86	86-87
III	*Kurnool Dist*										
	(a) Banaganapalli	48 (14.82)	99 (20.29)	54 (15.34)	256 (36.52)	139 (26.33)	390 (52.49)	230 (50.77)	226 (26.36)	275 (56.47)	244 (54.59)
	(b) Kurnool	36 (11.11)	41 (8.40)	61 (17.33)	81 (11.55)	96 (18.18)	93 (12.52)	58 (12.80)	88 (21.95)	68 (13.96)	71 (15.88)
	(c) Nandyal	240 (74.07)	348 (71.31)	237 (67.33)	364 (51.93)	293 (55.49)	260 (34.99)	165 (36.43)	87 (21.69)	144 (29.57)	132 (29.53)
	Total III	324 (100.0)	488 (100.0)	352 (100.0)	701 (100.0)	528 (100.0)	743 (100.0)	453 (100.0)	401 (100.0)	487 (100.0)	447 (100.0)
IV	*Anantapur Dist.*										
	(a) Dharmavaram	269 (25.43)	335 (22.51)	362 (24.18)	898 (39.35)	428 (33.13)	527 (26.32)	238 (30.36)	212 (31.93)	248 (26.19)	233 (29.20)
	(b) Hindupur	442 (41.78)	497 (33.40)	467 (31.20)	343 (15.03)	199 (15.40)	434 (21.68)	244 (31.12)	242 (36.45)	346 (36.54)	277 (34.71)
	(c) Tadpatri	347 (32.79)	656 (44.09)	668 (44.62)	1041 (45.62)	665 (51.47)	1041 (52.0)	302 (38.52)	210 (31.62)	353 (37.27)	288 (36.09)
	Total IV	1058 (100.0)	1488 (100.0)	1497 (100.0)	2282 (100.0)	1292 (100.0)	2002 (100.0)	784 (100.0)	664 (100.0)	947 (100.0)	798 (100.0)
	Total I+II+III+IV	4955	6605	7016	10116	3632	6391	3740	2299	3268	3102

Source: Based on Annual Reports of APCCADB various Issues.
Note: Figures in Brackets indicate percentage of District total.

The banks in Chittoor district had 34.35 per cent of beneficiaries over the region total in 1977-78 and 22.18 per cent in 1986-87. This shows a decline in number of beneficiaries. In 1980-81 the percentage of beneficiaries was 31.28 over the total. In Cuddapah district in 1977-78 the banks accounted 37.76 per cent of beneficiaries over the total of the region, and 37.69 in 1986-87; 28.66 per cent in 1978-79; 36.27 per cent in 1979-80; 39.23 per cent in 1980-81; 27.48 per cent in 1981-82; 24.32 per cent in 1982-83; 51.28 per cent in 1983-84; 28.10 per cent in 1984-85; 28.86 per cent in 1985-86; and 37.69 per cent in 1986-87.

The percentage share of beneficiaries recorded by the banks in Kurnool district over the total was 6.54 per cent in 1977-78; 7.39 per cent in 1978-79; 5.02 per cent in 1979-80; 6.93 per cent in 1980-81; 14.53 per cent in 1981-82; 11.63 per cent in 1982-83; 12.11 per cent in 1983-84; 17.44 per cent in 1984-85; 14.90 per cent in 1985-86; and 14.41 per cent in 1986-87.

The banks in Anantapur district showing 21.35 per cent in 1977-78; 22.53 per cent in 1978-79; 21.34 per cent in 1979-80; 22.56 per cent in 1980-81; 35.57 per cent 1981-82; 31.33 per cent in 1982-83; 20.96 per cent in 1983-84; 28.88 per cent in 1984-85; 28.98 per cent in 1985-86 and 25.73 per cent in 1986-87.

Percentage of Beneficiaries to Membership

The analysis of ratio of relationship between beneficiaries and membership shows some interesting characteristics. The percentage of beneficiaries to membership for the region was highest of 14.54 per cent in 1980-81 and the lowest percentage of beneficiaries to membership was 3.16 per cent only in 1984-85. In other years the percentage was 8.53 in 1977-78; 10.61 per cent in 1978-79; 10.89 per cent in 1979-80; 4.97 per cent in 1981-82; 8.21 per cent in 1982-83; 5.04 per cent in 1983-84; 4.46 per cent in 1985-86 and 4.22 per cent in 1986-87.

In 1977-78 the highest percentage of beneficiaries to membership was recorded by the banks in Chittoor district and lowest was 2.35 per cent represented by the banks in Kurnool district. 9.98 per cent was recorded by the banks in Cuddapah district and 8.28 in case of Anantapur district. The figure for the region as a whole was 8.53 per cent and Chittoor district above region's average. In Cuddapah district the Rajampet PCADB represented from the district having highest percentage of beneficiaries to members. In Chittoor district the Madanapalli PCADB and 22.29 per cent. In Anantapur district the Hindupur PCADB accounted 15.30 per cent as the highest. In Kurnool district the highest percentage of beneficiaries to membership was only 4.14 per cent.

Comparing these figures with the figures of 1986-87 the percentage of beneficiaries to membership had declined. Accordingly, it was only 3.55 per cent in Chittoor district, 5.70 per cent in Cuddapah district; 2.96 per cent in Kurnool district; and 4.33 per cent in Anantapur district; while for the region the figure was 4.22 per cent.

The comparative percentages of beneficiaries to membership over the period bank-wise and year-wise are given in Table 5.2.

Loaning Procedure

Before to analyse loaning operations, the following is the brief description of procedure generally followed in granting loans.

The farmer member who wants to take loan from the co-operative bank has necessarily to follow a prescribed procedure. It involves to fulfil the stipulated conditions. A prescribed loan application is to be duly filled in and submitted to the concerned bank accompanied by the exact scheme to be financed alongwith necessary documents. This is the first step in loan procedure. From this stage till a loan is disbursed a uniform procedure broadly is followed in all the co-operative banks with slight modifications, alterations to suit local conditions. The All India Rural Credit Review Committee, 1969 broadly classified between the receipt of a loan application and the disbursement of the first instalment of loan. To mention they are preliminary scrutiny, public enquiry, scrutiny into the purpose, submission to the board and transmission to the Central land development bank.

Loans are advanced on the mortgage of property. Land is the main security for grant of loans to the members. The next step is the procedure followed by the bank which makes a close and thorough scrutiny of the application, documents and in particular title deeds. The title to land is very important element in the case of agricultural development banks. The concerned field inspector or supervisor inspects loan applications and documents. The bank after scrutiny and following all formalities forwards the proposal to regional offices of the central land development bank. The Central land development bank has established regional offices in all most all districts. The regional

TABLE 5.2: Percentage of Beneficiaries to membership

(percentage)

Sl. No.	Name of the Bank	1977-78	78-79	79-80	80-81	81-82	82-83	83-84	84-85	85-86	86-87
1.	Chittoor	5.70	6.99	7.70	15.22	9.42	9.97	6.89	5.71	6.95	6.51
2.	Chandragiri	8.48	8.86	22.03	20.45	5.77	15.17	1.47	2.92	3.55	2.66
3.	Madanapalli	22.29	30.57	20.10	19.22	1.82	9.68	1.60	1.54	3.58	2.24
	Total	13.29	18.77	17.26	18.50	4.71	11.09	3.02	3.07	4.55	3.55
4.	Rajampet	13.83	12.76	15.23	30.02	4.56	4.98	11.13	0.21	0.34	3.79
5.	Cuddapah	8.46	7.75	7.95	9.31	3.91	5.26	3.88	4.56	5.25	4.57
6.	Proddatur	8.90	8.94	13.68	16.90	4.70	8.99	12.11	3.24	5.59	7.19
	Total	9.98	9.46	11.66	18.44	4.41	6.61	9.06	3.23	4.63	5.70
7.	Banaganapalli	0.92	1.86	1.13	5.72	3.06	7.76	5.25	5.03	6.00	5.44
8.	Kurnool	1.31	1.47	2.10	2.78	3.25	2.98	1.63	2.39	2.14	2.04
9.	Nandyal	4.14	5.46	3.74	5.34	4.33	3.68	2.35	1.22	1.98	1.85
	Total	2.35	3.37	2.51	4.93	3.70	4.88	3.03	2.62	3.24	2.96
10.	Dharmavaram	4.88	6.08	6.57	11.35	4.90	5.82	3.27	2.87	3.48	3.21
11.	Hindupur	15.30	15.87	14.35	9.36	5.31	10.32	5.62	6.51	8.89	6.95
12.	Tadpatri	7.93	14.42	14.53	20.14	10.41	14.98	4.28	2.90	4.82	4.00
	Total	8.28	11.29	11.20	13.63	6.85	9.91	4.20	3.62	5.16	4.33
	Region	8.53	10.61	10.89	14.54	4.97	8.21	5.04	3.16	4.46	4.22

offices in all most all districts. The regional offices discharge functions like undertaking the work of sanction and disbursement of loans, acting as a close liaison between APCCADB and its primary banks assisting member banks in scrutiny of loan applications, conducting field inspection and evaluating the hypothecation.

Though loan sanctioning is decentralised by establishing regional offices the procedure followed is still complicated and time consuming. This is the reason why loans are sanctioned with undue delay. A detailed examination of loan application, loan scheme and elaborate examination of the title to hypothecation, compliance of technical and legal aspects etc., are responsible for this cumbersome procedure which delay loan operations. The illiterate and ignorant farmers sometimes may feel uneasy about these loans. The rural credit survey committee recommended to follow a simplified procedure.

Credit Disbursement

In the matters of loaning operations the co-operative banks made a remarkable progress over the years. There has been a phenomenal increase in the amount of credit disbursement. The purposes of loans are according to schematic pattern of advances formulated by the apex bank. Purpose-wise classification of loans advanced covers wells; development of wells; pumpsets; tractors, power tillers and other types of agricultural machinery; Land development under irrigation projects including CAD; Horticulture; Diversified purposes (Dairy, sheep rearing poultry, pisciculture, Bullocks and Bullock carts); Sericulture; Gobar gas plants; Advances to cyclone affected areas; Advances to Andhra Pradesh State Electricity Board; other Development purposes (Tobacco barns, pipelines, shares in sugar factories, Lift Irrigation Schemes and Land Development Schemes etc.).

The major objective of the Central bank to classify schemes of lending is to develop the rural economy by providing long-term credit and other facilities for agriculture and other allied to agriculture and rural development which cover small farmers, marginal farmers, agricultural labourers, artisans and other entrepreneurs. Keeping this objective in view the apex bank and other central financing institutions have been confining their financial assistance to cover these schemes. The coverage of the weaker sections by the co-operative banks makes them as the small man's bank of their own and this sector is considered as the most distinguishing one. The NABARD – financed schemes are predominantly covered the land based activities. While co-operatives carrying on rural banking business, their lending operations are some what limited, because of the fact that their lending is confined to farmers.

Analysis of Loan Operations

Between 1977-78 and 1986-87 there was a phenomenal increase in the lending operations of co-operative banks. The quantum of loans issued have gone up to Rs. 434.14 lakhs in 1980-81 from Rs. 280.94 lakhs in 1977-78. In deployment of resources in the total, the districts particularly Cuddapah received the lion's share of Rs. 75.57 lakhs in 1986-87, Rs. 63.36 lakhs in case of Anantapur district. The amount of credit disbursement by the banks in Chittoor district accounted Rs. 60.13 lakhs and in Kurnool district Rs. 35.19 lakhs in the same year.

In Chittoor district the total amount advanced by these banks increased from Rs. 72.13 lakhs in 1977-78 to Rs. 112.18 lakhs in 1982-83; Rs. 127.46 lakhs in 1978-79; Rs. 129.43 lakhs in 1980-81 and to Rs. 131.23 lakhs in 1979-80. In other years the amount of loans disbursed ranged between Rs. 47.60 lakhs in 1984-85 to Rs. 76.86 lakhs in 1985-86. The banks in Chittoor district advanced 25.67 per cent of the total in the region in 1977-78; 34.85 per cent in 1978-79; 35.35 per cent 1979-80; 29.81 per cent in 1980-81; 22.76 per cent in 1981-82; 34.03 per cent 1982-83; 22.30 per cent in 1983-84; 25.86 per cent in 1984-85; 28.75 per cent in 1985-86; and 25.67 per cent in 1986-87.

The share of the banks in Cuddapah district in the total amount of credit was 41.78 per cent in 1977-78; 35.46 per cent in 1978-79; 34.66 per cent in 1979-80; 33.84 per cent in 1980-81; 26.43 per cent in 1981-82; 23.06 per cent in 1982-83; 36.97 per cent in 1983-84; 31.64 per cent 1984-85; 28.27 per cent in 1985-86; and 32.26 per cent in 1986-87.

The banks in Kurnool district accounted 4.87 per cent in 1977-78 (27.67 per cent in Anantapur district); 8.48 per cent in 1978-79 (21.21 per cent); 7.16 per cent in 1979-80 (22.83 per cent); 9.20 per cent in 1980-81 (27.15 per cent); 13.86 per cent in 1981-82 (36.95 per cent); 12.75 per cent in 1982-83 (30.16 per cent); 13.63 per cent in 1983-84 (27.10 per cent); 14.76 per cent in 1984-85 (27.80 per cent); 16.50 per cent in 1985-86 (26.68 per cent); and 15.02 per cent in 1986-87 (27.05 per cent).

TABLE 5.3: Disbursement

(Rupees in lakhs)

Sl. No.	Name of the Bank	1977-78	78-79	79-80	80-81	81-82	82-83	83-84	84-85	85-86	86-87
I	*Chittoor Dist*										
	(a) Chittoor	9.44	12.41	11.02	32.16	22.83	41.76	38.46	29.30	41.86	36.54
		(13.09)	(9.74)	(8.40)	(24.85)	(44.20)	(37.23)	(68.74)	(61.55)	(54.46)	(60.77)
	(b) Chandragiri	15.33	26.27	39.25	30.49	15.49	28.74	6.29	7.64	16.14	10.02
		(21.25)	(20.61)	(29.91)	(23.56)	(29.99)	(25.62)	(11.24)	(16.05)	(21.00)	(16.66)
	(c) Madanapalli	47.36	88.78	80.96	66.78	13.33	41.68	11.20	10.66	18.86	13.57
		(65.66)	(69.65)	(61.69)	(51.59)	(25.81)	(37.15)	(20.12)	(22.40)	(24.54)	(22.57)
	Total I	72.13	127.46	131.23	129.43	51.65	112.18	55.95	47.60	76.86	60.13
		(100.0)	(100.0)	(100.0)	(100.0)	(100.0)	(100.0)	(100.0)	(100.0)	(100.0)	(100.0)
II	*Cuddapah Dist.*										
	(a) Rajampet	46.24	47.53	40.78	63.89	21.50	17.70	16.45	0.68	3.73	6.95
		(39.40)	(36.64)	(31.70)	(43.49)	(35.85)	(23.28)	(17.73)	(1.16)	(4.94)	(9.20)
	(b) Cuddapah	31.06	36.72	35.83	32.18	15.52	18.41	23.57	24.10	34.00	27.22
		(26.46)	(28.31)	(27.85)	(21.90)	(25.88)	(24.21)	(25.41)	(41.28)	(44.99)	(36.02)
	(c) Proddatur	40.07	45.46	52.03	50.84	22.95	39.93	52.75	33.61	37.85	41.40
		(34.14)	(35.05)	(40.45)	(34.61)	(38.27)	(52.51)	(56.86)	(57.56)	(50.07)	(54.78)
	Total II	117.37	129.71	128.64	146.91	59.97	76.04	92.77	58.39	75.58	75.57
		(100.0)	(100.0)	(100.0)	(100.0)	(100.0)	(100.0)	(100.0)	(100.0)	(100.0)	(100.0)

TABLE 5.3 *Contd.*

Sl. No.	Name of the Bank	1977-78	78-79	79-80	80-81	81-82	82-83	83-84	84-85	85-86	86-87
III	*Kurnool Dist*										
	(a) Banaganapalli	2.04	9.57	9.46	12.66	10.24	13.71	16.49	11.89	16.54	14.97
		(14.90)	(80.84)	(35.58)	(31.71)	(32.55)	(32.62)	(48.20)	(43.65)	(37.49)	(42.54)
	(b) Kurnool	1.63	1.86	4.62	5.13	4.56	8.69	5.75	6.21	7.30	6.42
		(11.91)	(5.99)	(17.38)	(12.85)	(14.50)	(20.68)	(16.81)	(22.80)	(16.55)	(18.24)
	(c) Nandyal	10.02	19.60	12.51	22.13	16.66	19.63	11.97	9.14	20.28	13.80
		(73.19)	(63.17)	(47.04)	(55.44)	(52.95)	(46.70)	(34.99)	(33.55)	(45.96)	(39.22)
	Total III	13.69	31.03	26.59	39.92	31.46	42.03	34.21	27.24	44.12	35.19
		(100.0)	(100.0)	(100.0)	(100.0)	(100.0)	(100.0)	(100.0)	(100.0)	(100.0)	(100.0)
IV	*Anantapur Dist.*										
	(a) Dharmavaram	22.40	14.28	27.91	38.73	22.08	31.25	20.13	22.05	24.60	22.26
		(28.81)	(18.41)	(32.94)	(32.86)	(26.34)	(31.43)	(29.60)	(42.98)	(34.75)	(35.13)
	(b) Hindupur	30.33	24.23	22.69	23.78	11.55	21.25	13.17	12.32	20.93	15.47
		(39.01)	(31.24)	(26.78)	(20.17)	(13.78)	(21.37)	(19.37)	(24.02)	(29.57)	(24.42)
	(c) Tadpatri	25.02	39.06	34.14	55.37	50.21	46.94	34.70	16.93	25.26	25.63
		(32.18)	(50.35)	(40.28)	(46.97)	(59.88)	(47.20)	(51.03)	(33.00)	(35.68)	(40.45)
	Total IV	77.75	77.57	84.74	117.88	83.84	99.44	68.00	51.30	70.79	63.36
		(100.0)	(100.0)	(100.0)	(100.0)	(100.0)	(100.0)	(100.0)	(100.0)	(100.0)	(100.0)
	Total I+II+III+IV	280.94	365.77	371.20	434.14	226.92	329.69	250.93	184.53	267.35	234.25

Source: Based on Annual Reports of APCCADB, Various Issues.
Note: Figures in Brackets indicate percentage of District total.

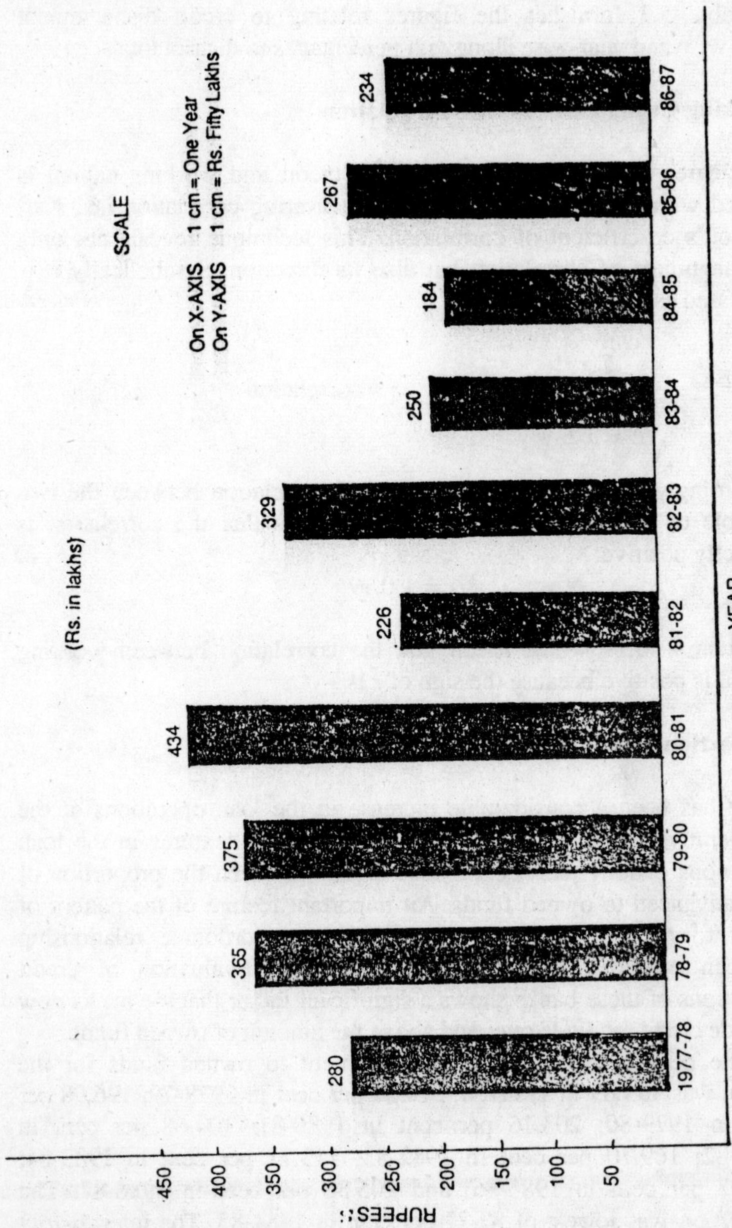

FIG. 5.1: Loan Disbursements

Table 5.3 furnishes the figures relating to credit disbursement bank-wise and year-wise alongwith pereentages to district total.

Working Capital and Credit Correlation

The degree of correlation between the credit and working capital is studied with mathematical method of measuring correlation i.e., Karl pearson's co-efficient of correlation. This technique reveals not only the magnitude of correlation but also its direction. Symbolically it is expressed as under:

$$r = \frac{\Sigma xy}{\sqrt{E\, x^2 \, x\, E\, y^2}} \qquad r = \text{correlation}$$

Accordingly the value of co-efficient of correlation between the two variable of working capital and credit shows that the correlation is perfectly positive.

$$r = +\, 0.19$$

Thus, + 0.19 would mean that the correlation between working capital is positive because the sign of r is + .

Proportion of Advances to owned funds

There has been a considerable increase in the loan operations of the co-operative banks. One of the most disquieting features in the loan operations of long-term cooperative banks has been the proportion of loan advanced to owned funds. An important feature of the pattern of funds to be lent to the members is disproportionate relationship between owned funds and loans advanced. Evaluation of credit operations of these banks shows a significant factor that the banks now provide credit facilities over and above the amount of owned funds.

The percentages of credit disbursement to owned funds for the region was 155.89 in 1971-78, 214.04 per cent in 1978-79; 196.98 per cent in 1979-80; 203.16 per cent in 1980-81; 104.68 per cent in 1981-82; 169.70 per cent in 1982-83; 113.73 per cent in 1983-84; 122.22 per cent in 1985-86; and 105.86 per cent in 1986-87. The proportion was lowest of 82.21 per cent in 1984-85. The inter district comparison of percentage of credit disbursement to owned funds shows that it was 195.74 per cent in Anantapur district, 167.62 per cent in Cuddapah district 165.36 per cent in Chittoor district and lowest of 50.97 per cent in Kurnool district in 1977-78. Their position in 1986-87 was 126.67 per cent in Kurnool district; 122.76 per cent in Cuddapah district; 93.95 per cent in Anantapur district and 93.22 per cent in Chittoor district.

The figure for the region was 105.86 per cent. Accordingly, the Chittoor district and Anantapur district have recorded less than region's average and Cuddapah and Kurnool districts have more percentage of credit disbursement to owned fund.

The individual bank-wise analysis of relationship between credit and owned funds discloses some distinguishing characteristics features. Accordingly, in 1977-78 there were 4 banks having 200 per cent and above percentage of credit to owned funds. In 1978-79 there were 5 such Banks. Among them the Madanapalli PCADB had 439.72 per cent of advances to owned funds. In 1979-80 4 banks had above 200 per cent of credit to owned funds. Again the Madanapalli PCADB had 346.72 per cent of credit disbursement to owned funds. There were 5 co-operative banks in 1980-81 with above 200 per cent of credit to owned funds. In 1981-82 only the Tadpatri PCADB had 219.64 per cent of credit to owned funds. The Chittoor PCADB bank in 1982-83, was the only bank among the banks in the region which had 266.64 per cent of advances to owned funds. In 1983-84 also the same bank represented 210.97 per cent and 209.51 per cent in 1985-86. It may be mentioned, that there was no bank in 1986-87 which had 200 and above per cent of credit disbursement to owned funds.

The co-operative bank-wise and year-wise percentage of credit disbursement to owned funds figures are shown in Table 5.4.

The table discloses that the co-operative banks suffer from inadequacy of funds. Bulk of the loans advanced by these banks consists of borrowed funds. The insufficiency of owned funds is only the main reason to depend more on borrowed funds. The small proportion of owned funds, due to poor capital base of the members and inadequacy of ploughing back of profits, made difficult for the banks to deploy adequate owned funds. Because of this fact the percentage of credit disbursement to owned funds in the loaning operations of these banks in many years and in respect of many banks have remained at a higher level.

TABLE 5.4: Percentage of Credit Disbursement to owned funds

(in percentage)

Sl. No.	Name of the Bank	1977-78	78-79	79-80	80-81	81-82	82-83	83-84	84-85	85-86	86-87
1.	Chittoor	77.57	101.06	82.55	240.90	163.19	266.64	210.97	160.28	209.51	194.05
2.	Chandragiri	176.82	241.45	292.91	198.37	100.45	142.14	32.04	39.36	193.53	63.46
3.	Madanapalli	207.90	439.72	346.72	241.61	48.23	137.06	37.70	35.46	63.12	45.41
	Total	165.36	294.03	269.02	229.65	90.53	168.62	82.80	70.26	132.06	93.22
4.	Rajampet	125.11	280.08	185.73	233.60	77.98	62.43	119.38	5.03	29.56	52.26
5.	Cuddapah	193.64	196.57	178.35	150.80	74.08	88.26	116.17	113.79	154.48	128.64
6.	Proddatur	235.43	228.21	231.35	201.03	91.76	158.08	198.76	124.99	135.86	152.77
	Total	167.62	233.42	199.32	198.58	81.56	102.11	153.06	94.82	120.95	122.76
7.	Banaganapalli	20.97	94.94	95.56	137.16	118.12	158.31	184.25	129.66	171.40	161.66
8.	Kurnool	27.58	33.10	85.56	93.96	79.44	145.81	104.55	100.98	119.67	108.45
9.	Nandyal	89.30	167.81	112.80	185.34	138.72	155.18	97.56	73.35	155.28	109.52
	Total	50.97	113.33	100.76	149.91	119.08	154.13	128.03	98.06	153.14	126.67
10.	Dharmavaram	140.97	86.99	157.06	188.65	108.18	140.01	91.21	96.20	103.71	97.21
11.	Hindupur	248.00	173.32	152.38	145.71	69.96	127.93	78.38	71.42	115.57	88.96
12.	Tadpatri	215.69	277.41	212.19	278.66	219.64	185.83	129.19	62.29	92.12	94.40
	Total	195.74	173.96	173.86	207.83	140.25	154.92	103.45	76.17	102.22	93.95
	Region total	155.89	214.04	196.98	203.16	104.68	169.70	113.73	82.21	122.22	105.86

Source: Tables 4.15 and 5.3.

Credit to working capital

The relationship between credit and funds can be calculated in a variant form. This is between credit to working capital. In general the percentage of credit to capital shows lower than the percentage of credit to owned funds. For the region as a whole the per cent of credit to working capital was 54.97 in 1977-78 (155.89 per cent credit to owned funds); 59.07 per cent in 1978-79 (214.04 per cent); 62.63 per cent in 1979-80 (196.98 per cent), 62.12 per cent in 1980-81 (203.16 per cent); 46.84 per cent in 1981-82 (104.68 per cent); 57.65 per cent in 1982-83 (169.70 per cent); 50.25 per cent in 1983-84 (113.73 per cent); 44.86 per cent in 1984-85 (82.21 per cent); 55.18 per cent in 1985-86 (122.22 per cent); and 50.37 per cent in 1986-87 (105.86 per cent).

The principal cause for lower percentage of credit disbursement to working capital is that working capital includes all sources of funds available for lending operations. The owned funds generally represent smaller amount in relation to credit advanced because of poor financial strength in terms of members 'paid-up share capital, free reserves, admission fees etc. To be self-reliant these banks should have higher proportion of, or equal proportion of owned funds to advances. Evidently, therefore, it is not possible in rural credit institutions like co-operative banks because of reasons identified and mentioned above. Table 5.5 depicts bank-wise percentage of credit disbursement to working capital.

Loans per Beneficiary and Member

Since in order to provide long-term finance, these banks have been established under the name land Mortgage Banks or Agriculture Development Banks. They have separate entity and exclusively responsible for the supply of long-term credit to the agriculturist. These banks advance loans to their members for the development of agriculture. The loans of these banks are meant to be utilised for improvement of land and methods of cultivation, construction of minor irrigation works consist of digging wells, tanks and other storage facilities, repairs renovation, deepening of owned wells, pumpsets, oil engines or electric motors installation, lift irrigation, levelling of land, drainage, reclamation, field channels and other allied to agriculture.

TABLE 5.5: Percentage of Credit Disbursement to Working Capital

Sl. No.	Name of the Bank	1977-78	78-79	79-80	80-81	81-82	82-83	83-84	84-85	85-86	86-87
1.	Chittoor	43.44	48.48	47.91	33.93	61.67	72.40	63.17	63.19	68.09	64.97
2.	Chandragiri	64.09	68.64	78.37	63.51	49.76	57.80	24.89	27.91	66.56	39.09
3.	Madanapalli	72.77	82.31	78.14	72.25	32.26	58.72	27.07	26.09	38.77	31.10
	Total	65.14	74.22	74.27	55.02	47.18	62.89	43.87	41.54	57.20	47.91
4.	Rajampet	56.03	74.82	63.98	70.75	24.59	37.60	54.29	4.82	22.34	34.12
5.	Cuddapah	66.25	31.27	65.10	59.24	41.33	45.23	54.03	53.60	59.46	56.02
6.	Proddatur	37.59	68.27	74.75	64.48	47.70	60.67	70.31	54.28	55.49	60.54
	Total	49.73	52.18	68.28	65.74	34.65	49.51	62.28	48.26	53.19	55.02
7.	Banaganapalli	15.63	48.58	49.32	59.13	52.35	48.51	73,91	58.40	65.82	66.24
8.	Kurnool	21.31	6.66	46.67	48.17	40.57	62.79	50.35	45.43	60.93	51.94
9.	Nandyal	46.80	60.18	54.25	62.20	58.27	59.50	48.46	41.12	65.13	53.04
	Total	32.51	38.69	51.00	59.02	52.97	55.98	58.55	48.42	64.65	57.71
10.	Dharmavaram	56.72	46.50	63.98	67.92	53.36	56.57	46.90	48.92	50.84	48.97
11.	Hindupur	68.64	64.84	27.70	58.43	41.09	56.49	44.22	40.88	53.93	47.01
12.	Tadpatri	64.94	75.58	68.44	74.05	68.73	65.26	37.83	38.22	48.00	40.76
	Total	63.62	64.77	48.31	68.34	58.82	60.34	41.36	42.93	50.63	44.86
	Region	54.97	59.07	62.63	62.12	46.84	57.65	50.25	44.86	55.18	50.37

Source: Tables 5.03 and 4.18

The quantum of credit disbursement depends upon the nature of scheme of loan applied for and it may also varies from district to district depending on land conditions and economic activity. For instance in deltaic areas and in dry upland areas the amount of loan required may be more than other areas. Thus generally the amount of loan required varies from Rs. 5,000 to Rs. 25,000.

Table 5.6 shows average amount of loan per member and beneficiary. The average loan per member usually shows less than the average loan per beneficiary. Because the number of beneficiaries are a few in number every year and membership includes total number of members of the bank. Thus average loan per user member or beneficiary in each year reveals reasonable average loan per beneficiary than average loan per member. In 1977-78 the average minimum loan per member was Rs. 100 in Kurnool district and maximum was Rs. 600 in other three districts. The figure for the region was Rs. 500. The figures for 1986-87 show Rs. 300 for the region; Rs. 400 for Cuddapah district; Rs. 300 for Chittoor and Anantapur district and Rs. 200 for Kurnool district. Over a period of 1977-78 to 1986-87 the minimum average loan per member in the entire region ranged between Rs. 200 to Rs. 600.

The minimum average loan per beneficiary in the region was Rs. 5,200 and maximum was Rs. 8000 during the period under study. However, there are instance where some co-operative banks recorded average loan per beneficiary to the extent of nearly Rs. 10,000. In 1983-84 in Chittoor district the banks recorded Rs. 9600 average loan per member. Similarly in 1984-85 in Cuddapah district the average loan per beneficiary was Rs. 9000 and Rs. 9100 average loan per member in 1985-86 in Kurnool district. The comparative figures relating to average loan per member and average loan per beneficiary for each district can be observed from the table

The statement of analysis discloses that the growth rate for the region in respect of beneficiaries was negative. The co-efficient of variation was highest in Chittoor district of 63.10. While the figure for the region 47.01. The C.V. was lowest in Kurnool district of 27.72. The analysis relating to credit disbursement for the region was 26.49 C.V. but for the Chittoor district it was highest of 40.13.

Location Quotient

The removal of regional disparities in the matters of rural credit distribution has been accepted as one of the objectives of economic

TABLE 5.6: Average loan per Member and Per Beneficiary

(Rs. in lakhs)

Year	Average loan per member					Average loan per Beneficiary				
	CHI	CU	KU	ANT	T	CHI	CU	KU	ANT	T
1977-78	0.006	0.006	0.001	0.006	0.005	0.042	0.063	0.042	0.073	0.057
1978-79	0.009	0.006	0.002	0.006	0.006	0.047	0.069	0.064	0.052	0.055
1979-80	0.009	0.006	0.002	0.006	0.006	0.050	0.051	0.076	0.057	0.053
1980-81	0.008	0.007	0.003	0.007	0.006	0.041	0.037	0.057	0.052	0.043
1981-82	0.003	0.003	0.002	0.004	0.003	0.063	0.060	0.060	0.065	0.062
1982-83	0.006	0.003	0.003	0.005	0.004	0.054	0.049	0.057	0.050	0.052
1983-84	0.003	0.004	0.002	0.004	0.003	0.096	0.048	0.076	0.087	0.067
1984-85	0.003	0.003	0.002	0.003	0.003	0.081	0.090	0.068	0.077	0.080
1985-86	0.004	0.004	0.003	0.004	0.004	0.086	0.080	0.091	0.075	0.082
1986-87	0.003	0.004	0.002	0.003	0.003	0.087	0.065	0.079	0.080	0.076

Source: Table 5.01; 5.03; 4.01.

CHI : Chittoor; CU : Cuddapah; KU : Kurnool; ANT : Anantapur; T : Total

Statement of Analysis

District	Beneficiaries				Credit Disbursement			
	Mean	CGR	LGR	CV	Mean	CGR	LGR	CV
Chittoor	1588.2	-15.40	-14.76	63.10	86.46	-7.01	-7.29	40.13
Cuddapah	1750.6	-10.17	-9.71	55.29	96.09	-7.48	-7.90	33.28
Kurnool	492.4	1.57	1.00	27.72	32.55	6.83	5.25	27.30
Anantapur	1291.2	-7.31	-6.66	42.22	79.47	-3.85	-3.65	23.68
Region	5112.4	-9.87	-9.48	47.01	294.57	-5.08	-2.04	26.49

CGR : Compound Growth Rate
LGR : Linear Growth Rate
CU : Coefficient of variation.,

development. A balanced regional development in India, however has been largely not achieved in several respects. Regional disparities manifest themselves both in the form of inter state disparities and intra-regional disparities. Disparities between districts within the region refers to intra regional disparities. The region under study is entirely delineated as drought affected tract and some of the areas as hardcore. An accelerated development of drought areas is one of the important objectives of rural development. The co-operative banks have been drawn attention to the problem areas and emphasised that the realisation of local potentials should be taken up on a priority basis in order to give a practical shape to the ideals of co-operative principles.

A balanced and adequate distribution of credit by these banks is the major problem in the balanced regional development. The long term co-operative credit plays an equal role to promote balanced development between the districts. It is with this object locational aspects of credit and borrowers is emphasised. The technique of location quotient is adopted with a view to identify imbalance, if any, in the distribution of credit in relation to borrowers. The tool of location quotient of credit indicates ratio of ratios. The results obtained under this technique help to know the imbalance in the credit distribution in relation to borrowers. The quotient is proportional or greater or less than the unit which respectively means distribution of credit is proportionate or greater or less than the borrowers i.e., beneficiaries.

Symbolically the location quotient may be expressed as

$$Cq = \frac{TC_d / TB_d}{TC / TB}$$

Where, TC = Total credit

TB = Total beneficiaries

d = District

Cq = Location quotient of credit.

Alongwith above technique in order to calculate the rate of change in credit distribution, the Elasticity co-efficient of credit is introduced. The change in credit distribution in the district is equal or not to the change in the number of borrowers, and hence whether the marginal increase would equal to average increase or otherwise can be determined.

Symbolically the Elasticity co-efficient of credit is expressed as:

$$Ce = \frac{\Delta c/C}{\Delta b/B}$$

Where,

Δc	=	Change in volume of credit
Δb	=	Change in number of beneficiaries
C	=	Total credit
B	=	Total beneficiaries
Ce	=	Elasticity Coefficient of Credit.

The figures of quotient and Elasticity co-efficient of credit are shown in Table 5.7.

Table 5.7 reflects that the co-operative banks well responded in the distribution of credit to borrowers. In the year 1981-82 the response of the increase of credit to increase in beneficiaries (Ce) the co-operative banks in all the districts except Anantapur district got more credit. In 1986-87 the distribution of credit in relation to beneficiaries showed less comparing to 1981-82. The elasticity co-efficient of credit for the region was 0.70 in 1981-82 and 0.46 in 1986-87. Except in 1978-79 and 1985-86 in Anantapur district the location quotient was to unit and more than unit. In case of co-operative banks in the district of Kurnool, the credit distribution in relation to borrowers in 1986-87 was more than unit which means the change in credit distribution was more than the change in a number of beneficiaries. The amount of credit distributed was very less in 1981-82 and 1986-87 comparing other districts and other years. The year-wise and district-wise Location quotient of credit and Elasticity co-efficient of credit comparatively can be better understood with the help of results worked out and arranged in Table.

Out-standing

Outstanding refers to that part of loan amount advanced to the members to be collected in instalments. When instalment amounts are repaid regularly the outstanding amount in the individual ledger account appears a gradual reduction. It is similar to written down value of the asset in the books. In this paragraphs it is proposed to observe the position of out-standing.

TABLE 5.7: Results of Credit Quotient and Credit Elasticity Co-efficient

Year	Chittoor		Cuddapah		Kurnool		Anantapur	
	Cq	Ce	Cq	Ce	Cq	Ce	Cq	Ce
1977-78	0.67		1.00		0.67		1.17	
1978-79	0.83		1.17		1.00		0.83	
1979-80	1.00		1.00		1.60		1.20	
1980-81	1.00		0.75		1.50		1.25	
1981-82	1.00	1.04	1.00	1.04	1.00	2.06	1.00	0.36
1982-83	1.00		1.00		1.20		1.00	
1983-84	1.43		0.71		1.14		1.29	
1984-85	1.13		1.13		0.88		1.00	
1985-86	1.13		1.00		1.23		0.88	
1986-87	1.13	0.28	0.75	0.95	1.00	4.13	1.00	0.76

Ce for the Region : 0.70 in 1981-82
0.46 in 1986-87

Cq = location quotient of credit
Ce = Elasticity co-efficient of credit.

Beneficiaries Outstanding

The number of beneficiaries outstanding were 53,500 in the region in 1978 which went up to 62844 in 1986-87 representing an increase of 1.17 times. The outstanding beneficiaries were more in 1980-81 of 64,916 in the region. The district-wise analysis shows that there were 13,142 in 1977-78 in Chittoor district which slowly and steadily reached to 17,220 in 1986-87 and were more in the district in 1980-81 of 17,628. The percentage of beneficiaries outstanding in this district over the region was 24.56 in 1977-78; 25.11 per cent in 1978-79; 27.29 per cent in 1985-86; 27.44 per cent in 1986-87. In Cuddapah district their position respectively was 33.48 per cent; 34.20 per cent in 1977-78 and 1978-79; 35.46 per cent and 34.48 per cent in 1985-86 and 1986-87. The banks in Kurnool district had 20.46 per cent in 1977-78; 19.40 per cent in 1978-79; 14.08 per cent in 1985-86; and 15.40 per cent in 1986-87. The percentage of beneficiaries outstanding over the region in Anantapur district was 21.50 in 1977-78; 21.29 in 1978-79; 23.17 in 1985-86 and 22.71 in 1986-87.

Year-wise figures as to beneficiaries outstanding bank-wise are indicated in Table 5.8.

TABLE 5.8: Beneficiaries Outstanding

Sl. No. Name of the Bank	1977-78	78-79	79-80	80-81	81-82	82-83	83-84	84-85	85-86	86-87
I *Chittoor Dist*										
(a) Chittoor	3740	3330	3037	3247	3106	3084	3574	3754	3821	3716
	(28.46)	(23.45)	(19.56)	(18.42)	(19.60)	(18.20)	(20.97)	(21.69)	(22.08)	(21.58)
(b) Chandragiri	3475	3296	3765	4269	2679	3075	2818	2805	2852	2826
	(26.44)	(23.21)	(24.25)	(24.22)	(16.91)	(18.15)	(16.53)	(16.21)	(16.48)	(16.41)
(c) Madanapalli	5927	7575	8723	10112	10061	10787	10652	10750	10633	10678
	(45.10)	(53.34)	(56.19)	(57.36)	(63.49)	(63.65)	(62.50)	(62.10)	(61.14)	(62.01)
Total I	13142	14201	15525	17628	15846	16946	17044	17309	17306	17220
	(100.0)	(100.0)	(100.0)	(100.0)	(100.0)	(100.0)	(100.0)	(100.0)	(100.0)	(100.0)
II *Cuddapah Dist.*										
(a) Rajampet	5308	5696	6590	8088	8107	8370	5717	3609	3107	4144
	(29.63)	(29.45)	(31.46)	(33.85)	(34.08)	(35.96)	(27.89)	(16.38)	(13.82)	(19.12)
(b) Cuddapah	7781	8116	8322	8643	8537	8105	7299	7298	8171	7589
	(43.44)	(41.96)	(39.73)	(36.17)	(35.88)	(34.82)	(35.62)	(33.12)	(36.34)	(35.02)
(c) Proddatur	4823	5532	6034	7166	7146	6801	7479	11127	11207	9938
	(26.93)	(28.59)	(28.81)	(29.98)	(30.04)	(29.22)	(36.49)	(50.50)	(49.84)	(45.86)
Total II	17912	19344	20946	23897	23790	23276	20495	22034	22485	21671
	(100.0)	(100.0)	(100.0)	(100.0)	(100.0)	(100.0)	(100.0)	(100.0)	(100.0)	(100.0)

TABLE 5.8 *Contd.*

Sl. No. Name of the Bank	1977-78	78-79	79-80	80-81	81-82	82-83	83-84	84-85	85-86	86-87
III *Kurnool Dist*										
(a) Banaganapalli	4432	4261	3559	3023	2874	2960	2618	2661	2804	2694
	(40.50)	(38.82)	(35.59)	(31.64)	(30.77)	(32.06)	(26.14)	(26.37)	(31.41)	(27.84)
(b) Kurnool	2053	1919	1703	1689	1651	1494	2833	2779	1329	2314
	(18.76)	(17.49)	(17.03)	(17.68)	(17.68)	(16.18)	(28.29)	(27.54)	(14.89)	(23.91)
(c) Nandyal	4459	4795	4737	4841	4814	4779	4564	4651	4795	4670
	(40.74)	(43.69)	(47.38)	(50.68)	(51.55)	(51.76)	(45.57)	(46.09)	(53.70)	(48.25)
Total III	10944	10975	9999	9553	9339	9233	10015	10091	8928	9678
	(100.0)	(100.0)	(100.0)	(100.0)	(100.0)	(100.0)	(100.0)	(100.0)	(100.0)	(100.0)
IV *Anantapur Dist.*										
(a) Dharmavaram	4963	4944	4552	5450	5503	5898	4333	4471	4456	4420
	(43.15)	(41.05)	(36.85)	(39.38)	(38.98)	(38.41)	(31.27)	(31.32)	(30.32)	(30.96)
(b) Hindupur	3333	3504	3802	3630	3440	3692	3763	4005	4351	4040
	(28.98)	(29.10)	(30.78)	(26.23)	(24.37)	(24.04)	(27.16)	(28.06)	(29.61)	(28.30)
(c) Tadpatri	3206	3595	3999	4758	5173	5765	5760	5798	5888	5815
	(27.87)	(29.85)	(32.37)	(34.39)	(36.65)	(37.55)	(41.57)	(40.62)	(40.07)	(40.74)
Total IV	11502	12043	12353	13838	14116	15355	13856	14274	14695	14275
	(100.0)	(100.0)	(100.0)	(100.0)	(100.0)	(100.0)	(100.0)	(100.0)	(100.0)	(100.0)
Total I+II+III+IV	53500	56563	58823	64916	63091	64810	61410	63708	63414	62844

Source : Based on Annual Reports of APCCADB, Various Issues.

The relationship between the number of beneficiaries during each year and number of beneficiaries outstanding shows disproportionately more. Beneficiaries out-standing ratios to number of beneficiaries during each year district-wise are given in Table 5.9.

Table 5.9 reveals ratios of beneficiaries out-standing to beneficiaries. The ratios indicate the relationship between the number of beneficiaries outstanding to beneficiaries during the last 10 years. This ratio reflects increasing trend of beneficiaries outstanding. In this region the ratio of beneficiaries outstanding to beneficiaries in 1977-78 was 10.80: 1. It indicates with the addition of one beneficiary, the number of beneficiaries outstanding represented nearly 11. In the year 1978-79 and 79-80 their relationship was 8.56:1 and 8.38:1 respectively. It indicates reduction in number of beneficiaries outstanding. The ratio was highest in 1984-85 of 27.71:1 and in 1986-87 it was 20.26:1. The banks in Chittoor district recorded ratios of 29.14 in 1983-84 and 29.44 in 1984-85 revealing over and above the region. In 1979-80 in Kurnool district the ratio was 28.41:1. The figures for other years and districts can be seen from Table 5.9.

TABLE 5.9: Ratios of Beneficiaries outstanding to Beneficiaries

Year	Chittoor	Cuddapah	Kurnool	Anantapur	Region
1977-78	7.72:1	9.57:1	46.77:1	10.87:1	10.80:1
1978-79	5.19:1	10.22:1	22.49:1	8.09:1	8.56:1
1979-80	5.92:1	8.23:1	28.41:1	8.25:1	8.38:1
1980-81	5.57:1	6.02:1	13.63:1	6.06:1	6.42:1
1981-82	19.47:1	23.84:1	17.69:1	10.93:1	17.37:1
1982-83	8.10:1	14.98:1	12.43:1	7.67:1	10.14:1
1983-84	29.14:1	10.69:1	22.11:1	17.67:1	16.42:1
1984-85	29.44:1	34.11:1	25.16:1	21.50:1	27.71:1
1985-86	19.42:1	23.84:1	18.33:1	15.52:1	19.40:1
1986-87	25.03:1	18.54:1	21.65:1	17.89:1	20.26:1

Source: Table 5.1 and Table 5.8.

Loan Amount Outstanding

The mean of loan amount outstanding for the region was Rs. 1763.713. Over a period of decade there has been a steady progress in the amount outstanding. These figures show a similar steady increase in the amount of loan disbursed. The amount of loan outstanding was Rs. 1239.71 lakhs in 1977-78 which raised to Rs. 2167.74 lakhs in 1984-95 and marginally fell down to Rs. 1922.55 lakhs in 1986-87. In Chittoor district the proportion of loan amount outstanding to total outstanding in the region was 20.64 per cent in 1977-78 and 26.76 per cent in 1986-87. In Cuddapah district the co-operative banks recorded 38.24 per cent of outstanding over the total of the region in 1977-78 and 32.54 per cent in 1986-87. In 1986-87 the banks in Kurnool district had 11.59 per cent while the same was 15.58 per cent in 1977-78 indicating a decrease in the amount of outstanding by 3.99 per cent. 25.55 per cent of outstanding represented by the banks in Anantapur district in 1977-78, 27.73 per cent in 1982-83 and 29.11 per cent in 1986-87.

In Chittoor district the Madanapalli PCADB accounted 45.17 per cent of outstanding over the district aggregate outstanding. In all the 10 years this co-operative bank had taken high proportion of outstanding comparing other two co-operative banks in the district. The percentage of outstanding was 45.17 in 1977-78; 54.84 in 1978-79; 58.56 in 1979-80; 58.60 in 1980-81; 56.45 in 1981-82; 54.30 in 1982-83; 51.52 in 1983-84; 50.15 in 1984-85; 36.11 in 1985-86; and 46.65 in 1986-87.

In Cuddapah district, the Proddatur PCADB accounted high percentage of loan amount outstanding in 1977-78; 78-79; 79-80; 80-81. In 1981-82 the Rajampet PCADB represented highest percentage of 37.00 and also in 1982-83 of 37.83 per cent. From 1983-84 to 1986-87 again the Proddatur PCADB ranked first in having highest amount of outstanding in the district. The percentages respectively were 46.09 per cent; 66.09 per cent; 47.73 per cent and 55.39 per cent.

The Nandyal PCADB in Kurnool district had more proportion of loan amount outstanding comparing the other two co-operative banks in the district under study. During this period the percentage of loan amount outstanding ranged from lowest of 43.07 per cent in 1977-78 to highest of 51.52 per cent in 1981-82. In the last two years the percentages of outstanding remained constant though there had been variation in absolute terms.

In Anantapur district the Dharmavaram PCADB represented 35.91 per cent in 1977-78; in 1978-79 the Hindupur PCADB of 34.66 per cent; 34.68 per cent by Tadpatri PCADB in 1979-80. From 1980-81 to 1986-87 the Tadpatri PCADB represented from the district which had highest percentage of loan amount outstanding. The difference during this period ranged from 41.43 per cent in 1981-82 and 43.83 per cent in 1983-84. Table 5.10 depicts bank-wise and year-wise loan amount outstanding.

Relationship of owned Funds To Outstanding

The aggregate of outstanding amount comprises both of owned funds and debt funds. Owned funds and borrowings put together constitute bulk amount in the outstandings. Among these two funds the proportion of borrowed funds has been more than owned funds. Table 5.11 furnishes indices of owned funds and borrowings to outstanding. The percentage of owned funds to outstanding in four district put together in 1977-78 was 58.27, divided into 17.05 per cent in Chittoor district; 14.77 per cent in Cuddapah district; 13.91 per cent in Kurnool district; 12.54 per cent in Anantapur district. While the figure for the region was 14.54 per cent. A comparison of these figures with other districts figures reveals higher percentage of owned funds to outstanding of 17.05 per cent represented by Chittoor district and 14.77 per cent in Cuddapah district. The other two district per had percentages less than average.

The borrowed funds, however, claim higher percentage to outstanding amount. In 1977-78 the percentage of debt funds to outstanding was 85.30 per cent distributed, 26.23 per cent in Chittoor district; 25.13 per cent in Cuddapah district; 7.90 per cent in Kurnool district and 26.04 per cent in Anantapur district. While the figure for the region was 22.90 per cent. Except Kurnool district the other three districts accounted high percentage of borrowed funds over the average of the region. The percentage of borrowings to outstanding was 7.90 only in Kurnool district.

In 1986-87 both the percentages of owned funds to outstanding and borrowings to outstanding declined to 46.89 per cent and 50.28 per cent respectively. In 1978-79 the percentage of borrowings to outstanding exceeded 100 per cent i.e., 100.56 representing 38.05 per cent in Chittoor district; 24.23 per cent in Cuddapah district; 17.11 per cent in Kurnool district; 21.17 per cent in Anantapur district, whereas it was 25.78 for the region as a whole. The total percentage of borrowed funds to outstanding was 91.57 per cent in 1980-81 divided into 25.05 per cent in Chittoor district, 22.01 per cent in Cuddapah district, 20.80 per cent in Kurnool district and 23.71 per cent in

TABLE 5.10: Amount Outstanding

(Rs. in lakhs)

Sl. No.	Name of the Bank	1977-78	78-79	79-80	80-81	81-82	82-83	83-84	84-85	85-86	86-87
I	*Chittoor Dist*										
	(a) Chittoor	76.67	73.39	68.25	87.92	97.18	121.00	135.49	147.77	157.26	146.84
		(29.97)	(21.75)	(16.42)	(17.08)	(19.03)	(20.82)	(24.63)	(26.63)	(35.85)	(28.54)
	(b) Chandragiri	63.60	78.97	103.99	125.22	125.20	144.61	131.16	128.84	123.00	127.67
		(24.86)	(23.41)	(25.02)	(24.32)	(24.52)	(24.88)	(23.85)	(23.22)	(28.04)	(24.81)
	(c) Madanapalli	115.56	185.01	243.34	301.70	288,16	315.66	283.34	278.37	158.45	240.05
		(45.17)	(54.84)	(58.56)	(58.60)	(56.45)	(54.30)	(51.52)	(50.15)	(36.11)	(46.65)
	Total I	255.83	337.37	415.58	514.84	510.54	581.27	549.99	554.98	438.71	514.56
		(100.0)	(100.0)	(100.0)	(100.0)	(100.0)	(100.0)	(100.0)	(100.0)	(100.0)	(100.0)
II	*Cuddapah Dist.*										
	(a) Rajampet	142.58	174.38	192.00	240.72	237.43	244.30	107.09	100.94	86.95	98.33
		(30.08)	(32.89)	(33.12)	(35.44)	(37.00)	(37.83)	(20.98)	(12.19)	(16.17)	(15.72)
	(b) Cuddapah	151.68	169.12	178.33	195.21	180.04	175.17	168.14	179.87	194.15	180.72
		(32.00)	(31.89)	(30.76)	(28.74)	(28.06)	(27.13)	(32.93)	(21.72)	(36.10)	(28.89)
	(c) Proddatur	179.76	186.77	209.35	243.28	224.19	226.29	235.33	547.40	256.77	346.50
		(37.92)	(35.22)	(36.12)	(35.82)	(34.94)	(35.04)	(46.09)	(66.09)	(47.73)	(55.39)
	Total II	374.02	530.27	579.68	679.21	641.66	645.76	510.56	828.21	537.87	625.55
		(100.0)	(100.0)	(100.0)	(100.0)	(100.0)	(100.0)	(100.0)	(100.0)	(100.0)	(100.0)

TABLE 5.10 *Contd.*

Sl. No.	Name of the Bank	1977-78	78-79	79-80	80-81	81-82	82-83	83-84	84-85	85-86	86-87
III	*Kurnool Dist*										
	(a) Banaganapalli	71.04	68.45	62.51	65.65	61.64	63.13	65.76	78.44	75.73	73.31
		(36.78)	(35.35)	(34.45)	(33.29)	(31.04)	(29.85)	(31.42)	(34.65)	(32.53)	(32.90)
	(b) Kurnool	38.92	34.45	32.78	34.68	34.64	39.67	39.18	42.96	45.24	42.46
		(20.15)	(17.79)	(18.07)	(17.59)	(17.44)	(18.75)	(18.72)	(18.98)	(19.43)	(19.06)
	(c) Nandyal	83.17	90.71	86.14	96.88	102.32	108.72	104.35	104.95	111.86	107.05
		(43.07)	(46.86)	(47.48)	(49.12)	(51.52)	(51.40)	(49.86)	(46.37)	(48.04)	(48.04)
	Total III	193.13	193.61	181.43	197.21	198.60	211.52	209.29	226.35	232.83	222.82
		(100.0)	(100.0)	(100.0)	(100.0)	(100.0)	(100.0)	(100.0)	(100.0)	(100.0)	(100.0)
IV	*Anantapur Dist.*										
	(a) Dharmavaram	113.75	112.77	122.76	161.49	151.46	168.75	162.82	173.64	180.29	172.25
		(35.91)	(31.76)	(31.47)	(33.07)	(30.10)	(30.57)	(29.96)	(31.11)	(31.23)	(30.78)
	(b) Hindupur	111.22	123.08	132.05	147.11	143.26	149.60	142.42	148.00	157.21	149.21
		(35.12)	(34.66)	(33.85)	(30.12)	(28.47)	(27.10)	(26.21)	(26.51)	(27.24)	(26.66)
	(c) Tadpatri	91.76	119.21	135.27	179.76	208.47	233.61	238.22	236.56	239.72	238.16
		(28.97)	(33.58)	(34.68)	(36.81)	(41.43)	(42.33)	(43.83)	(42.38)	(41.53)	(42.56)
	Total IV	316.73	355.06	390.08	488.36	503.19	551.96	543.46	558.20	577.22	559.62
		(100.0)	(100.0)	(100.0)	(100.0)	(100.0)	(100.0)	(100.0)	(100.0)	(100.0)	(100.0)
	Total I+II+III+IV	1239.71	1416.31	1566.77	1879.62	1853.99	1990.51	1813.30	2167.74	1786.63	1922.55

Source: Based on Annual Reports of APCCADB, Various Issues.
Note: Figures in brackets indicate percentage to District total.

TABLE 5.11: Indices of owned funds and borrowings to outstanding

(in percentage)

Year	Chittoor		Cuddapah		Kurnool		Anantapur		Total		Region	
	OFO	BO	OFO	BO	OFO	BO	OFO	BO	OFO	BO	OFO	BO
1977-78	17.05	26.23	14.77	25.13	13.91	7.90	12.54	26.04	58.27	85.30	14.54	22.90
1978-79	12.85	38.05	10.48	24.23	14.14	17.11	12.56	21.17	50.03	100.56	12.07	25.78
1979-80	11.74	30.78	11.13	21.37	14.55	14.24	12.49	21.29	49.91	87.68	12.03	23.02
1980-81	10.95	25.05	10.89	22.01	13.50	20.80	11.61	23.71	46.95	91.57	11.37	23.16
1981-82	11.17	10.28	11.46	9.07	13.30	16.60	11.88	16.45	47.81	52.40	11.69	12.21
1982-83	11.45	19.24	11.53	12.25	12.89	22.61	11.63	17.65	47.50	71.75	9.76	16.89
1983-84	12.29	10.90	11.87	17.30	12.77	15.15	12.09	12.68	49.02	56.03	12.17	13.73
1984-85	12.21	8.44	7.44	7.18	12.27	12.58	12.07	9.34	43.99	37.54	10.35	8.63
1985-86	12.69	17.36	11.62	14.80	12.37	16.94	11.99	12.23	48.67	61.33	12.24	14.88
1986-87	12.53	11.85	9.84	12.12	12.47	14.90	12.05	11.41	46.89	50.28	11.51	12.17

OFO: Percentage of owned Funds to outstandings; *BO*: Percentage of borrowings to outstandings.
Source: Table 4.15; 5.10 and 4.7

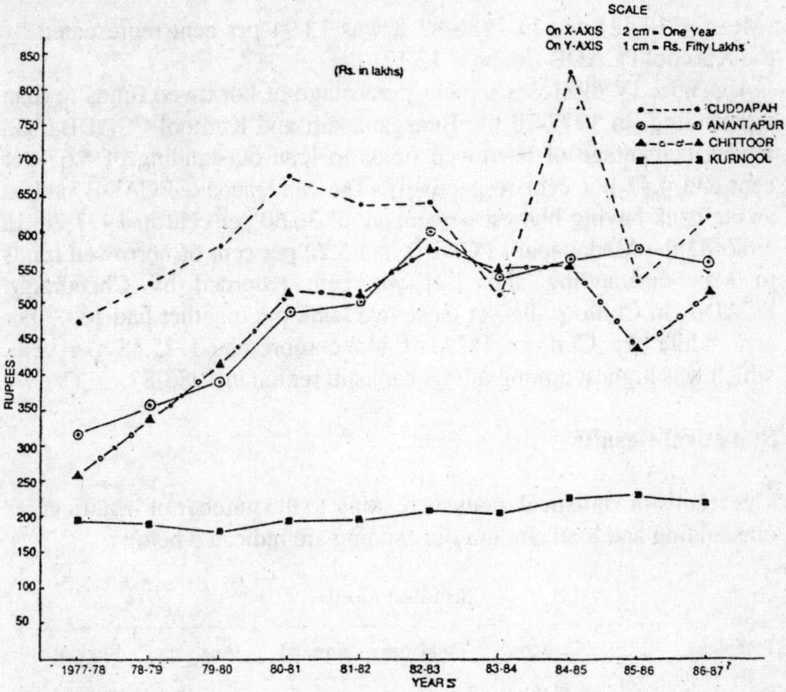

FIG. 5.2: Loans Outstanding

Anantapur district. Indices of percentages of owned and borrowings to outstanding district wise, year-wise along with total and figures for region are indicated in Table. Bank-wise results of proportion of owned funds the outstanding are given in Appendix -III. It shows that it was 25.92 per cent in 1977-78 in Rajampet PCADB; the mean for the region was 14.60 per cent. The individual bankwise analysis of banks having highest per cent of owned funds to out-standing reveals 16.31 per cent represented by Kurnool PCADB in 1978-79 (Mean = 12.89), 17.63 per cent in 1979-80 accounted by Chittoor PCADB (Mean = 13.03), 15.74 per cent represented by Kurnool PCADB (Mean 12.19) in 1980-81, and 16.57 per cent (Mean = 12.42) by the same bank in 1981-82, again in 1982-83 the same bank claimed highest per cent of 15.02 (Mean = 12.25). In 1983-84 in Chittoor district the Chandragiri PCADB accounted 14.97 per cent (Mean = 12.60), in 1984-85 the same bank claimed 15.07 per cent (Mean = 11.88), 18.86 per cent by the Madanapalli PCADB from the same district in 1985-86

(Mean = 12.42) and in 1986-87 it was 13.94 per cent represented by the Kurnool PCADB (Mean = 12.12).

Appendix IV discloses indices percentage of borrowed funds to loan outstanding. In 1977-78 the Banaganapalli and Kurnool PCADBs had lowest percentage of borrowed funds to loan outstanding of 4.67 per cent and 4.47 per cent respectively. The Madanapalli PCADB ranked as the bank having highest percentage of 36.60 per cent in 1977-78. In 1986-87 the Madanapalli PCADB had 5.72 per cent of borrowed funds to loan outstanding and 7.71 per cent recorded by Chandragiri PCADB. In Chittoor district these two bank put together had 13.43 per cent while the Chittoor PCADB alone represented 25.48 per cent, which was highest among all the banks in region in 1986-87.

Statistical Results

The results of statistical analysis relating to the number of beneficiaries outstanding and loan amount outstanding are indicated below:

Statistical Analysis

,Technique	Chittoor		Cuddapah		Kurnool		Anantapur		Region	
	BO	LO	BO	LO	BO	LO	BO	LO	BO	LO
R	0.65	0.47	0.23	0.15	0.42	0.80	0.67	0.85	0.51	0.59
C.G.R	2.66	6.18	1.55	2.16	1.43	2.41	2.59	6.72	1.53	4.44
C.V.	9.36	22.44	9.03	17.02	6.90	8.08	9.18	19.69	6.22	5.80
L.G.R.	2.49	5.07	1.42	2.16	-1.47	2.39	2.48	6.00	1.46	4.01

CGR : Compound Growth Rate
LGR : Linear Growth Rate
CV : Co-efficient of variation
R : Correlation
LO : Loan Amount outstanding
BO : Beneficiaries outstanding

OR Due to and Due by

The abbreviation OR stands for outstanding ratio. In the financial management of rural financial institutions the area of outstanding due to and due by indicates the relationship between the primary banks and the apex bank and between the beneficiaries and primary banks. The primary banks have been always showing in their ledgers outstanding amount due to apex bank. This represents the borrowed amount repayable by the co-operative banks in turn have ledger balances of loan amount outstanding due by the members to the primary banks. Thus the study of outstanding due to, and outstanding due by, highlights the co-operative banks' financial relations of loaning operations between the beneficiaries, primary banks and the apex bank.

Generally the amount of loan outstanding due by the beneficiaries to the primary banks is more than the amount of borrowing outstanding due to apex banks by the primary banks. In some years the outstanding due to and due by has been in increase relations. Under this paragraph it is attempted to measure the relationship between outstanding, due to and outstanding due by with the help of technique of outstanding Ratio and Elasticity Co-efficient of outstanding. Symbolically the outstanding ratio is expressed as follows:

$$OR = OD_t / OD_b$$

where,

OR = Outstanding Ratio
OD_t = Outstanding Due to
OD_b = Outstanding Due by

Similarly the elasticity co-efficient of outstanding explains the rate of change. It may be more or less than the unit or it may be equal to unit. If it is not equal to unit it may be inferred the existence of variation in the amount of outstanding due to and due by. If it is equal to unit if reflects change in the outstanding amount due to and amount of outstanding due by is equal.

Symbolically the elasticity co-efficient of outstanding is studied with the help of

$$O_e = \frac{\Delta OD_t / OD_t}{\Delta OD_b / OD_b}$$

Where,

O_e = Elasticity Co-efficient of outstandings
OD_t = Outstanding Due to
OD_b = Outstanding Due by

$\Delta\ OD_t$ = Change in outstanding Due to
$\Delta\ OD_b$ = Change in outstanding Due by
Due to = The amount of borrowing outstanding due to, by the primary bans to the apex bank.
Due by = The amount of loan amount outstanding due by the beneficiaries to the primary banks.

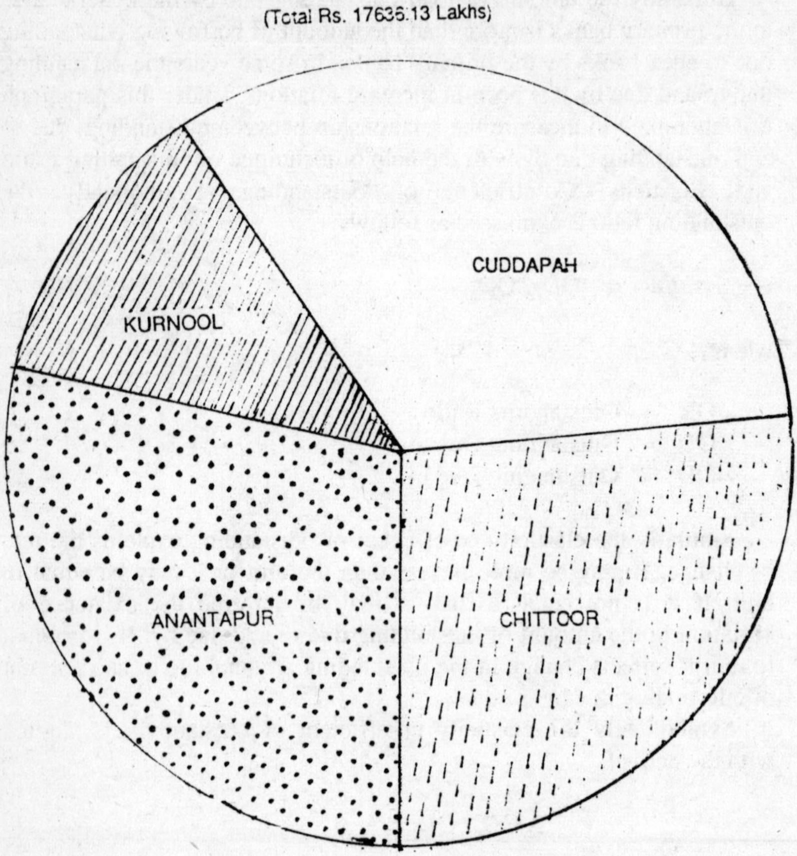

FIG. 5.3: Loans Outstanding

The results of outstanding ratios alongwith elasticity co-efficient of outstanding are presented in Table 5.12. The outstanding ratio (OR) indicates the amount outstanding due to the apex bank for every one rupee outstanding due by the members. The OR may be greater or lesser or equal to unit i.e., one. If OR is greater or lesser than the unit it reflects that outstanding due to is more or less than the outstanding due by.

The analysis given in Table 5.12 discloses the ratio of outstanding due to, to outstanding due by. In the year 1977-78, accordingly, for every one rupee of outstanding due by, the outstanding due to was ninety seven paise. In other words the amount of outstanding due by was more by Rs. 32.44 lakhs. In 1980-81 the OR was nearly equal to unit.

TABLE 5.12: Outstanding Ratios and Elasticity Co-efficient of Outstanding

Year	Chittoor	Cuddapah	Kurnool	Anantapur	Region
1977-78	0.98	0.95	1.02	0.98	0.97
1978-79	0.97	1.01	1.01	0.96	0.99
1979-80	0.96	0.99	1.03	0.96	0.98
1980-81	1.00	1.01	1.05	0.95	1.00
1981-82	0.99	1.02	1.07	0.99	1.01
1982-83	1.01	1.02	1.11	0.98	1.02
1983-84	1.00	1.28	1.11	0.99	1.09
1984-85	1.01	0.80	1.12	1.00	0.94
1985-86	1.24	1.27	1.12	1.01	1.16
1986-87	1.07	1.06	1.12	1.00	1.05
Mean	1.02	1.04	1.08	0.98	1.02
O_e	1.20	1.50	1.80	1.05	1.24

It means there was a difference of Rs. 9.25 lakhs more due by. The due to was Rs. 1870.37 lakhs and due by was Rs. 1879.62 lakhs. In the year 1986-87 the OR was 1.05 :1 lakhs and it may be inferred from this ratio that the proportion of outstanding amount due to was more than the amount outstanding due by. In the region the outstanding ratios was more than unit in 1981-82; 1982-83 1983-84; 1985-86 and 1986-87. The mean outstanding ratio for the region was 1.02, while elasticity co-efficient of outstanding was 1.24. The Co-operative banks in all the districts except the banks in Anantapur district had mean OR more than one. The significant feature is that the Kurnool district had OR ratio more than one in all ten years, while the elasticity co-efficient of outstanding was 1.80. Year-wise and district-wise OR and O_e results can be pursued from Table.

Instalment Demand

An instalment demand refers to a demand or call made by the bank on the beneficiaries to pay a part of instalment amount due for payment during the year. When the loan is granted by the banks to the beneficiaries, they seldom collect full amount along with interest by equal instalments distributed over a period of years. It is part of outstanding amount on the loan, is a debt due by the members to the bank. It is a liability for payment arises when instalment amount due is called by the bank. The terms and conditions of payment of instalment money are governed by the bye-laws and the agreement of loan.

The total instalment demand recoverable from member borrowers during the co-operative year 1977-78 aggregated to Rs. 311.75 lakhs, which represents 25.15 per cent to outstanding. In 1981-82 the demand was Rs. 672.77 lakhs, Rs. 693.89 lakhs in 1982-83 and it marginally fell down to Rs. 657.46 lakhs in 1986-87. The percentage of instalments demand to outstanding was highest in 1983-84 in the region of 41.93 per cent, 38.14 per cent in 1985-86, 34.20 per cent in 1986-87. Table 5.13 gives details of instalment demand bank-wise and year-wise. The mean percentage of instalment demand to outstanding was 38.38 per cent in 1981-82; 43.05 per cent in 1983-84 and 40.36 per cent in 1985-86. The percentage of instalment demand decreased by 3.55 per cent in 1986-87. The individual bank-wise performance of percentage of instalment demand to outstanding as well as mean value results are arranged in Appendix V.

Loan Recoveries

Loan recovery means the actual recover of money as against instalment demand. Recovery is the most crucial area of financial management in co-operative banks to judge soundness and effectiveness of these banks in their financial performance. Thus the importance of recovery cannot be overemphasised. As a matter of fact the success of long-term co-operative credit movement is largely dependent on the recovery performance. The poor recovery performance not only leads to chronic overdue problem but also effects eligibility to draw fresh loans from apex and other financing agencies like NABARD.

TABLE 5.13: Instalment Demand

Sl. No.	Name of the Bank	1977-78	78-79	79-80	80-81	81-82	82-83	83-84	84-85	85-86	86-87
I	*Chittoor Dist*										
(a)	Chittoor	22.45	22.87	22.25	21.98	27.31	31.02	33.50	37.30	53.29	41.36
		(36.42)	(31.77)	(25.10)	(20.88)	(15.70)	(16.06)	(15.30)	(25.42)	(26.15)	(21.78)
(b)	Chandragiri	17.23	19.99	23.75	28.28	44.20	46.78	51.30	34.56	53.96	46.61
		(27.95)	(27.77)	(26.79)	(26.86)	(25.41)	(24.22)	(23.42)	(23.55)	(26.47)	(24.55)
(c)	Madanapalli	21.96	29.13	42.65	55.01	102.41	115.37	134.22	74.88	96.57	101.89
		(35.63)	(40.46)	(48.11)	(52.26)	(58.89)	(59.72)	(61.28)	(51.03)	(47.38)	(53.67)
	Total I	61.64	71.99	88.65	105.27	173.92	193.17	219.02	146.74	203.82	189.86
		(100.0)	(100.0)	(100.0)	(100.0)	(100.0)	(100.0)	(100.0)	(100.0)	(100.0)	(100.0)
II	*Cuddapah Dist.*										
(a)	Rajampet	24.13	31.72	43.13	44.22	43.15	32.03	43.67	32.35	32.28	36.10
		(25.16)	(25.71)	(26.19)	(26.35)	(18.03)	(14.42)	(18.08)	(19.65)	(16.48)	(17.99)
(b)	Cuddapah	37.04	47.70	60.92	60.90	92.90	92.53	102.85	68.97	77.95	83.26
		(38.62)	(38.66)	(36.99)	(36.29)	(38.82)	(41.67)	(42.58)	(41.90)	(39.79)	(41.49)
(c)	Proddatur	34.74	43.97	60.66	62.70	103.24	97.51	95.05	63.27	85.67	81.33
		(36.22)	(35.63)	(36.82)	(37.36)	(43.15)	(43.91)	(39.34)	(38.44)	(43.73)	(40.52)
	Total II	95.91	123.39	164.71	167.82	239.29	222.07	241.57	164.59	195.90	200.69
		(100.0)	(100.0)	(100.0)	(100.0)	(100.0)	(100.0)	(100.0)	(100.0)	(100.0)	(100.0)

(Contd.)

TABLE 5.13 *Contd.*

Sl. No.	Name of the Bank	1977-78	78-79	79-80	80-81	81-82	82-83	83-84	84-85	85-86	86-87
III	*Kurnool Dist*										
(a)	Banaganapalli	25.89	23.18	27.49	23.61	31.69	30.70	33.16	25.04	32.43	30.21
		(34.44)	(31.49)	(32.99)	(36.02)	(35.67)	(32.54)	(32.20)	(27.41)	(27.89)	(29.17)
(b)	Kurnool	17.05	18.98	18.85	13.49	17.41	18.23	20.58	18.04	22.82	20.48
		(24.00)	(25.78)	(22.62)	(20.58)	(19.59)	(19.32)	(19.98)	(19.74)	(19.62)	(19.78)
(c)	Nandyal	28.11	31.46	36.98	28.44	39.75	45.42	49.24	48.29	61.04	52.86
		(39.56)	(42.73)	(44.39)	(43.39)	(44.74)	(48.14)	(47.82)	(52.85)	(52.49)	(51.05)
	Total III	71.05	73.62	83.32	65.54	88.85	94.35	102.98	91.37	116.29	103.55
		(100.0)	(100.0)	(100.0)	(100.0)	(100.0)	(100.0)	(100.0)	(100.0)	(100.0)	(100.0)
IV	*Anantapur Dist.*										
(a)	Dharmavaram	35.85	39.81	44.37	42.85	63.86	66.40	83.17	54.99	67.52	68.56
		(43.11)	(43.44)	(40.08)	(38.44)	(37.41)	(36.03)	(43.25)	(43.01)	(40.82)	(41.97)
(b)	Hindupur	26.13	26.33	33.53	35.42	54.53	56.88	50.07	27.96	40.40	39.48
		(31.43)	(28.73)	(30.29)	(31.78)	(31.94)	(30.86)	(25.44)	(21.87)	(24.43)	(24.17)
(c)	Tadpatri	21.17	25.50	32.80	33.19	52.32	61.02	63.59	44.90	57.47	55.32
		(25.46)	(27.83)	(29.63)	(29.78)	(30.65)	(33.01)	(32.31)	(35.12)	(34.75)	(33.86)
	Total IV	83.15	91.64	110.70	111.46	170.71	184.30	196.83	127.85	165.39	163.36
		(100.0)	(100.0)	(100.0)	(100.0)	(100.0)	(100.0)	(100.0)	(100.0)	(100.0)	(100.0)
	Total I+II+III+IV	311.75	360.64	447.38	450.09	672.77	693.89	760.40	530.55	681.40	657.46

Source : Based on Annual Reports of APCCADB, various Issues.
Note: Figures in brackets indicate percentage to sub total.

The study of experience of these banks in recoveries discloses some interesting events on the recovery front. The figures relating to recovery performance of these banks over the years in respect of many banks do not indicate effective recovery from the members. One of the most disquieting characteristics of these banks in the management of loan operation has been the problem of unsatisfactory recovery trends. The primary banks could not genuinely recovering from their borrowers though the banks have been increasingly advancing loans. Poor recovery may also affect the working capital availability at bank level and leads to inadequate repaying capacity of the banks to the apex bank and other financial institutions. The Maclagen committee correctly pointed out that "unless loans are repaid punctually, co-operation is both financially and educationally an illusion".

Of the instalment demand the primary co-operative banks were able to collect Rs. 263.07 lakhs in the region in 1977-78 and retained a balance of Rs. 48.68 lakhs as against Rs. 335.03 lakhs retained as at the end of 1986-87. The percentage of recovery to instalment demand as at the end of 1986-87 works out to 49.04 per cent as compared to that of 84.38 per cent in 1977-78, 73.94 per cent in 1978-79; 73.55 per cent in 1979-80. In majority of years the percentage of recovery had been less than 50 per cent. In Chittoor district in 1977-78 the percentage of recovery to instalment demand was 59.39 per cent while it was 57.47 per cent in 1986-87. The banks in cuddapah district could recover 65.14 per cent to demand in 1977-78 and 45.28 per cent to instalment demand in 1986-87, thereby showing a fall in the percentage of recovery to the extent of 19.86 per cent during the period. The co-operative banks in Kurnool district in 1977-78 were able to collect 72.55 per cent to demand and 39.34 per cent in 1986-87. The recovery experience in respect of these banks in Anantapur district also has been of no difference. 79.78 per cent of loans recovered as against instalment demand of Rs. 83.15 lakhs in 1977-78 as against Rs. 163.36 lakhs in 1986-87 and retained a balance of nearly 50 per cent. Table 5.14 gives a detailed information regarding individual bank-wise loan recoveries, alongwith percentage of recoveries to instalment demand.

The proportion of recovery to outstanding loan in the region was only 21.22 per cent in 1977-78, decreased to 16.77 per cent in 1986-87. The percentage recovery to loan amount outstanding fluctuated widely during the period.

TABLE 5.14: Loan Recoveries

(Rs. in Lakhs)

Sl. No.	Name of the Bank	1977-78	78-79	79-80	80-81	81-82	82-83	83-84	84-85	85-86	86-87
	1	2	3	4	5	6	7	8	9	10	11
1.	Chittoor	21.86	21.76	21.60	18.36	23.73	24.72	27.87	24.67	45.51	32.68
		(97.37)	(95.15)	(97.08)	(83.53)	(86.89)	(79.69)	(83.19)	(66.14)	(85.40)	(79.01)
2.	Chandragiri	14.75	15.64	17.36	13.68	25.26	13.36	26.69	14.00	33.32	24.67
		(85.61)	(78.24)	(71.83)	(48.37)	(57.15)	(28.56)	(52.03)	(40.51)	(61.75)	(52.93)
3.	Madanapalli	—	—	38.60	14.06	49.68	23.07	73.21	24.24	57.83	51.76
		(100)	(100)	(90.50)	(25.56)	(48.51)	(20.00)	(54.54)	(32.37)	(59.88)	(50.80)
4.	Rajampet	—	26.05	33.58	19.02	28.94	11.76	22.30	9.70	22.55	18.18
		(100)	(81.84)	(77.86)	(43.01)	(67.07)	(36.72)	(51.06)	(29.99)	(69.86)	(50.36)
5.	Cuddapah	28.86	31.13	39.62	20.58	46.94	34.66	43.55	18.46	27.84	29.95
		(77.92)	(65.26)	(65.04)	(33.79)	(50.53)	(37.46)	(42.34)	(26.67)	(35.72)	(35.97)
6.	Proddatur	33.62	35.86	47.47	22.89	63.50	51.95	58.01	30.03	40.18	42.74
		(96.78)	(81.56)	(78.26)	(36.51)	(61.51)	(53.28)	(61.03)	(46.46)	(46.99)	(27.96)
7.	Banaganapalli	21.06	16.31	21.08	10.26	19.57	16.45	18.19	11.53	14.25	14.66
		(81.34)	(70.36)	(76.68)	(43.46)	(61.75)	(53.58)	(54.86)	(46.05)	(43.94)	(48.53)

(Contd.)

TABLE 5.14 *Contd.*

1	2	3	4	5	6	7	8	9	10	11
8. Kurnool	8.29	8.41	8.73	4.12	7.83	5.52	9.11	2.72	9.62	7.15
	(48.62)	(44.31)	(46.31)	(30.54)	(44.97)	(30.28)	(44.27)	(15.08)	(42.16)	(34.91)
9. Nandyal	22.20	20.27	25.92	14.46	19.88	18.22	24.05	12.93	19.79	18.93
	(78.98)	(64.43)	(70.09)	(50.84)	(50.01)	(40.11)	(48.84)	(26.78)	(32.42)	(35.81)
10. Dharmavaram	24.45	22.69	25.36	12.29	32.12	19.32	40.06	14.13	25.34	26.51
	(68.20)	(57.00)	(57.16)	(28.68)	(50.30)	(29.10)	(48.17)	(25.70)	(37.53)	(38.67)
11. Hindupur	24.53	19.83	22.79	11.68	30.35	20.83	29.90	9.58	15.02	18.17
	(93.88)	(75.31)	(67.97)	(32.98)	(55.66)	(36.62)	(59.72)	(34.26)	(37.18)	(46.02)
12. Tadpatri	17.36	19.21	26.92	16.97	35.35	37.08	46.24	29.67	35.18	37.03
	(82.00)	(75.33)	(82.07)	(51.13)	(67.56)	(60.77)	(72.72)	(66.08)	(61.22)	(66.94)
Region	263.07	266.29	329.03	178.37	383.15	276.94	419.18	201.66	346.43	322.43
	(84.38)	(73.84)	(73.55)	(39.63)	(56.95)	(39.91)	(55.13)	(38.00)	(50.84)	(49.04)
Mean	18.08	19.76	27.42	14.86	31.93	23.08	34.93	16.81	28.87	26.87

Note: Figures in bracket indicate percentage of recovery of instalment demand.
Source: Based on Annual Reports and Table 5.13

It was only 9.49 per cent in 1980-81 and 9.30 per cent in 1984-85. The position of the co-operative banks in this respect was satisfactory in the year 1983-84 in which percentage of recovery to outstanding was highest of 23.12 per cent during this period. One of the most unsatisfactory features of these banks is in respect of many banks being less than 10 per cent of recovery to outstanding. From a small figure percentage of 4.81 recovery to outstanding up to 10 per cent also there are many banks. There is decreasing trend of percentage of recovery in respect of many banks.

The individual bank-wise analysis shows that the percentage of recovery to outstanding recorded by Banaganapalli PCADB was 29.65 in 1977-78, whose recovery performance has been not satisfactory by passing of years. For instance the percentage of recovery to outstanding decreased to 14.70 per cent in 1984-85; 18.82 per cent in 1985-86; and 20.00 per cent in 1986-87. This shows a difference of 9.65 per cent down trend over the period. Similarly the Hindupur PCADB which had 22.06 per cent of recovery to outstanding accounted in 1977-78 which gradually fell down to 13.92 per cent in 1982-83; to 6.47 per cent in 1984-85; to 9.55 per cent in 1985-86 and marginally increased to 12.18 per cent in 1986-87. The main reasons for lower percentage of recovery to instalment due and outstanding are cyclical drought conditions, crop failures etc. Appendix VI gives bank-wise percentage of recover to outstanding. It discloses that the mean percentage of recovery of outstanding was 19.13 in 1977-78, 11.53 per cent in 1980-81, 25.61 per cent in 1983-84 and 15.93 per cent in 1986-87.

The following Table 5.15 shows the size of recovery performance to demand.

Overdue Management

A timely recovery of loans advanced is a matter of serious concern in overdue management. It is a main branch of financial management in co-operative rural banks. The extent to which recovery of loans not made it leads to deterioration of working capital and ultimately causes an obstacle to uninterrupted flow of credit to the needy members. If the overdues exceed a specific percentage of demand, may impair the banks capacity to draw funds either from the apex bank or central financing agencies. Though there has been considerable increase in the loan operations of these banks both in respect of expansion and coverage, there has been no corresponding results in the recovery. The working of co-operative banks in long-term credit in this region shows to some extent lack of punctuality in the repayment of loans advanced. The results of this trend has been a steady rise in the amount of overdues. In respect of many banks the problem of high overdues has assumed serious proportion. It has been causing serious concern particularly to the primary banks and apex bank. The overdues in these banks have been rising steadily in this region over the past five years. The scarce owned funds of these banks are at present blocked up because of the backlog of long overdues.

TABLE 5.15: Size of Recovery Performance to Demand

Year	Up to 20%	Between 21%-40%	Between 41%-60%	Above 60%	Total
1977-78	2 (5)	- (7)	1 (-)	9 (-)	12(12)
1978-79	1 (8)	- (4)	2 (-)	9 (-)	12(12)
1979-80	- (4)	- (8)	2 (-)	10 (-)	12(12)
1980-81	- (11)	6 (1)	5 (-)	1 (-)	12(12)
1981-82	- (4)	- (8)	7 (-)	5 (-)	12(12)
1982-83	1 (10)	7 (2)	2 (-)	2 (-)	12(12)
1983-84	- (2)	- (9)	9 (1)	3 (-)	12(12)
1984-85	1 (12)	6 (-)	3 (-)	2 (-)	12(12)
1985-86	- (7)	4 (4)	4 (1)	4 (-)	12(12)
1986-87	- (10)	5 (1)	5 (1)	2 (-)	12(12)

Note: Figures in bracket indicate percentage of recovery to outstanding.

Table 5.16 shows the trends in overdues of co-operative agricultural development banks in this region since 1977-78 to 1986-87. It is evident from the table that there has been a significant increase in the amount of overdues. In the region as a whole covering 12 sample units the amount of overdues in case of agricultural development banks increased from Rs. 48.68 lakhs in 1977-78; to Rs. 94.35 lakhs in 1978-79; to Rs. 118.35 lakhs in 1979-80; to Rs. 271.72 lakhs in 1980-81; to Rs.289.62 lakhs in 1981-82; to Rs. 416.95 lakhs in 1982-83; to Rs. 341.22 lakhs in 1983-84; to Rs. 328-89 lakhs in 1984-85, to Rs. 334.97 lakhs in 1985-86, and to Rs. 335.03 lakhs in 1986-87, while the percentage of overdues to instalment demand moved from 15.62 per cent in 1977-78 to 50.96 per cent in 1986-87. These banks also experienced that percentage of overdues to instalment demand was more than 60 per cent. For instance in 1980-81 in this region the percentage of overdues to instalment demand was 60.37 per cent; in 1982-83 60.09 per cent and in 1984-85 62.00 per cent.

The banks which have 60 per cent and above overdues to instalment demand were the Cuddapah PCADB (66.21 per cent), the Proddatur PCADB (63.49 per cent), Kurnool PCADB (69.46 per cent), Dharmararam PCADB (71.32 per cent), Hindupur PCADB (67.02 per cent) in 1980-81, while the average for the region was 60.37 per cent. In 1984-85 such banks were Madanapalli PCADB (67.63 per cent), the incidence of percentage of overdues to outstandings had shot up year after year. In the region as a whole of sample banks the mean proportion of overdues to outstanding moved from 5.23 per cent in 1977-78; 8.60 per cent in 1978-79; 9.49 per cent in 1979-80; 15.23 per cent in 1980-81; 16.59 per cent in 1981-82; 21.74 per cent in 1982-83; 19.98 per cent in 1985-86; and 19.46 per cent in 1986-87.

Overdue size

The analysis of distribution of co-operative banks according to overdue size reveals some additional information on overdue aspects and the number of banks. In overdue size below 25 per cent there were 10 banks in 1977-78; 8 banks in 1978-79; and 7 banks in 1979-80 and remaining years 1 bank in each year from 1980-81 to 1986-87. In other words, it means there was only one bank in 1977-78 between overdue size of 26 per cent — 40 percentage, represented by Kurnool district. Between 41 per cent and above the same district represented which had one bank in this range. Gradually the distribution of banks in the overdue size of 41 per cent and above constituted major proportion. To refer as against 12 total units there were Rajampet PCADB (70.01 per cent), Cuddapah PCADB (73.33 per cent), Kurnool PCADB (84.92 per cent), Nandyal PCADB (73.22 per cent), Dharmavaram PCADB (74.30 per cent) and Hindupur PCADB (65.74 per cent). In this year the percentage for the region was 62.00. There were five banks in 1986-87 having percentage of overdue to instalment demand more than 60 per cent. To mention by name they were Cuddapah PCADB (64.03 per cent), Proddatur PCADB (72.04 per cent), Kurnool PCADB (65.09 per cent), Nandyal PCADB (64.19 per cent), and in Anantapur district Dharmavaram PCADB (61.33 per cent). The serious magnitude of overdues in these banks can be gauged from table, bank-wise.

TABLE 5.16: Overdues

(*Rs. in Lakhs*)

Sl. No.	Name of the Bank	1977-78	78-79	79-80	80-81	81-82	82-83	83-84	84-85	85-86	86-87	t-test
	1	2	3	4	5	6	7	8	9	10	11	12
1.	Chittoor	0.59	1.11	0.65	3.62	3.58	6.30	5.63	12.63	7.78	8.68	
		(2.63)	(4.85)	(2.92)	(16.47)	(18.11)	(20.31)	(16.81)	(33.86)	(14.60)	(20.99)	
2.	Chandragiri	2.48	4.35	6.39	14.60	18.94	33.42	24.61	20.56	20.64	21.94	
		(14.39)	(21.76)	(28.17)	(51.63)	(42.85)	(71.44)	(47.97)	(59.49)	(38.25)	(47.07)	
3.	Madanapalli	—	—	4.05	40.95	52.73	92.30	61.01	50.64	38.74	50.13	
		(—)	(—)	(9.50)	(74.44)	(51.49)	(80.00)	(45.46)	(67.63)	(40.12)	(49.20)	
4.	Rajampet	(—)	5.67	9.55	25.20	14.21	20.27	21.37	22.65	9.73	17.92	
			(18.16)	(22.14)	(56.99)	(32.93)	(63.28)	(48.94)	(70.01)	(30.14)	(49.64)	
5.	Cuddapah	8.18	16.57	21.30	40.32	45.96	57.87	59.30	50.51	50.11	53.31	
		(22.08)	(34.74)	(34.96)	(66.21)	(49.47)	(62,54)	(57.66)	(73.33)	(64.28)	(64.03)	
6.	Proddatur	1.12	8.11	13.19	39.81	39.74	45.56	37.04	33.24	45.49	38.59	
		(3.22)	(18.44)	(21.74)	(63.49)	(38.49)	(46.72)	(38.97)	(53.54)	(53.01)	(72.04)	
7.	Banaganapalli	4.83	6.87	6.41	13.35	12.12	14.25	14.97	13.51	18.18	15.55	
		(18.66)	(29.64)	(23.32)	(56.54)	(38.25)	(46.42)	(45.14)	(53.95)	(56.06)	(51.47)	

(*Contd.*)

TABLE 5.16 *Contd.*

1	2	3	4	5	6	7	8	9	10	11	12
8. Kurnool	8.76	10.57	10.12	9.37	9.58	12.71	11.47	15.32	13.20	13.33	
	(51.38)	(55.69)	(53.69)	(69.46)	(55.03)	(69.72)	(55.73)	(84.92)	(57.84)	(65.09)	
9. Nandyal	5.91	11.19	11.06	13.98	19.87	27.20	25.19	35.36	41.25	33.93	
	(21.02)	(35.57)	(29.91)	(49.16)	(49.99)	(59.89)	(51.16)	(73.22)	(67.58)	(64.19)	
10. Dharmavaram	11.40	17.12	19.01	30.56	31.74	47.08	43.11	40.86	42.18	42.05	
	(31.80)	(43.00)	(42.84)	(71.32)	(49.70)	(70.90)	(51.83)	(74.30)	(62.47)	(61.33)	
11. Hindupur	1.60	6.50	10.74	23.74	24.18	36.05	20.17	18.38	25.38	21.31	
	(6.12)	(24.69)	(32.03)	(67.02)	(44.34)	(63.38)	(40.28)	(65.74)	(62.82)	(53.98)	
12. Tadpatri	3.81	6.29	5.88	16.22	16.97	23.94	17.35	15.23	22.29	18.29	
	(18.00)	(24.67)	(17.93)	(48.87)	(32.44)	(39.23)	(27.28)	(33.92)	(38.78)	(33.06)	
Region	48.68	94.35	118.35	271.72	289.62	416.95	341.22	328.89	334.97	335.03	-16.48*
	(15.62)	(26.16)	(26.45)	(60.37)	(43.05)	(60.09)	(44.87)	(62.00)	(49.16)	(50.96)	
Mean	4.06	7.86	9.86	22.64	24.14	34.75	28.44	27.41	27.91	27.92	

Note: Figures in brackets indicate percentage of overdues to instalment demand.

Source: Based on Annual reports of APCCADB, various issued.

For 9 Degree of Freedom the table value of t at 5 per cent level of significance (t 0.05)=2.262

* Difference is significant.

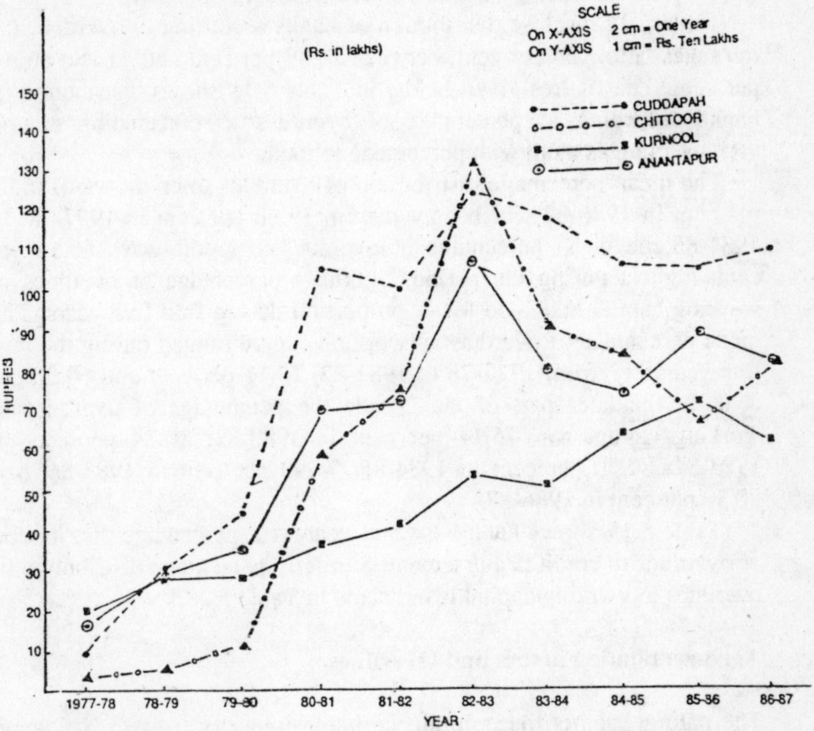

FIG. 5.4: Overdues

It is also more relevant to observe proportional relationship of overdues to outstandings. The percentage of overdues to outstanding, bank-wise and year-wise figures, during a decade are arranged in a statement appended (Appendix VII). The appendix discloses evidently that there has been a significant increase in the percentage of overdues to outstanding. The proportion of overdues to outstanding had gone up from 3.93 per cent in 1977-78, to 20.95 per cent in 1982-93 and subsequently decreased to 17.43 per cent of overdues to outstanding in 1986-87 in the region. This region's analysis shows that there were 11 units in the overdue size of 41 per cent and above in 1980-81; 7 units in 1981-82; 10 units in 1982-83; 8 units in 1983-84; 10 units in 1984-85; 7 units in 1985-86 and 10 units in 1986-87. The percentage of overdue size to total units below 25 per cent was 83.33; between 26-40 per cent range 8.33; and 41 and above per cent it was 8.34 in 1977-78. By the end of decade their position had been in quite inverse respectively 8.33 per cent; 8.33 per cent and 83.34 per cent.

Table 5.17 disclose distribution of banks according to overdue size in ranges below 25 per cent, between 26.40 per cent and 41 and above per cent. The figures given below in Table 5.18 shows distribution of banks according to percentage of overdues to outstanding among various a ranges alongwith percentage to total.

The mean percentage distribution of overdues to credit was 176.20 per cent in 1986-87 which moved from 79.68 per cent in 1977-78. In 1984-85 the mean percentage of overdues to credit was 466.52 per cent, highest during the period. Similarly percentage of overdues to working capital had been lower proportion during first five years. The mean percentage of overdues to working capital ranged during the first five years i.e., from 1977-78 to 1981-82, 20.11 per cent and 68.50 per cent. In the later part of the decade the percentage of overdues to working capital was 75.14 per cent in 1982-83; 80-54 per cent in 1983-84; 89.70 per cent in 1984-85; 74.99 per cent in 1985-86; and 80.32 per cent in 1986-87.

Table 5.19 shows bank-wise and year-wise percentage distribution of overdues to credit disbursement. Similarly percentage distribution of overdues to working capital is indicated in Table 5.20.

Agro-economic Factors and Overdues

The natural factors like rainfall, cropping intensity, pattern, irrigation etc., are directly influencing factors in the farm economics. Among them rainfall is basic ingredient for better yield and output. As it has been already discussed earlier that delay, failure and inadequate rainfall are the characteristic features in this region. This may cause to affect production and in turn makes the farmer earn lower income and thereby commits default in payment of credit. Raising two or more crops during a year is known as cropping intensity. The commercial crops like cotton, sugarcane, groundnut etc., yield more income comparing to food crops. The agroeconomic factors like rainfall, cropping intensity, irrigation and commercial crops ensure more production and thereby higher income which enable the farmer to repay the loans. The impact of these factors is verified with the help of data given in Table 5.21.

TABLE 5.17: Distribution of Banks According to Overdue Size

Year	Below 25%					Between 26-40					41% and above					Total Units
	AN	CHI	CU	KU	T	AN	CHI	CU	KU	T	AN	CHI	CU	KU	T	
1977-78	2	3	3	2	10	—	—	—	1	1	—	—	—	1	1	12
1978-79	3	3	2	—	8	—	—	1	2	3	—	—	—	1	1	12
1979-80	1	3	2	1	7	1	—	1	1	3	1	—	—	1	2	12
1980-81	—	1	—	—	1	—	—	—	—	—	3	2	3	3	11	12
1981-82	—	1	—	—	1	1	—	2	1	4	2	2	1	2	7	12
1982-83	—	1	—	—	1	1	—	—	—	1	2	2	3	3	10	12
1983-84	—	1	—	—	1	2	—	1	—	3	1	2	2	3	8	12
1984-85	—	—	—	—	—	1	1	—	—	2	2	2	3	3	10	12
1985-86	—	1	—	—	1	1	2	1	—	4	2	—	2	3	7	12
1986-87	—	1	—	—	1	1	—	—	—	1	2	2	3	3	10	12
Percentage of overdue size to total units																
1977-78		83.33 %				8.33 %						8.34 %				100.00%
1978-79		66.67 %				25.00 %						8.33 %				100.00%
1979-80		58.33 %				25.00 %						16.67 %				100.00%
1980-81		8.33 %				00.00 %						91.67 %				100.00%
1981-82		8.33 %				33.33 %						58.34 %				100.00%
1982-83		8.33 %				8.33 %						83.34 %				100.00%
1983-84		8.33 %				25.00 %						66.67 %				100.00%
1984-85		0.00 %				16.67 %						83.33 %				100.00%
1985-86		8.33 %				33.33 %						58.34 %				100.00%
1986-87		8.33 %				8.33 %						83.34 %				100.00%

AN : Anantapur; CHI : Chittoor; CU : Cuddapah; KU : Kurnool; T : Total

TABLE 5.18: Percentage of overdues to outstanding

Year	Up to 20%	Between 21% - 40%	Between 41% - 60%	Above 60%	Total
1977-78	11 (91.67)	1 (8.33)	- (-)	- (-)	12 (100.00)
1978-79	11 (91.67)	1 (8.33)	- (-)	- (-)	12 (100.00)
1979-80	11 (91.67)	1 (8.33)	- (-)	- (-)	12 (100.00)
1980-81	10 (83.33)	2 (16.67)	- (-)	- (-)	12 (100.00)
1981-82	9 (75.00)	3 (25.00)	- (-)	- (-)	12 (100.00)
1982-83	4 (33.33)	8 (66.67)	- (-)	- (-)	12 (100.00)
1983-84	6 (50.00)	6 (50.00)	- (-)	- (-)	12 (100.00)
1984-85	7 (58.33)	5 (41.67)	- (-)	- (-)	12 (100.00)
1985-86	6 (50.00)	6 (50.00)	- (-)	- (-)	12 (100.00)
1986-87	6 (50.00)	6 (50.00)	- (-)	- (-)	12 (100.00)

The table reveals that the value of co-efficient of correlation of the banks' overdues with that of agro-economic like rainfall, cropping intensity, irrigated are to net area sown, commercial crops area to net area sown are (-) 0.66; (-) 0-89; (-) 0.46; and (-) 0.87 in the district of Anantapur respectively. The results indicates a negative relationship between overdues and agro-economic factors. The relation of overdues with the four agro-economic factors in the district of Chittoor; (-) 0.48; (-) 0.93; (-) 0.46; and (-) 0.22; in the district of Cuddapah (-) 0.4; (-) 0.94; (-) 0.51; and (-) 0.95; in the district of Kurnool (-) 0.54; (-) 0.88; (-) 0.53 and (-) 0.6. The above figures show the existence of inverse relationship of agroeconomic factors and overdues position. One of our hypotheses is that the relationship between agro-economic factors and overdues is positive. But the results shows relationship between them as negative.

Regression Co-efficients

Here it is attempted to study regression co-efficients of influencing agro-economic factors of overdues. This phenomenon is explained by fitting in the Regression Co-efficient Analysis; ($Y = a + b^x$). The independent variables are working capital, rainfall, cropping intensity, irrigated area to net area sown and commercial crops area to net area (x), and depend variable is overdues of the banks (Y). The adopted variables of agroeconomic factors and overdues are as under :

$$Y = a+b_1 x_1 + b_2 x_2 + b_3 x_3 + b_4 x_4 + b_5 x_5$$

TABLE 5.19: Percentage Distribution of Overdues to Credit Disbursements

(*Percentage*)

Name of the Bank	1977-78	78-79	79-80	80-81	81-82	82-83	83-84	84-85	85-86	86-87
1. Chittoor	6.25	8.94	5.90	11.26	15.68	15.09	14.64	43.11	18.59	23.75
2. Chandragiri	16.18	16.56	16.28	47.88	122.27	116.28	391.26	269.11	127.88	218.96
3. Madanapalli	0	0	5.00	61.32	395.57	221.45	544.73	475.05	205.41	369.42
4. Rajampet	0	11.93	23.42	39.44	66.09	114.52	129.91	3330.88	260.86	257.84
5. Cuddapah	26.34	45.13	59.45	125.30	296.13	314.34	251.59	209.59	147.38	195.85
6. Proddatur	2.80	17.84	25.35	78.30	173.16	115.00	70.22	98.90	120.18	93.21
7. Banaganapalli	236.76	71.79	67.76	105.45	118.36	103.94	90.78	113.62	109.92	103.87
8. Kurnool	537.42	568.28	219.05	182.65	210.09	146.26	199.48	246.70	180.82	207.63
9. Nandyal	58.98	57.09	83.41	63.17	119.27	136.56	210.44	386.87	203.40	245.87
10. Dharmavaram	50.89	119.89	68.11	78.91	143.75	150.56	214.16	185.31	171.46	188.90
11. Hindupur	5.28	26.83	47.33	99.83	209.35	169.65	153.15	149.19	121.26	137.75
12. Tadpatri	15.23	16.10	17.22	29.29	33.80	51.00	50.00	89.85	88.24	71.36
Mean (X)	79.68	80.03	53.61	76.90	158.63	137.90	193.36	466.52	146.23	176.20

TABLE 5.20: Percentage Distribution of Overdues of Working Capital

(*Percentages*)

Name of the Bank	1977-78	78-79	79-80	80-81	81-82	82-83	83-84	84-85	85-86	86-87
1. Chittoor	2.72	4.34	2.83	3.82	9.67	10.92	9.25	27.24	12.65	15.43
2. Chandragiri	10.37	11.37	12.76	30.41	60.84	67.22	97.39	75.12	85.11	85.60
3. Madanapalli	—	—	3.91	44.30	127.61	130.04	147.44	123.94	79.65	114.90
4. Rajampet	—	8.92	14.98	27.90	16.25	43.06	70.52	160.52	58.26	87.97
5. Cuddapah	17.45	14.11	38.70	74.23	122.40	142.19	135.95	112.34	87.63	110.13
6. Proddatur	1.05	12.18	18.95	50.49	82.60	69.23	49.37	53.68	66.69	56.43
7. Banaganapalli	37.01	34.44	33.42	62.35	61.96	50.42	67.10	66.36	72.34	68.81
8. Kurnool	114.51	37.83	102.22	87.98	85.23	91.83	100.43	112.07	110.18	107.85
9. Nandyal	27.60	34.36	47.96	39.29	69.50	82.45	101.98	159.06	132.47	130.40
10. Dharmavaram	28.87	55.75	43.58	53.60	76.70	85.23	100.44	90.66	87.17	92.50
11. Hindupur	3.62	17.39	13.11	58.33	86.02	95.83	67.73	60.98	65.40	64.75
12. Tadpatri	9.89	12.17	11.79	21.69	23.23	33.28	18.92	34.38	42.36	29.09
Mean (X)	20.11	20.24	28.68	46.20	68.50	75.14	80.54	89.70	74.99	80.32

TABLE 5.21: Agro-economic Factors and Overdues

Year	Anantapur					Chittoor					Cuddapah					Kurnool				
	R	CI	I	CC	O	R	CI	I	CC	O	R	CI	I	CC	O	R	CI	I	CC	O
1969-70	45	117	13	51	8.45	60	116	30	47	0.78	56	118	34	44	1.83	55	113	14	51	10.32
1972-73	58	116	17	49	25.22	52	117	29	41	3.13	54	115	27	43	1.49	58	122	21	56	26.92
1975-76	67	115	18	43	36.75	83	119	26	44	5.84	80	117	24	40	9.59	81	117	24	53	25.98
1978-79	52	117	15	36	188.81	98	112	24	40	34.38	82	120	21	42	62.94	74	113	19	46	110.60
1981-82	51	107	14	39	285.15	70	107	21	38	330.14	55	103	19	38	270.62	55	110	17	52	158.48
1984-85	42	103	18	40	304.60	66	109	34	54	299.99	56	102	29	34	371.15	59	105	15	36	230.01
1986-87	40	102	10	32	424.42	67	104	12	32	353.74	58	102	14	34	418.40	55	104	15	48	310.05
r(-)	0.66	0.89	0.46	0.87		0.48	0.93	0.46	0.22		0.4	0.94	0.51	0.95		0.54	0.88	0.53	0.6	

Sources: 1.Andhra Pradesh Year Book, 1986.
2.Government of Andhra Pradesh, Planning and Development of Backward Regions — A Case of Rayalaseema Vol. I, 1970.
3.Government of Andhra Pradesh, Statistical Abstracts, 1981.
4.Overdues Management in Co-operative Banks, Dr. C.R. Reddy.

R = Rainfall in cms during three years ended; CC = Commercial crops area to net area (in%)
I = Irrigation area to net area (in%)
O = Overdues (Rs. in lakhs)
CI = Cropping Intensity (in %)

Where,

$Y =$ Overdues
$x_1 =$ Working capital
$x_2 =$ Rainfall
$x_3 =$ Cropping intensity
$x_4 =$ Irrigated area to net area sown
$x_5 =$ Commercial crops area to net area sown
b_1, b_2, b_3, b_4 and b_5 = co-efficients
a = Intercept.

The collective impact of these influencing factors is observed by fitting to regression analysis to explain overdues. To achieve this object the figures relating to independent variables (X) pertain to the entire district, not necessarily sample units. The district-wise data of the influencing agroeconomic factors co-efficients are given below:

Anantapur

$$Y = 1022.1111 + 0.5034\,X_1 - 1.8369\,X_2 - 2.1130\,X_3 - 14.9840\,X_4 - 10.5197\,X_5$$

F- Value = 24.15 C.D = 0.9757

Chittoor

$$Y = 2648.6442 + 0.1402\,X_1 - 4.6453\,X_2 - 24.2823\,X_3 - 11.0631\,X_4 + 17.2681\,X_5$$

F - value = 2.64 C.D. = 0.8919

Cuddapah

$$Y = 2002.2635 - 0.3975\,X_1 + 0.9953\,X_2 - 9.1395\,X_3 - 16.4032\,X_4 = 9.8815\,X_5$$

F - value = 6.0724 C.D. = 0.9100

Kurnool

$$Y = 1247.5525 + 1.1466\,X_1 - 3.9407\,X_2 - 0.1031\,X_3 - 7.7396\,X_4 - 17.1955\,X_5$$

F - value = 3.0580 C.D = 0.8360

Region

$$Y = 1720.9759 + 0.2461 X_1 - 0.3766 X_2 - 0.0348 X_3 - 1.1974 X_4 - 1.5034 X_5$$

F - value = 3.42 C.D. = 0.8387

The co-efficient of determination (R^2) for overdues and agroeconomic factors works out 0.9757, 0.8149, 0.9100 and 0.8360 respectively for Anantapur, Chittoor, Cuddapah and Kurnool districts. The overdues were explained by the independent variables at 97.57 per cent, 81.49 per cent, 91.00 per cent and 83.60 per cent respectively. For the region as a whole overdues are being explained by 83.87 per cent. The contribution of individual characteristics to total overdues are calculated and are given in Appendix VIII.

Inter-Regional Variation

Comparison of sample units' total percentage of loan recovery to instalment demand with that of Rayalaseema region's (39 Co-operative banks) percentage of recovery to instalment demand shows that loan recovery performance of sample units has been better comparing the region's average. In 1977-78 the percentage of loan recovery of 12 units was 84.38 per cent while of 39 units' percentage of recovery was 74.3 per cent. In 1985-86 their position respectively was 50.84 and 41.6 per cent. The comparative references year-wise can be observed through Table 5.14 and Table 5.22. Table 5.22 also reveals inter regional variations of instalment demand and loan recoveries in respect of Rayalaseema, Telangana and Coastal Andhra. In so far as recovery experience is concerned the banks in coastal Andhra have been better comparing banks in Rayalaseema region as well as Telangana region. The most disquieting feature of co-operative banks in Rayalaseema region has been that since 1980-81 till 1985-86 no bank secured 100 per cent recovery as against 40 primary banks working in this region. In 1979-80 as against 39 banks in this region only one bank secured 100 per cent recovery, 2 banks in 1978-79 and 6 banks in 1977-78.

Out of 205 banks in the entire state only 24 banks were able to secure 100 per cent recovery. The State figures relating to number of banks which secured 100 per cent recovery were 23 out of 218 in 1985-86, 19 banks in 1984-85 out of 218 banks, 28 banks in 1983-84 out of 218 banks in the state, in 1982-83 22 banks out of the same number and 21 banks in 1981-82 out of 218 banks. In 1980-81, 20 banks only could secure 100 per cent recovery as against 206 banks in the state. The table discloses particulars of number of banks which secured 100 per cent recovery, percentage of recovery to instalment demand, reflecting inter-regional variations.

Foreclosed Loans

The number of cases and the amount under foreclosed loans are more, is another important hypothesis grounded to be tested. The problem is foreclose has serious implications. The co-operative banks have experienced with the problems of poor recovery and overdues. Consequently, therefore, the loans have been closed either on accounts of arrears of instalments or on account of alienation. If the property is mortgaged as security for a loan which the borrower unables to repay the loan the bank can foreclose on the mortgage. The bank is entitled to sell the security and indemnity out of the proceeds to the extent of loan. Sometimes in the course of recovery of amounts of the foreclosed loans the banks have to purchase the lands.

During earlier years of the decade the primary banks closed only a few loans comparing the later part of the decade. At the beginning of the year 1978-79 there were 918 number of foreclosed loans. The banks have further closed 59 cases during 1978-79. In 1982-83 there were 1,093 foreclosed loans which moved to 1,402 in 1986-87. In Chittoor district the number of foreclosed loans outstanding were 458 in 1984-85 constituting 32.57 per cent of the region. In Cuddapah district the number of, foreclosed loans outstanding were more in 1985-86 accounting 736 representing 42.20 per cent. In Kurnool district the number of foreclosed loans outstanding had been more from 1977-78 to 1981-82 ranged between 181 and 259. From 1982-83 to 1986-87 the closed loans ranged between 151 and 167. In Anantapur district the maximum number of foreclosed loans outstanding were 511 in 1984-85 accounting 36.64 per cent to total, in 1985-86 there were 453 accounting 25.97 per cent to total. The trend of foreclosed loans outstanding figures are shown in Table 5.23.

The table value of t at 5 per cent level of significance (t 0.05) = 2.262. For the region the difference is significant. It is also significant in respect of all the districts except the Chittoor district, where the difference is insignificant.

The amount on foreclosed loans outstanding was Rs. 24.09 lakhs in

1977-78 on 918 foreclosed loans. The amount recoverable was Rs. 64.10 lakhs in 1986-87 on 1402 closed loans. In 1985-86 the number of closed loans outstanding were maximum during the decade. The banks recorded 1744 cases involving a sum of Rs. 75.43 lakhs on this outstanding loans. Table 5.24 indicates bank-wise and year-wise amount on foreclosed loans outstanding.

The test statistics t, shows that the difference is significant for the region and for Chittoor, Cuddapah and Anantapur districts and it is insignificant in case of Kurnool district.

Working Results

The study of financial results of co-operative banks in terms of profit earned and losses incurred enables us to know the operational efficiency and viability of these banks. This paragraph is devoted on this area of financial performance of the bank, in order to achieve one of the objectives of the work. Hypothesis also grounded that, the most of the co-operative sector banks have been running on losses. In order to measure the soundness of their working results it would be desirable to know the figures relating to profits earned or loss sustained. This is the deciding factor as to the availability of dividends to the members. By observation of these figures for the last few years, a fairly sound assessment of the financial performance of these banks can be worked out.

Table 5.25 shows net profit earned or loss sustained resulting from business operations over a period of 10 years, and their comparative performance over the years would reveal in general their economic viability. Besides the members who are owners of the bank, the outsiders like creditors, financial institutions and perspective investors are also interested in their financial soundness. The mobilisation of resources, declaration of reasonable rate of dividend, to plough back of profits, the operating efficiency of the bank etc., would depend upon the extent of ultimate present profits and future earning.

The table reveals that the Chittoor PCADB incurred loss for 7 years during 10 years with an amount of loss ranged between Rs. 0.32 lakhs and Rs. 2.03 lakhs. The Chandragiri PCADB sustained loss continuously for 9 years from 1978-79 to 1986-87. The amount of loss sustained was heaviest of Rs. 11.42 lakhs. In Chittoor district this bank functioning with losses. The Madanapalli PCADB recorded losses for four years during 10 years. The amount of loss was Rs. 0.15 lakhs in 1981-82 lowest, Rs. 11.26 lakhs in 1985-86 highest.

TABLE 5.22: Inter-Regional Variations of Instalment Demand and Recoveries

(*Amount Rs. in Lakhs*)

Year	Rayalaseema			Telangana			Coastal Andhra		
	Instalment Demand	% of Recoveries	No. of Banks which secured 100% recovery	Instalment Demand	% of Recoveries 100% recovery	No. of Banks which secured	Instalment Demand	% of Recoveries	No. of Banks which secured 100% recovery
1977-78	926	74.3	6	1229	71.6	4	1721	69.2	27
1978-79	1073	63.1	2	1560	66.2	3	2311	68.6	18
1979-80	1307	64.4	1	1981	66.3	3	2709	75.7	20
1980-81	1222	31.7	—	2082	55.3	—	2598	71.9	20
1981-82	1937	51.2	—	2965	56.7	—	3254	71.0	21
1982-83	2057	31.9	—	3506	50.6	—	3636	62.0	22
1983-84	2257	47.1	—	3763	57.5	—	4066	69.3	28
1984-85	1655	27.2	—	3233	45.5	—	3795	56.8	19
1985-86	2053	41.6	—	4860	51.6	—	4533	62.7	23

Source: Based on Annual Reports of APCCADB, various issues.

TABLE 5.23: Number of Foreclosed Loans Outstanding

(Nos.)

Sl. No. Name of the Bank	1977-78	78-79	79-80	80-81	81-82	82-83	83-84	84-85	85-86	86-87
I *Chittoor Dist*										
(a) Chittoor	74	70	61	45	43	42	81	79	54	71
	(26.62)	(19.45)	(20.54)	(16.85)	(16.67)	(16.41)	(29.35)	(17.25)	(13.47)	(18.78)
(b) Chandragiri	54	53	49	48	48	47	44	44	32	40
	(19.42)	(14.72)	(16.50)	(17.98)	(18.60)	(18.36)	(15.94)	(9.61)	(7.98)	(10.58)
(c) Madanapalli	150	237	187	174	167	167	151	335	315	267
	(53.96)	(65.83)	(62.96)	(65.17)	(64.73)	(65.23)	(54.71)	(73.14)	(78.55)	(70.64)
Total I.	278	360	297	267	258	256	276	458	401	378
	(100.0)	(100.0)	(100.0)	(100.0)	(100.0)	(100.0)	(100.0)	(100.0)	(100.0)	(100.0)
II *Cuddapah Dist.*										
(a) Rajampet	13	47	42	31	187	187	96	110	569	258
	(7.18)	(25.68)	(22.70)	(18.24)	(58.08)	(46.06)	(32.32)	(38.46)	(77.31)	(58.77)
(b) Cuddapah	81	69	74	73	70	96	90	84	88	87
	(44.75)	(37.71)	(40.00)	(42.94)	(21.74)	(23.65)	(30.30)	(29.37)	(11.96)	(19.82)
(c) Proddatur	87	67	69	66	65	123	111	92	79	94
	(48.07)	(36.61)	(37.30)	(38.82)	(20.18)	(30.29)	(37.38)	(32.17)	(10.73)	(21.41)
Total II	181	183	185	170	322	406	297	286	736	439
	(100.0)	(100.0)	(100.0)	(100.0)	(100.0)	(100.0)	(100.0)	(100.0)	(100.0)	(100.0)

(Contd.)

TABLE 5.23 *Contd.*

Sl. No.	Name of the Bank	1977-78	78-79	79-80	80-81	81-82	82-83	83-84	84-85	85-86	86-87
III	*Kurnool Dist*										
(a)	Banaganapalli	27	61	54	54	54	54	53	51	42	48
		(11.64)	(23.55)	(23.18)	(24.22)	(29.83)	(32.34)	(33.54)	(33.77)	(27.27)	(31.17)
(b)	Kurnool	85	84	77	77	74	68	68	65	61	65
		(36.64)	(32.43)	(33.05)	(34.53)	(40.89)	(40.72)	(43.04)	(43.05)	(39.61)	(42.21)
(c)	Nandyal	120	114	102	92	53	45	37	35	51	41
		(51.72)	(44.02)	(43.77)	(41.25)	(29.28)	(26.94)	(23.42)	(23.18)	(33.12)	(26.62)
	Total III	232	259	233	223	181	167	158	151	154	154
		(100.0)	(100.0)	(100.0)	(100.0)	(100.0)	(100.0)	(100.0)	(100.0)	(100.0)	(100.0)
IV	*Anantapur Dist.*										
(a)	Dharmavaram	124	82	55	53	32	26	20	[illegible]	183	134
		(54.63)	(46.86)	(45.83)	(17.04)	(11.15)	(9.85)	(6.08)	(38.94)	(40.40)	(31.09)
(b)	Hindupur	58	54	39	101	98	91	174	166	138	159
		(25.55)	(30.86)	(32.50)	(32.48)	(34.15)	(34.47)	(52.89)	(32.49)	(30.46)	(36.89)
(c)	Tadpatri	45	39	26	157	157	147	135	146	132	138
		(19.82)	(22.28)	(21.67)	(50.48)	(54.70)	(55.68)	(41.03)	(28.57)	(29.14)	(32.02)
	Total IV	227	175	120	311	287	264	329	511	453	431
		(100.0)	(100.0)	(100.0)	(100.0)	(100.0)	(100.0)	(100.0)	(100.0)	(100.0)	(100.0)
	Total I+II+III+IV	918	977	835	971	1048	1093	1060	1406	1744	1402

Note: Figures in Brackets indicate percentage to district total.
Source: Based on Annual Reports of APCCADB, various issues.
For 9 Degree of Freedom the table value of t at 5 per cent level of significance, (t 0.05) = 2.262; * Difference is significant.

TABLE 5.24: Amount on Foreclosed Loans Outstanding

(Rs. in lakhs)

Sl. No.	Name of the Bank	1977-78	78-79	79-80	80-81	81-82	82-83	83-84	84-85	85-86	86-87
I	*Chittoor Dist*										
	(a) Chittoor	1.40	1.30	1.12	0.96	0.94	0.87	1.87	1.84	1.53	1.75
		(26.67)	(18.90)	(18.70)	(16.93)	(17.90)	(17.16)	(33.94)	(11.35)	(10.09)	(14.24)
	(b) Chandragiri	1.12	1.07	1.02	0.98	0.98	0.87	0.76	0.76	0.62	0.71
		(21.33)	(15.55)	(17.03)	(17.28)	(18.67)	(17.16)	(13.79)	(4.69)	(4.09)	(5.78)
	(c) Madanapalli	2.73	4.51	3.85	3.73	3.33	3.33	2.88	13.61	13.01	9.83
		(52.00)	(65.55)	(64.27)	(65.79)	(63.43)	(65.68)	(52.27)	(83.96)	(85.82)	(79.98)
	Total I	5.25	6.88	5.99	5.67	5.25	5.07	5.51	16.21	15.16	12.29
		(100.0)	(100.0)	(100.0)	(100.0)	(100.0)	(100.0)	(100.0)	(100.0)	(100.0)	(100.0)
II	*Cuddapah Dist.*										
	(a) Rajampet	0.27	1.13	1.00	0.74	6.75	6.75	4.95	4.51	17.83	9.10
		(5.40)	(22.56)	(20.41)	(17.21)	(64.59)	(28.60)	(24.90)	(24.03)	(58.96)	(39.62)
	(b) Cuddapah	2.99	2.54	2.59	2.39	2.31	7.95	7.46	7.26	7.47	7.40
		(59.80)	(50.70)	(52.86)	(55.58)	(22.11)	(33.69)	(37.53)	(38.68)	(24.70)	(32.22)
	(c) Proddatur	1.74	1.34	1.31	1.17	1.39	8.90	7.47	7.00	4.94	6.47
		(34.80)	(26.74)	(26.73)	(27.21)	(13.30)	(37.71)	(37.57)	(37.29)	(16.34)	(28.16)
	Total II	5.00	5.01	4.90	4.30	10.45	23.60	19.88	18.77	30.24	22.97
		(100.0)	(100.0)	(100.0)	(100.0)	(100.0)	(100.0)	(100.0)	(100.0)	(100.0)	(100.0)

(Contd.)

TABLE 5.24 *Contd.*

Sl. No.	Name of the Bank	1977-78	78-79	79-80	80-81	81-82	82-83	83-84	84-85	85-86	86-87
III	*Kurnool Dist*										
(a)	Banaganapalli	0.87	1.86	1.80	1.76	1.74	1.70	1.62	1.91	1.29	1.61
		(12.32)	(24.09)	(25.25)	(25.96)	(31.58)	(35.79)	(36.90)	(42.44)	(15.07)	(27.47)
(b)	Kurnool	1.97	1.91	1.86	1.85	1.75	1.58	1.57	1.56	1.51	1.55
		(27.90)	(24.74)	(26.09)	(27.29)	(35.79)	(33.26)	(35.76)	(34.67)	(17.64)	(26.63)
(c)	Nandyal	4.22	3.95	3.47	3.17	1.40	1.47	1.20	1.03	5.76	2.66
		(59.78)	(51.17)	(48.66)	(46.75)	(28.63)	(30.95)	(27.34)	(22.89)	(67.29)	(45.70)
	Total III	7.06	7.72	7.13	6.78	4.89	4.75	4.39	4.50	8.56	5.82
		(100.0)	(100.0)	(100.0)	(100.0)	(100.0)	(100.0)	(100.0)	(100.0)	(100.0)	(100.0)
IV	*Anantapur Dist.*										
(a)	Dharmavaram	2.95	2.63	1.63	1.28	0.83	1.09	0.65	9.64	6.82	5.70
		(43.51)	(42.97)	(39.47)	(12.40)	(7.71)	(10.91)	(3.33)	(34.35)	(31.77)	(24.76)
(b)	Hindupur	2.78	2.51	1.77	5.65	6.68	5.84	15.93	15.04	11.50	14.16
		(41.00)	(41.01)	(42.86)	(54.75)	(62.08)	(58.46)	(81.61)	(53.60)	(53.56)	(61.51)
(c)	Tadpatri	1.05	0.98	0.73	3.39	3.25	3.06	2.94	3.38	3.15	3.16
		(15.49)	(16.02)	(17.67)	(32.85)	(30.20)	(30.63)	(15.06)	(12.05)	(14.67)	(13.73)
	Total IV	6.78	6.12	4.13	10.32	10.76	9.99	19.52	28.06	21.47	23.02
		(100.0)	(100.0)	(100.0)	(100.0)	(100.0)	(100.0)	(100.0)	(100.0)	(100.0)	(100.0)
	Total I+II+III+IV	24.09	25.73	22.15	27.07	31.35	43.41	49.30	67.54	75.43	64.10

Note: Figures in brackets indicate percentage to district total.
Source : Based on Annual Reports of APCCADB, various issues.
For 9 Degree of Freedom the table value of t at 5 per cent level of significane (t 0.05) = 2.262.
* Difference is significant.

TABLE 5.25: Banks on Profit/Loss Line

(*Rs. in Lakhs*)

Sl. No.	Name of the Bank	1977-78	78-79	79-80	80-81	81-82	82-83	83-84	84-85	85-86	86-87
1.	Chittoor	0.44 (–)	0.50 (–)	0.65 (–)	0.32 (–)	— (0.70)	— (0.67)	1.13 (–)	— (0.80)	2.03 —	1.05 —
2.	Chandragiri	— (0.17)	0.60 (–)	0.80 (–)	5.85 (–)	5.26 (–)	0.76 (–)	3.71 (–)	11.42 (–)	9.62 (–)	8.25 (–)
3.	Madanapalli	— (0.40)	— (0.40)	— (0.45)	— (0.05)	0.15 (–)	— (0.18)	— (0.15)	0.25 (–)	11.26 (–)	3.84 (–)
4.	Rajampet	— (0.90)	— (0.39)	— (0.20)	— (0.37)	— (0.20)	— (0.20)	0.10 (–)	0.45 (–)	4.39 (–)	1.65 (–)
5.	Cuddapah	— (0.25)	0.75 (–)	3.40 (–)	6.00 (–)	1.63 (–)	3.86 (–)	4.36 (–)	18.21 (–)	31.23 (–)	17.93 (–)
6.	Proddatur	— (0.60)	— (1.05)	0.62 (–)	2.00 (–)	0.65 (–)	5.00 (–)	0.50 (–)	6.00 (–)	11.86 (–)	6.12 (–)
7.	Banaganapalli	— (0.38)	— (0.02)	— (0.01)	4.35 (–)	1.75 (–)	1.90 (–)	3.75 (–)	1.74 (–)	12.40 (–)	5.96 (–)
8.	Kurnool	3.25 (–)	4.56 (–)	4.59 (–)	1.40 (–)	1.67 (–)	2.03 (–)	3.03 (–)	5.69 (–)	3.36 (–)	4.03 (–)
9.	Nandyal	1.91 (–)	1.58 (–)	1.53 (–)	1.90 (–)	3.83 (–)	5.81 (–)	3.36 (–)	7.14 (–)	12.75 (–)	7.75 (–)
10.	Dharmavaram	3.16 (–)	3.96 (–)	4.64 (–)	5.20 (–)	6.73 (–)	16.11 (–)	15.03 (–)	16.89 (–)	37.51 (–)	23.14 (–)
11.	Hindupur	— (0.25)	— (0.10)	— (0.13)	8.00 (–)	4,75 (–)	11.70 (–)	0.25 (–)	20.13 (–)	26.07 (–)	15.48 (–)
12.	Tadpatri	— (0.50)	0.71 (–)	— (0.62)	2.48 (–)	— (0.40)	1.84 (–)	1.27 (–)	3.54 (–)	— (3.29)	1.60 (–)
	Total	8.76 (3.45)	12.66 (1.96)	16.23 (1.41)	37.50 (0.42)	26.42 (1.30)	49.01 (1.05)	36.49 (0.15)	91.46 (0.80)	162.48 (3.29)	96.80 (–)

Source: Based on Annual Reports of APCCADB

Note: Figures in bracket indicate profit earned.

TABLE 5.26: Number of Banks on Loss Lines

Year	Chittoor	Cuddapah	Kurnool	Anantapur	Region	t-test
1977-78	1(2)	-(3)	2(1)	1(2)	4(8)	
1978-79	2(1)	1(2)	2(1)	2(1)	7(5)	
1979-80	2(1)	2(1)	2(1)	1(2)	7(5)	
1980-81	2(1)	2(1)	3(-)	3(-)	10(2)	
1981-82	2(1)	2(1)	3(-)	2(1)	9(3)	
1982-83	1(2)	2(1)	3(-)	3(-)	9(3)	33.12*
1983-84	2(1)	3(-)	3(-)	3(-)	11(1)	
1984-85	1(2)	3(-)	3(-)	3(-)	10(2)	
1985-86	3(-)	3(-)	3(-)	2(1)	11(1)	
1986-87	3(-)	3(-)	3(-)	3(-)	12(-)	

Note: Figures in bracket indicate the number of banks on profit line.
Source: Table 5.25
For 9 degree of freedom the table value of t at 5 per cent level of significance (t 0.05) = 2.262. Since the calculated value of t is more than the table value.
* Significant.

In Cuddapah district, the Rajampet PCADB showing losses only for the last 4 years i.e., from 1983-84 to 1986-87. The Cuddapah PCADB incurred losses continuously for 9 years out of 10 years observation. The amount of loss was Rs. 31.23 lakhs in 1985-86, Rs. 18.21 lakhs in 1984-85 and the lowest was Rs. 0.75 lakhs in 1978-79. The Proddatur PCADB except for the years 1977-78 and 1978-79 the bank continuously incurred losses.

In Kurnool district, the Banaganapalli PCADB has been better comparing other two banks because the other two banks incurred losses for 10 years. While Banaganapalli PCADB did not sustain loss during 1977-78, 1978-79 and 1979-80.

In Anantapur district, the Dharmavaram PCADB sustained loss for 10 years, Hindupur PCADB for 7 years and Tadpatri PCADB for 4 years.

Even the banks which have been earning profit, the amount of profit has been only in thousands of rupees. The observation of profit figures shows that no bank had earned profit of one lakh except Proddatur PCADB which earned profit of Rs. 1.05 lakhs. A comparative glance about number of banks on profitable lines, and loss line along with the amount of profit and loss can be had from table.

The co-operative banks have been providing both financial and other services at comparatively low cost. Even though one of the principles of co-operation is not to earn profit but to render service to the members to promote their economic interest. But they are not expected to sustain losses heavily and continuously which eats away internal resources, cannot build up funds by retaining a part of profits to strengthen resources and ultimately makes the bank financially weak. The financing agencies also measure their financial soundness on the basis of profits as one of the criteria for extending loans. Though profit earning is not aimed at in case of rural banks of this sector but must earn the reasonable surplus to strengthen the bank financially, slowly and steadily to be self-reliant.

6

APEX BANK

Laws for Restricting the operations of money lenders have completely failed.

— Agrarian Reforms Committee

In the preceeding chapters we have discussed in a bit detail the financial relations between the primary banks and the Central co-operative agricultural Development Bank. In this chapter it is attempted to study the working of the Apex Bank in general to have full coverage of co-operative Banks in agricultural development.

Regional Apex Banks

(A) *Andhra Co-operative Central Mortgage Bank (ACCMB)*

In Andhra Pradesh, as already stated, there is a two-tier federal structure of land development banking. At State level there is an Apex land Development institution. It is primarily the association of the primary land development banks which are, essentially by virtue of their relations, affiliated to the Apex Bank. The need for a Central Co-operative land development bank was long felt to raise adequate long-term funds to finance primary land development member banks affiliated to it.

The history of the establishment of central land development bank in the state goes back to composite Madras state. The then Registrar of Co-operative Societies of the Madras State Mr. F.R. Hemingway, suggested a scheme to issue debentures to raise long-term funds. He viewed in 1919 that the provincial Co-operative Bank should issue debentures. In 1927, the Townsend Committee appointed by the Madras Government found that the primary banks were unable to make progress without the help of Central land mortgage bank and to raise and finance the primary banks. The Royal Commission on Agriculture, 1928 also suggested the formation of Central land development banks.

So, the Central Land Mortgage Bank was formed in 1929. For successful working of these institutions the Centre Land Mortgage Bank Act, 1934 came into being in the Composite Madras State.

The Bank was organically connected with basic and secondary institutions. Thus its division became inevitable with the policy of the Government. The Andhra State Act facilitated the separation of Andhra Area from the composite Madras State in Act, 1953. The Madras Government facilitated the division of the Madras Central Land Mortgage Bank by promulgating on 4th September, 1953 an ordinance No. 2, 1953, known as the Madras Co-operative Societies (Reorganisation and Formation) Ordinance, 1953. It facilitated and provided for the registration of the Andhra Co-operative Central Land Mortgage Bank. The Registrar of Co-operative Societies (Madras) placed before the general body of the Bank, a scheme for the division of the Madras Central Land Mortgage Bank (MCLMB). The scheme was finally accepted with minor modifications as suggested by the members.

Accordingly, the Andhra Central Land Mortgage Bank was carved out of the old Madras Central Land Mortgage Bank, registered on 5th September, 1953 and started from 7th September 1953, In 1953 with the formation of separate state of Andhra region, the Andhra Central Land Mortgage Bank assumed as Apex Bank for primary banks located in eleven telugu speaking districts. However, the Bank continued to function till 1962 when it was first amalgamated with the another regional bank for Telangana area, namely the Hyderabad Central Land Mortgage Bank.

On the bifurcation of Composite Madras Co-operative Land Mortgage Bank and on the formation of the Andhra Co-operative Central Land Mortgage Bank on 5th September, 1953 debentures for a sum of Rs. 276.94 lakhs were allotted to its shares by the composite Co-operative Central Land Mortgage Bank. Since its inception till its amalgamation with the Hyderabad Co-operative Central Land Mortgage Bank, the Andhra Co-operative Central Land Mortgage issued debentures for a sum of Rs. 688.06 lakhs.

Under the scheme of productive credit it was agreed that the Government of India and the Reserve Bank of India should together purchase the debenture of Andhra Co-operative Central Land Mortgage Bank up to a maximum limit of 40 per cent. During 1953-54 the Bank issued first series of debentures of Rs. 60.00 lakhs for 20 years at 4.50 per cent.

In the wake of the recommendations of the All India Rural Credit Survey Committee that the loaning policy of the land mortgage bank should be reoriented in order to provide loans for improvement, development and reclamation of lands, purchase of agricultural machinery and equipments and other productive purposes with a view to achieve the object of increasing agricultural production. The Andhra Co-operative Central Land Mortgage Bank had been following this policy of providing loans for productive purpose. The Bank had successfully implemented the recommendations of the All India Rural Credit Survey Committee.

(B) *Hyderabad Co-operative Central Land Mortgage Bank (HCCLMB)*

The land mortgage banking movement was conceived in 1952 in Telangana region which was then a part of the erstwhile state of Hyderabad. The Central Land Mortgage Bank in Telangana area was established in 1953, namely the Hyderabad Co-operative Central Land Mortgage Bank LTD; Hyderabad. There were 12 primary land mortgage banks affiliated to this Bank in 1957.

The Hyderabad Co-operative Central Land Mortgage Bank successfully functioned for nine years before its merger. There had been a significant progress in the working of the bank. There were 29 primary land mortgage banks affiliated to this Bank in 1960. During 1960-61 six more primary land banks were affiliated to it bringing the total number banks on rolls to 35 in the year of its amalgamation. The paid-up share capital stood at Rs. 5.61 lakhs. Pending amalgamation of the Bank with the Andhra Co-operative Central Land Mortgage Bank, the Bank did not issue debentures and the Government continued to provide funds by way of temporary accommodation to carry on its loaning operations to the member banks.

Formation of APCCADB

At the end of the first year of the Second Five Year Plan, in the State there were two Central Land Development Banks working in two regions, namely; the Andhra Central Co-operative Land Mortgage Bank looking after the credit needs of the primary banks located in Andhra area and the Hyderabad Central Co-operative Land Mortgage Bank for the Primary banks working in Telangana area. In response to the recommendations of the informal conference convened by the Reserve Bank of India 1956, that there should be only one Apex land mortgage bank in each of the reorganised states. The State Legislature was under way for the merger of the two regional Apex Banks into one single State level Apex Bank.

Accordingly, the Andhra Pradesh Co-operative Central Land Mortgage Bank (APCCLMB) was formed as a result of amalgamation of the Andhra Co-operative Central Land Mortgage Bank and the Hyderabad Co-operative Central Land Mortgage Bank under the Andhra Pradesh Co-operative Central Land Mortgage Bank (Formation) Act, 1961. In accordance with the provisions of the Act a scheme for the amalgamation of the two Banks was prepared and placed before the bodies of the two banks which met on 4th March 1962. The scheme was unanimously approved by the general bodies of the two banks and in accordance with the provisions of the Act, the bye-laws of the Andhra Pradesh Co-operative Central Land Mortgage Bank were registered and the Bank was started working on the same day to serve the entire State of Andhra Pradesh.

Now the name of the Bank is the Andhra Pradesh Co-operative Central Agricultural Development Bank LTD., formerly known as the Andhra Pradesh Co-operative Central Land Mortgage Bank LTD. The registered office is situated at Hyderabad (Andhra Pradesh) and the area of operation extends to the whole State of Andhra Pradesh. The Land Mortgage Banks are also being registered under the Andhra Pradesh Co-operative Societies Act, 1946 and are subjected to the provisions of the Act, it is considered that there is no advantage in retaining separately the Co-operative Land Mortgage Banks Act on the statute Book. Consequently, the special provision required for Co-operative Land Mortgage Banks were embodied in a separate chapter in the Andhra Pradesh Co-operative Societies Act, 1964 repealing the said Land Mortgage Banks, Act.

Section 4 of the Andhra Pradesh (Andhra Area) Land Mortgage Banks Act, provided that the value of debentures in circulation at any time shall not exceed the amount of loans due to the banks. Another development was that Andhra Pradesh Ceiling on Agriculture Holding Act, 1961 exempted co-operative societies including land mortgage Banks from its provisions in respect of land held by it as a result of purchase in satisfaction of a decree obtained against a member, with a view to ensure that the banks are not confronted with the provisions of the Tenancy Act in respect of land leased by it, it was necessitated to exempt the Bank from the provisions of the Tenancy Act.

The Rural Credit Survey Committee suggested that Land Mortgage Bank should undertake financing the farmers for the reclamation of the land under the project areas to enable the farmers to reclaim their lands and raise irrigation crops. In Nalgonda district of Telangana area a dam was constructed across the river Musi to provide irrigation facilities for the production of paddy in about 32,348 acres of land. The land mortgage banks of this region could take up the scheme for reclamation. The full Finance scheme in the Musi project area was drawn up and it received the approval of the Government in 1961. The features of the scheme in so far as long-term credit concerned were as follows:

(1) The loan for the full amount required for reclamation of land which was estimated at not more than Rs. 300 per acre may be advanced by the land mortgage bank. For the purpose of potential value of land may be taken at Rs. 600 per acre and loan of Rs. 300 may be advanced.
(2) In view of the difficulties in tracing the title in Telangana area and the need for reclamation finance in time, loan may be advanced to the owners and occupants of land on the basis of Khasera Pahani (Records of Rights) prepared by the Government in the year 1954-55.
(3) Any loss arising on account of defective title of the Musi project area was to be shared by the Government and the bank in equal proportion.
(4) In the first two years of the loan interest will be collected and thereafter the full amount of the instalments together with the interest be recovered in 12 annual equal instalments.
(5) Government guarantee a cash credit amount of Rs. 25 lakhs per year for a period of three years till the completion of the scheme.
(6) The Andhra Pradesh Co-operative Land Mortgage Bank should float development debentures to cover the loans advanced for the reclamation work in the Musi project area, the RBI to subscribe up to 75 per cent of the amount of such debentures, to secure from the market.
(7) Government to provide free cost of necessary staff required for the purpose.

The APCCADB gained much popularity and extended its area of operations. All round progress in the financial position and soundness of the Bank was also recorded within a short period. The most significant event that took place in 1965-66 was that the Government had taken a decision to channelise all long-term taccavi loans through land mortgage banks. This was a radical change because hitherto these loans were advanced through the agency of Panchayat Samithis. The Government also agreed to subscribe to the debentures. Due to severe drought conditions prevailed in many parts of the state in Telangana and Rayalaseema, the Apex Bank sanctioned a total sum of Rs. 1122.01 lakhs during 1965-66. In view of the restrictions placed on the amount of debentures to be floated with the support of life Insurance Corporation etc., the Government felt that there was a need to utilise the available funds to the best advantage in the order of priority to be followed by the Bank in sanction of loans.

Membership

The membership of the Bank is openced to:

(a) Agricultural Development Banks registered or deemed to have been registered under the Andhra Pradesh Co-operative societies Act, 1964.
(b) The Government of Andhra Pradesh.
(c) Such other institutions as the board may with the approval of the Government determines from time to time.

As on 30th June 1962, the Bank had membership stood at 113 of primary land banks and the Government of Andhra Pradesh. The progress in the membership of the Bank is shown in Table 6.1

During the year 1975-76 the bank registered total membership of 202. During the year 1976-77 the total number of primary banks affiliated to the apex bank were 205. No new Primary Agricultural Development Bank was registered during the Years 1977-78 to 1979-80 and as such the membership of the bank continued at 205. During the year 1980-81, the Voyalpadu Co-operative Agricultural Development Bank was organised in Chittoor district and was admitted as a member and thus the membership of the bank increased to 206 excluding Government of Andhra Pradesh.

TABLE 6.1: Membership of APCCADB

Year	No. of Banks	Year	No. of Banks
1961-62	113	1974-75	190
1962-63	122	1974-76	202
1963-64	126	1976-77	205
1964-65	163	1977-78	205
1965-66	173	1978-79	205
1966-67	178	1979-80	205
1967-68	178	1980-81	206
1968-69	180	1981-82	218
1969-70	181	1982-83	218
1970-71	181	1983-84	218
1971-72	182	1984-85	218
1972-73	184	1985-86	218
1973-74	184	1986-87	218

Source: Annual Reports of the APCCADB.

The year 1981-82 was a significant year because in that year 12 Co-operative Agricultural Development Banks were registered. They are Pondur (Srikakulam), Narsipatnam (Visakhapatnam), Nagari (Chittoor), Kodur (Cuddapah), Jedcherla (Mahabub nagar) Kodad (Nalgonda), Wankidi (Adilabad), Wardhannapet (Warangal), Eturunagaram (Warangal), Cheriyal (Warangal), Husnabad (Karimnagar). Mahadevpur (Karimnagar). Thus the membership of the bank increased to 218 and including Government of Andhra Pradesh 219. Since then there has been no change in membership because no new Primary Co-operative Agricultural Development Banks (PCADB) were registered, till 31st March 1987, the last year of the period of our study. It is because of the fact, introduction of single Window Rural Credit Delivery scheme. Obviously, therefore, no new bank was permitted to be organised and registered due to re-organisation of co-operative credit structure. In the year 1977-78 the Andhra Pradesh State Electricity Board (APSEB) was admitted as a nominal member of the bank to enable it to advance loans to the board towards the cost of energisation of pumpsets of farmers. The admission of the board as a member would help the borrowers of members banks to a great extent to secure energisation of wells in a large measure.

Powers

In order to fulfil such objects, the Bank has the following powers, among other things:

(a) to accept deposits;
(b) to borrow funds by issue of debentures or otherwise;
(c) to organise Agricultural Development Banks (ADB) and to constitute a centralised service of such categories of employees of Agricultural Development Banks as may be prescribed from time to time for their efficient management;
(d) to grant loans to Agricultural Development Banks and other members on such terms as the Board may decide including providing of temporary cash credit accommodation and or over draft;
(e) to advise, develop, assist, co-ordinate, supervise and inspect functioning of Agricultural Development Banks;
(f) to establish Regional Offices, Branches or suboffices within or outside the area of operations of the Bank;
(g) to buy, sell or deal with securities and bonds, scripts or other forms of securities on its own behalf or on;
(h) to endorse and transfer Promissory Notes, debentures, negotiable instruments and other securities standing in the name of or held by the bank;
(i) to acquire and hold immovable properties and construct buildings as it may consider necessary for the conduct of its business and deal with in any manner as may be found expedient;
(j) to act as an agent of the Government or any institution in financing for agricultural development and to accept and administer any fund created for such purposes;
(k) to do all such other things and acts as are necessary, conductive and incidental to the attainment of the foregoing objects.

Regional Offices of APCCADB

The Andhra Pradesh Co-operative Central Agricultural Development Bank has established its branches throughout the state in all most all districts. In 1975-76, however, the name of the branch has been changed over to Regional Offices. As such there were only eight regional offices of the Bank in the state in 1971-72, 10 in 1975-76, and raised to 13 in 1979-80. Thus today, there were 22 Regional offices. The functions of the Regional Offices are as follows:

(1) To undertake the work of sanction and disbursement of loans.
(2) To decentralise the functions of the Apex Bank.
(3) To act as a close liaison between the APCCADB and its primaries affiliated.
(4) To assist the primaries in their recovery of loan instalments.
(5) To secure effective liaison in the formulation and implementation of schemes under ARDC/IDA.
(6) To assist the banks in scrutiny of loan applications.
(7) To conduct field inspection.
(8) To evaluate the hypothecation.
(9) To review the performances of the banks periodically.
(10) To implement the targetted advances.

Sources of Finance

The following are the principal sources of finance or working capital of the APCCADB:

(1) Share capital.
(2) Debentures.
(3) Deposits.
(4) Loans from the State Government and Government of India.
(5) Refinance from ARDC/NABARD.
(6) Borrowing otherwise than by issue of debentures.
(7) Loans on the Guarantee of the State Government.
(8) Admission fees.
(9) Grants and subsidies.
(10) Investments by the primary banks in APCCADB.
(11) Loans, cash credits and overdraft accommodations from the Scheduled banks with the permission of the Registrar and the State Government.

Share Capital

The APCCADB raises its share capital by issuing shares to the members in certain proportion. As a matter of fact the Principal subscribers to the shares of the Bank are primary agricultural development banks. But today, the Andhra Pradesh Government has been contributing substantially as state participation as partnership in agricultural development movement. The paid-up share capital of the

Bank as on 1st July 1962 was Rs. 97.18 lakhs divided into Rs. 46.18 lakhs contributed by the primaries and the share of the state Government was Rs. 51.00.

In 1971-72, the authorised share capital of the Bank was Rs. 10.00 crores divided into 10,00,000 shares of Rs. 100 each, of which 5,03,651 shares of Rs. 100 each were issued to the primary banks and 1,06,002 shares of Rs. 100 each issued to the Government of Andhra Pradesh. However, the authorised share capital was subsequently raised. The present position of authorised capital is Rs. 20.00 crores divided into 20,00,000 shares of Rs. 100 each. As against them 11,16,982 shares of Rs. 100 each were stand allotted to the primary agricultural development banks, 1,06,002 shares of Rs. 100 each to the Government of Andhra Pradesh, and one share to the Andhra Pradesh State Electricity Board.

The paid-up share capital, however, increased from Rs. 708.77 lakhs in 1976-77 divided into Rs. 602.76 lakhs of primary bank's and Rs. 106.00 lakhs of the state Government Contribution, to Rs. 1116.98 lakhs contributed by the member banks and Rs. 106.00 lakhs held by the Government of Andhra Pradesh as on 30th June 1983. The paid-up share capital of the Bank as on 30th June 1984 was Rs. 13.76 crores, divided into 12,69,502 shares of Rs. 100 each allotted to primary agricultural development banks of Rs. 12,69,50,200, 1,06,022 shares allotted to the state Government of Rs. 1,06,00,200 and one shares purchased by Andhra Pradesh State Electricity Board of Rs. 100 each. According to the byelaws of the Bank every member other than Government has to take at least one share and its value is to be payable in full on the allotment. Similarly no member other than Government is permitted to withdraw any share or shares held in the bank except as a result of bifurcation or amalgamation under section 12 and 15 of the Andhra Pradesh Co-operative societies Act, 1964. Share can be transferred only to a member, but no such transfer can be made unless the member has held such shares for not less than one co-operative year i.e, the period commencing on the first day of the July of any year and ending with the 30th June of the succeeding years.

While the authorised share capital remain unchanged at Rs. 10.00 crores, the paid-up share capital of the bank increased from Rs. 7.76 crores in 1978 to Rs. 9.04 crores in 1979. Of which Rs. 7.98 crores was held by members banks and Rs. 1.06 crores held by the Government of Andhra Pradesh. The general body of the bank in 1980 effected a change in the authorised share capital by enhancing it to Rs. 20.00

crores from Rs. 10.00 crores. Thus by amending the bye-laws the authorised share capital was increased to Rs. 20.00 crores during 1980-81. This way the margin available for allotment of further share capital to member banks became wide and found adequate to meet the requirement of member banks in the wake of increased lending operations.

The paid up share capital, however, increased from Rs. 14.45 crores as on 30th June 1985 to Rs. 15.44 crores as on 30th June 1986. Of the total paid-up share capital Rs. 14.39 crores was held by the member banks and Rs. 1.06 crores held by the Government of Andhra Pradesh. One share of Rs. 100/- each was held by A.P. State Electricity Board, A.P.State Irrigation Development Corporation, A.P. State Meat and Poultry Development Corporation and A.P. State Co-operative Rural Irrigation Corporation Limited.

Table 6.2 show the progress in the paid-up share capital of the Bank.

TABLE 6.2: Progress in the Paid up Share Capital of the APCCADB

(*Rs. in lakhs*)

Year	Amount	Growth rate	year	Amount	Growth rate
1962	97.18	-	1975	623.73	1.11
1963	130.81	34.61	1976	644.12	3.27
1964	147.29	12.60	1977	708.77	10.04
1965	175.96	19.47	1978	775.85	9.46
1966	247.76	40.80	1979	904.00	16.52
1967	295.26	19.17	1980	972.08	7.53
1968	344.33	16.62	1981	1078.42	10.94
1969	407.58	18.37	1982	1173.11	8.78
1970	502.77	23.35	1983	1222.99	4.25
1971	558.00	10.99	1984	1375.50	12.47
1972	609.65	9.26	1985	1445.00	5.05
1973	614.02	0.72	1986	1544.99	6.92
1974	616.88	0.47			

Source: Annual Reports of the APCCADB.

Reserves and Funds

Reserve Fund, Reserve for Bad and Doubtful Debts, Investment Fluctuation Reserves, Debenture Redemption Reserve, Agricultural Credit stabilisation fund, Common Good Fund, Subsidy Fund, Building

Fund, Gratuity Fund, Dividend, Subsidy for failed wells, contingency Reserve, Establishment Reserve, Depreciation Reserve, Dividend Equalisation Fund, Staff Benefit Fund are the various types of reserves and funds that the Bank has been maintaining. The reserves of the Bank registered an appreciable increase to Rs. 2205.93 crores in 1982-83, whereas it was Rs. 37.71 lakhs in 1961-62, Rs. 266.77 lakhs in 1971-72, Rs. 1388.14 lakhs in 1979-80, Rs. 2205.93 lakhs in 1982-83. The year-wise position of reserves of the APCCADB is shown in Table 6.3

TABLE 6.3: Reserves of the APCCADB

(*Rs. in lakhs*)

Year	Amount	Growth rate	Year	Amount	Growth rate
1962	37.71	-	1975	618.04	25.13
1963	43.38	15.04	1976	752.28	21.72
1964	48.00	10.65	1977	910.88	21.08
1965	55.37	15.35	1978	1070.64	17.54
1966	62.64	13.13	1979	1289.15	20.41
1967	75.50	20.55	1980	1388.14	7.68
1968	93.28	23.55	1981	1774.91	27.86
1969	116.43	24.82	1982	2041.35	15.01
1970	142.77	22.62	1983	2205.93	8.06
1971	191.11	33.86	1984	2586.25	17.24
1972	266.77	39.59	1985	2824.00	9.19
1973	399.56	49.78	1986	3037.36	7.56
1974	493.91	23.61			

Source: annual Reports of the APCCADB.

Deposits

The deposits of various types constitute another important source of working capital of the APCCADB. Fixed Deposits, Individuals, Security Deposits of staff, Debenture Deposit Special, Debenture Deposits Ordinary, and rural are the different five categories of deposits presently being maintained by the Bank. The balance of deposits as at the end of 1981 was Rs. 48.15 lakhs, Rs. 51.23 lakhs in 1982 and Rs. 59.58 lakhs in 1983.

The year-wise position of deposits during last five years along with particulars are given in Table 6.4.

TABLE 6.4: Deposits Position of APCCADB

(*Rs. in lakhs*)

Sl. No.	Particulars	1979	1980	1981	1982	1983	1984	1985	1986
1.	Debenture Deposit Rural	0.55	0.08	0.08	0.08	0.08	0.08	0.08	0.08
2.	Debenture Deposit ordinary	0.12	0.02	-	0.20	-	-	-	0.004
3.	Debenture Deposit Special	-	-	-	Neg	0.69	0.21	0.21	0.21
4.	Fixed Deposits individuals	30.06	29.30	30.59	23.59	21.83	20.91	20.17	20.28
5.	Security Deposit of C.A.D.B. Staff	10.44	10.93	17.47	27.35	36.98	50.33	54.05	55.77
	Total	41.17	40.33	48.15	51.23	59.58	71.53	74.52	76.34

Source: Annual Report of APCCADB.

Government Guarantee

The Government of Andhra Pradesh has been extending guarantee to the debentures issued by the APCCADB since the inception of the bank. In G.O.Ms. No. 1739 Food and Agriculture dated 1-9-1962, the maximum amount of guarantee to the debentures issued by the bank was fixed at Rs. 1500 lakhs. On the request of the bank the Government enhanced the maximum amount of guarantee to Rs. 2500 lakhs in 1963. The Government guarantee for the repayment of principal and payment of interest on debentures issued by the bank stood at Rs. 150.00 crores from 1971. The Government Guarantee for interim accommodation facility with Andhra Pradesh State Co-operative Bank of a sum of Rs. 4 crores expired in 1974 and on request the Government was pleased to extend the guarantee for a further period of three years.

The State Government guarantee for the debenture issues of the bank was increased to Rs. 200.00 crores from 1976. As against the said guarantee, the debenture issued by the bank and in circulation as at the close of the year 1976-77 aggregate to Rs. 180.97 crores. It also enhanced the guarantee of Rs. 4 crores for availing of the interim accommodation facility with A.P. State Co-operative Bank to Rs. 6.00 crores. The bank, however, moved the proposal for enhancing the guarantee from Rs. 200 crores to 300 crores. Considering the inadequacy of the amount of guarantee, the Government further enhanced the same to Rs. 300 crores from 1978.

As the guarantee limit to Rs. 300 crores was found to be inadequate to meet the increased lending operation and floating of debentures of the Bank on request the Government was pleased to pass orders increasing the guarantee to Rs. 350 crores vide G.O.Ms.No. 59 of 1981. The Government guarantee in respect of debentures issued to the extend of Rs. 350 crores continued to be in operation till 16-3-1984 in which the limits of guarantee enhanced to Rs. 500 crores. The credit of Rs. 6.00 crores on Government guarantee with A.P. State Co-operative Bank continued to be in operation. The Government further extended guarantee for Rs. 500 crores, of this guarantee the debentures issued and in circulation as at 30-6-1984 aggregated to Rs. 367.16 crores. The guarantee was again enhanced to Rs. 700.00 crores in 1985. As against the guarantee the debentures issued and in circulation as at 306-86 aggregated to Rs. 397.78 crores.

ARDC/NABARD's Refinance

The Agricultural Refinance Corporation was established in 1963 under Agricultural Refinance Corporation Act. The said Act was amended in 1975 and the name of the Corporation was altered and is now named as Agricultural Refinance and Development Corporation. The APCCADB is the principal agency through which ARDC's refinance is routed to ultimate beneficiaries. The refinance of the Corporation channelled through the Apex Bank for financing special development schemes for increasing agricultural production. The ARDC is primarily a refinance agency extending medium and long term finance on approved schemes, land development, reclamation, soil conservation, development of animal husbandry, dairy farming, pisciculture, fisheries, poultry farming, development of crops like arecanut, coconut, cashewnut, cardamom, coffee, tea, rubber forestry, storage etc.

Prior to the establishment of National Bank for Agricultural and Rural Development (NABARD) the ARDC was the main agency providing refinance to the Bank. With the establishment of NABARD, it has taken over the functions of ARDC. It has been now acting as

APEX refinancing institution for these activities and will combine the development and financial roles which are hitherto performed by the RBI and ARDC. It may be seen from the figures of the Table 6.5, that advances under ARDC refinance scheme have been on steep increase from year to year. The table reveals that the advances under normal loaning programme has been declining where fragmented lending was practiced. During 1977-78 the total advances under ARDC schemes accounted for Rs. 3999.26 lakhs as against Rs. 871.31 lakhs in 1974-75. It can also be seen from the Table that advances during the year 1982-83 under Normal loaning programme of the Bank was substantially improved when compared to the previous years. The Bank has been advancing on scientific evaluation of investment credit and its utilisation.

TABLE 6.5: ARDC/NABARD's Refinances

(*Rs. in lakhs*)

Year	Total Achievements				
	Normal	% to total	ARDC/ NABARD	% to total	Total
1974-75	1002.24	53.49	871.31	46.51	1873.55
1975-76	1207.35	40.64	1763.23	59.36	2970.58
1976-77	1169.86	34.92	2179.90	65.08	3349.76
1977-78	922.84	18.75	3999.26	81.25	4922.10
1978-79	685.75	11.56	5245.03	88.44	5930.78
1979-80	652.10	11.14	5201.48	88.86	5853.58
1980-81	798.58	11.22	6316.07	88.76	7114.65
1981-82	522.78	10.87	4288.09	89.13	4810.87
1982-83	843.35	12.12	6115.04	87.88	6958.39
1983-84	431.88	6.86	5866.23	93.14	6298.11
1984-85	901.39	17.36	4290.36	82.64	5191.75
1985-86	718.56	11.38	5595.16	88.62	6313.72

Source : Annual reports of APCCADB.

The advances even under Normal Loaning programme (NLP) were encouraged only on schematic basis and on a scientific evaluation of investment credit and its utilisation. The advances under NLP declined as many of the purposes for which investment credit was sanctioned were covered under Agricultural Re-finance and Development Corporation (ARDC). During the year 1979-80 the drawal from ARDC accounted for Rs. 45.39 crores as against Rs. 42.83 crores during the previous year. Thus advances under ARDC refinance scheme continued to register a steep increase till NABARD is formed. The advances under Normal and NABARD refinance schemes also the progress has been impressive. The figures relating to normal, ARDC/NABARD's refinance details can be seen from the Table 6.5. The Table reveals that the advances during the year 1982-83 under NLP of the bank has substantially improved when compared to the previous year 1981-82. But during 1983-84 the advances have substantially decreased when compared to 1982-83. This is because of other areas were covered by schematic lending and on a scientific evaluation of the schemes.

Debenture Loans

The apex bank has power to borrow which is the main source of working capital. Borrowing of the bank may be of two types i.e. borrowing by issue of debenture and borrowing otherwise than by issue of debenture. The word debenture has not been defined by the Co-operative societies Act, 1964. The word debenture is derived from the Latin word 'debere'. It means an instrument issued in writing, signed and executed under the common seal of the bank acknowledging the indebtedness. It is a certificate generally issued in series. The debenture holder is not a member of the society but merely a creditor and has no voting right. Section 2 (12) of the Companies Act, 1956 defines, debenture includes debenture stock, bonds and any other securities of a company, whether constituting a charge on the assets of the company or not.

Borrowing by issue of debenture by the APCCADB is the only principal source of borrowing method from outside which constitutes a bulk share to working capital. The RBI/NABARD has been approving an ordinary debenture programme of huge amount for every co-operative year to enable the bank to advance loans under its normal loaning programme. Accordingly the bank has been able to issue ordinary debentures.

Types of Debentures

The debentures issued by the APCCADB are of three types, viz.,

(1) Ordinary Debentures

(2) Rural Debentures
(3) Special Development Debentures.

Ordinary Debenture

The ordinary debentures are issued by the APCCADB for subscription to raise funds to meet the normal loaning requirements. These debentures are floated to the general public, institutions and individuals. The state Government is giving guarantee on this debenture loans. Government of India, Government of Andhra Pradesh, Reserve bank of India, Sister Land Development Bank, Life Insurance Corporation, Commercial Banks, State Bank of India, State Bank of Hyderabad, Co-operative Institutions, local bodies etc. have been presently subscribing to the debenture issued by the APCCADB.

Thus the Apex Bank has been floating debentures for the purpose of raising long-term funds, to extend adequate funds to the affiliated member banks. The bank in the first year of its existence it issued three series of ordinary debentures and one series of rural debentures. The first series of ordinary debentures for Rs. 200.00 lakhs was issued in October, 1962. Subsequently, the bank has been floating debentures with substantially increased amount every year. The RBI/NABARD has been approving ordinary debenture programme for normal loaning programme. Accordingly, it was Rs. 9.00 crores in 1977-78; Rs. 12.00 crores in 1978-79; Rs. 9.00 crores for the financial year 1979-80; Rs. 9.00 crores for 1980-81; Rs. 9.00 crores for 1981-82; Rs. 9.45 crores for 1982-83; Rs. 9.50 crores for 1983-84; Rs. 10.00 crores for 1984-85 and Rs. 7.00 crores for 1985-86.

As against the said approval programme the bank could able to issue ordinary debentures for an aggregate amount of Rs. 11.50 crores in 1977-78. The original approval was only Rs. 9.00 crores. However, in order to enable the bank to advance loans to the farmers in cyclone affected areas for their rehabilitation on additional lending and debenture programme for Rs. 3.60 crores was approved in February 1978. It, thus, taking the ordinary debenture programme of the bank of Rs. 12.60 crores, Rs. 10.00 crores in 1978-79; Rs. 6.50 crores in 1979-80; Rs. 7.00 crores in 1980-81; Rs. 7.00 crores in 1981-82; Rs. 7.00 in 1982-83; Rs. 6.50 crores in 1983-84; Rs. 6.50 crores in 1984=85; and Rs. 6.20 crores in 1985-86.

The sister central land Development Banks, Life Insurance Corporation of India (LIC) Commercial Banks, State Bank of India

(SBI) and other Co-operative Institutions take bulk investment in the ordinary debentures floating by APCCADB. The percentage of investment by the LIC in 1985-86 was 30.89 per cent over the total. While the share of sister land development banks was 28.90 per cent. The SBI invested 10.50 per cent. 9.94 per cent accounted by Commercial banks. The investment by other co-operative institutions constituted 8.29 per cent. Investor wise investment in ordinary debenture figures are given in Table 6.6

Special Development Debentures (SDD)

The scheme of floating special development debentures was introduced by Agricultural Refinance and Development Corporation. These debentures are meant to raise funds to get refinance for providing finance to the agriculturist under special agricultural development or land improvement programme. Under this scheme the Corporation has been subscribing 90% of the value of the special debentures and the rest of 10% is to be subscribed either by public or the Government.

The Central Government, Government of Andhra Pradesh, ARDC, LIC, SBI, SBH, other Commercial Banks, L.D. Banks and a negligible by others have been supporting special development debentures. It may be mentioned that as the portfolio of advances under special development programmes assisted by ARDC/NABARD has been expanding appreciably the issue of special development debentures has correspondingly registered an increase. The SDDs issued were of the order of Rs. 36.93 crores during 1977-78 as against Rs. 35.00 crores originally anticipated. The pattern of support by the Government of India on matching basis for SDDs, issues of the bank continued to be regular feature every year and their participation made by debenture issue a success. The SDDS issues were of the order of Rs. 49.80 crores in 1978-79; Rs. 53.95 crores in 1979-80; Rs. 59.04 crores in 1980-81; Rs. 37.62 crores in 1981-82; Rs. 57.30 crores in 1982-83; Rs. 51.55 crores in 1983-84; Rs. 51.14 crores in 1984-85 and Rs. 55.24 crores in 1985-86. The investor-wise subscription of SDDs details are indicated in Table 6.7.

Rural Debentures

In order to mobilise the rural savings the rural debentures are issued by the APCCADB. This scheme was formulated by the Reserve Bank of

TABLE 6.6: Investment of ordinary Debentures Floated by APCCADB

(*Rs. in lakhs*)

Sl.No.	1977	1978	1979	1980	1981	1982	1983	1984	1985	1986
1. Government of India	471	486	526	385	350	359	343	345	375	320
2. Government of Andhra Pradesh	1718	1448	1048	935	807	451	418	407	375	320
3. Reserve Bank of India	765	1355	1370	1243	1142	1096	1072	1018	776	337
4. Sister Central Land Development Bank	2467	3483	3518	3433	3214	2955	2962	2741	2676	2469
5. Agricultural Refinance & Development Corporation	-	-	-	-	-	-	-	-	-	-
6. Life Insurance Corporation	1684	1660	1865	1980	2166	2396	2593	2782	2611	2639
7. Commercial Banks	1543	1260	1167	849	709	687	762	806	870	849
8. State Bank of India	591	427	387	511	608	688	758	809	821	897
9. Co-operative Institutions	1105	782	862	798	754	833	887	886	888	708
10. Local Bodies, Trusts etc.	295	23	19	15	10	10	10	6	6	2
11. Individuals	-	-	-	-	-	-	-	-	-	-
12. Others	93	2	2	3	3	3	3	4	2	1
13. Banks own Debentures	52	13	3	neg.	neg.	-	-	-	-	-
Total	10783	10939	10768	10152	9763	9480	9808	9804	9400	8542

Neg: Negligible
Source: Annual Reports of the APCCADB

TABLE 6.7: **Special Development Debentures Subscriptions**

(*Rs. in lakhs*)

Sl. No.	Name of the Inventor	1980	1981	1982	1983	1984	1985	1986
1.	Central Govern-ment	427.802 (7.93)	436.732 (7.40)	238.342 (6.34)	288.612 (5.04)	297.846 (5.78)	288.957 (5.65)	298.787 (5.41)
2.	Andhra Pradesh Government	427.802 (7.93)	436.732 (7.40)	238.342 (6.34)	288.612 (5.04)	297.846 (5.78)	288.957 (5.65)	298.787 (5.41)
3.	ARDC/ NABARD	4538.961 (84.14)	5030.313 (85.20)	3285.413 (87.32)	5153.101 (89.92)	4559.783 (88.44)	4536.516 (88.70)	4927.015 (89.18)
	Total	5394.565 (100.00)	5903.777 (100.0)	3762.098 (100.0)	5730.325 (100.0)	5155.475 (100.0)	5114.466 ((100.0)	5524.589 (100.0)

Figures in brackets shows percentage to total
Source : Annual Reports of APCCADB.

India in 1957. It was in accordance with the recommendations of the rural credit survey committee. Under this scheme the bank has to sanction loans to agriculturists for productive purposes for a period of 6 to 7 years on the mortgage of land. In the rural debenture, the Reserve Bank of India alone has been making a sizeable contribution of APCCADB's scheme of floating rural debentures.

The Rural Debentures in circulation as subscribed by the RBI was Rs. 122.78 lakhs in 1977-78; Rs. 118-76 lakhs in 1978-79; Rs. 116.75 lakhs in 1979-80; Rs. ·84.34 lakhs in 1980-81; Rs. 68.34 lakhs in 1981-82; Ea. 68.34 lakhs in 1982-83; R. 68.34 lakhs in 1983-84; Rs. 52.34 lakhs in 1984-85; Rs. 26.90 lakhs in 1985-86. The year-wise figures relating to total value of debentures issued and in circulating are arranged in Table 6.8.

Advances

The regional offices of the bank have been the chanellising agents of the bank's advances. Besides disbursing loans to the members banks, it has been advancing loans to the APEB towards energisation of pumpsets. During the year 1977-78, the Regional offices of the Bank (ROB) sanctioned an aggregate advance of Rs. 4922.09 lakhs. The number of loans were 59.788. Loans advanced in 1985-86 went up to Rs. 6305.91 lakhs. The percentage of advances to loans outstanding was 34.26 in the year of its inception. While their relationship showed a steep ups and downs. It was 26.40 per cent in 1963; 39.62 per cent in 1966; 27.04 in 1970; 18.38 in 1975; 25.62 in 1980; 22.02 in 1983 and 17.31 per cent in 1986. The number of loans, the amount of loans advanced, outstandings alongwith growth rate particulars of the banks since its inception are given in Table 6.9. Table 6.10 shows purpose-wise classification of loans during period under study.

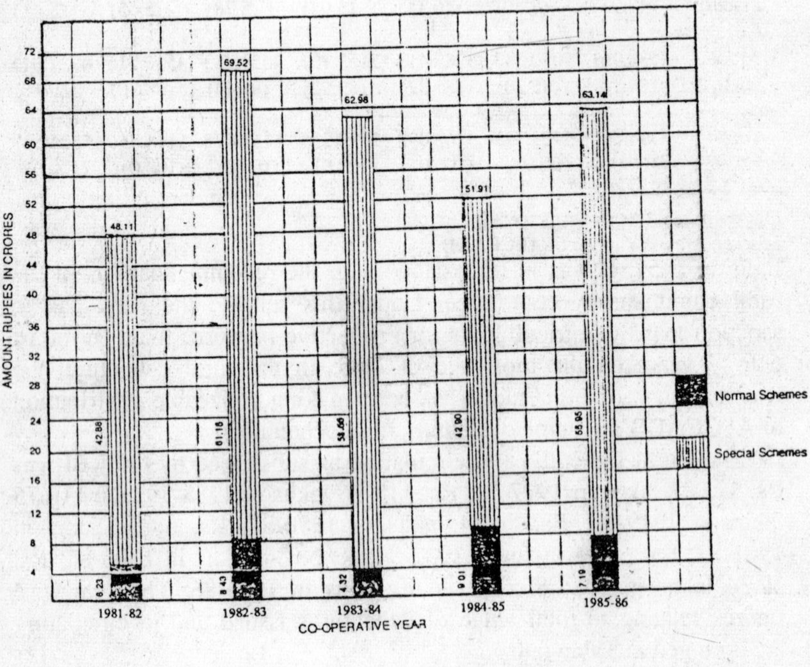

FIG. 6.1: Advances under Normal and Special Schemes

Removal of Regional Imbalances

Andhra Pradesh State has three economic regions, namely, Andhra, Rayalaseema and Telangana. The APCCADB has been endeavouring to remove economic imbalance between the regions. In order to provide investment credit for balanced regional development the Bank fixed ratios of advances in the ratio of 40:20:40 respectively for Andhra, Rayalaseema and Telangana Regions. The advances could not confirm to the ratios fixed in 1979-80. The advances by banks in Rayalaseema and Telangana did not reach the level of 20 and 40 per cent of investment in 1982-83. It was only 16% and 38% respectively in Rayalaseema and Telangana regions.

TABLE 6.8: Debentures Issued and in Circulation

(*Rs. in lakhs*)

Year	Debentures Issued	Debentures in circulation	% of Issue over circulation
1962	232.84	953.25	24.43
1963	471.70	1411.94	33.41
1964	254.95	1660.30	15.36
1965	553.70	2197.61	25.20
1966	1058.02	3179.51	33.28
1967	883.12	3993.47	22.11
1968	1037.85	4970.81	20.88
1969	1449.18	6397.78	22.65
1970	2258.27	8547.61	26.42
1971	2008.08	10340.28	19.42
1972	1620.82	11833.46	13.70
1973	1177.40	12234.79	9.62
1974	912.38	12679.15	7.20
1975	1412.97	13573.22	10.41
1976	2291.40	15634.48	14.66
1977	2874.19	18096.84	15.88
1978	4842.65	21431.16	22.60
1979	5925.97	25343.52	23.38
1980	6044.56	28768.86	21.01
1981	6603.78	31967.18	20.66
1982	4476.72	32306.24	13.86
1983	6430.33	35033.79	18.35
1984	5805.48	36715.18	15.81
1985	5764.47	37782.55	15.26
1986	6144.59	39777.64	15.45

Source: Annual Reports of APCCADB

It may be observed from the Table 6.11 that the advances in Telangana region have crossed the ratio fixed by 1 per cent and the advances in Rayalaseema just touched the ratio fixed. The ratios of advances have been fixed by the bank in order to provide investment credit for balanced regional development. However, the advances during the years 1979-80 — 1985-86 could not confirm to the ratio set for Rayalaseema region. The steps taken to bring equality between the regions could not be achieved. The advances made by the primary banks in Rayalaseema could not reach the level of 20 per cent investment ratio. The main reason for this un-satisfactory State of affairs has been due to heavy overdues by majority of the banks and consequentially restricted eligibility of banks. In 1980-81 the advances fell short by 2 per cent. But in 1984-85 the region could reach only 50 per cent of ratio fixed.

TABLE 6.9: Loans Advanced and Outstanding Since Inception

(*Rs. in lakhs*)

Year	Loans Advanced				Loans Outsta-nding	Growth Rate
	No.	Growth	Amount	Growth rate		
1962	10,800	-	333.89	-	974.57	-
1963	17,897	+65.71	322.54	-3.40	1221.81	+23.37
1964	13,778	-23.01	483.15	+49.80	1526.66	+24.95
1965	14,988	+8.07	445.73	-7.75	1848.11	+21.06
1966	47,015	+213.68	1122.02	+151.73	2832.09	+53.24
1967	42,903	-8.75	1018.72	-9.21	3653.95	+29.02
1968	43,098	+0.45	1194.82	+17.29	4589.11	+25.60
1969	65,179	+51.23	1803.07	+50.91	6077.25	+32.43
1970	70,113	+7.57	2068.21	+14.70	7649.57	+25.87
1971	63,134	-9.95	1980.08	-4.26	8983.94	+17.44
1972	46,268	-26.71	1518.47	-23.31	9701.16	+7.98
1973	9,031	-80.48	684.63	-54.91	9571.96	-1.33
1974	12,605	+39.57	1175.15	+71.65	9622.22	+0.53
1975	29,929	+137.74	1880.86	+60.05	10230.59	+6.32
1976	33,505	+11.95	2970.58	+57.94	11709.69	+14.46
1977	42,598	+27.14	3349.76	+12.76	13267.35	+13.30
1978	59,788	+40.35	4922.09	+46.94	16325.60	+23.05
1979	53,109	-11.17	5930.78	+20.49	20056.50	+22.85
1980	53,769	+1.24	5853.49	-1.30	22847.25	+13.91
1981	70,456	+31.04	7114.71	+21.55	27274.31	+19.38
1982	35,239	-49.98	4810.67	-32.38	28371.69	+4.02
1983	45,161	+28.16	6958.81	+44.65	31599.51	+11.38
1984	29,904	-33.78	6298.31	-9.49	33142.19	+4.88
1985	-	-	5192.19	-17.56	34841.21	+5.13
1986	-	-	6305.91	+21.45	36435.07	+4.57

Source : Annual Reports of the APCCADB.

TABLE 6.10: The Advances Classified purpose-wise

Sl. No.	Purpose	1977-78	1978-79	1979-80	1980-81	1981-82	1982-83	1983-84	1984-85	1985-86
	1		2	3	4	5	6	7	8	9
1.	Wells	1228.44	1206.10	1323.98	1583.97	970.40	1217.90	877.41	585.59	988.19
2.	Dev. of wells	128.75	112.48	175.04	497.02	220.33	356.27	205.50	165.61	230.10
3.	Pumpsets	928.19	747.77	669.49	712.89	492.56	604.51	542.65	405.42	642.29
4.	Tractor, power tillers and other types of agricultural machinery	626.65	828.98	724.44	997.92	1261.99	1096.05	1263.06	1110.13	1003.16
5.	Land Development under irrigation projects including CADA	187.38	243.35	147.84	227.38	254.07	399.00	597.87	626.09	816.19
6.	Horticulture	51.96	101.02	149.26	231.38	228.79	334.96	298.09	391.64	756.65

(Contd.)

TABLE 6.10 *Contd.*

1		2	3	4	5	6	7	8	9
7. Diversified	62.94	146.88	200.73	198.21	161.23	187.79	182.95	142.21	179.30
purposes									
a) Dairy									
b) Sheep rearing	105.27	146.66	193.04	384.12	193.78	400.36	251.56	178.35	244.01
c) Poultry	1.10	21.84	98.34	166.65	78.29	84.39	87.21	213.44	252.23
d) Pisciculture	24.13	31.93	28.90	39.58	34.07	28.25	16.65	26.77	68.71
e) Bullocks &	-	-	201.64	258.06	164.88	548.64	328.23	304.95	221.84
Bullock carts									
8. Sericulture	-	-	130.49	194.14	113.36	212.18	92.91	53.55	80.51
9. Gobar gas plants	-	-	7.80	7.00	4.70	17.36	16.47	16.78	55.21
10. Advances to APSE	919.36	1786.00	833.09	1194.50	366.59	990.38	679.47	158.96	408.00
Board									
11. Other Develop-	374.23	557.77	379.93	421.83	265.63	480.35	858.02	812.25	367.33
mental purposes									
12. Advances in	283.69	-	592.57	-	-	-	-	-	-
cyclone Affected									
areas									
	4922.09	5930.78	5853.58	7114.65	4810.67	6958.39	6298.11	5191.75	6313.72

Source : Annual Reports of APCCADB

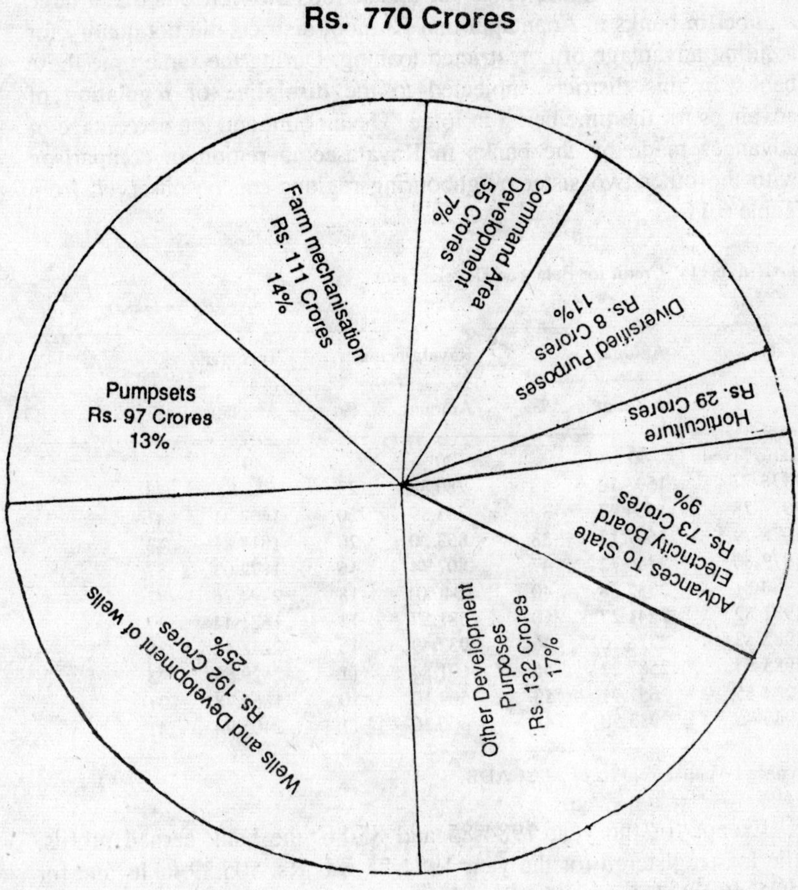

FIG. 6.2: Aggregate Advances — Purposewise till 30-6-1986

In 1983-84 and 1985-86 the banks in this region just reached 1 per cent more of 50 per cent of ratio fixed. The increased advances in Coastal Andhra has correspondingly reduced the percentage of advances in Rayalaseema. On the other had the advances by the primary banks in Rayalaseema region declined by Rs. 45.26 lakhs in 1979-80 when compared to the previous year 1978-79. The strong reason that can be attributable for this serious difference is that a large number of banks in Anantapur and Kurnool districts did not qualify for availing advantage of unrestricted loaning. During the same time these banks in this districts subjected to the discipline of regulation of advances for the time being in force. The amount and the percentage of advances made by the banks in Rayalaseema region in comparison with the other two sister neighbouring regions can be observed from Table 6.11.

TABLE 6.11: Credit for Balanced Development

(*Rs. in lakhs*)

Year	Andhra		Rayalaseema		Telangana	
	Amount	%	Amount	%	Amount	%
Ratio Fixed	40		20		40	
1976-77	1593.12	48	780.87	23	958.82	29
1977-78	1564.27	39	783.89	20	1663.41	41
1978-79	1607.13	38	853.00	20	1818.81	43
1979-80	2340.72	47	807.74	16	1872.03	37
1980-81	2385.38	40	1040.01	18	2494.76	42
1981-82	2241.27	50	581.57	13	1621.44	37
1982-83	2776.10	46	933.49	16	2258.42	38
1983-84	2587.22	46	601.84	11	2429.58	43
1984-85	2657.91	53	509.10	10	1865.78	37
1985-86	2933.50	48	666.20	11	2405.94	41

Source : Annual Reports of APCCADB.

Except for the year 1984-85 and 85-86, the bank earned profits. The loss registered for the year 1984-85 was Rs. 505.39 lakhs and for 1985-86 Rs. 156.47 lakhs Sustaining a net loss during these two year, the total cumulative net loss accounted to Rs. 661.86 lakhs as at the commencement of the year 1987. Table 6.12 indicates year-wise earning of profits since its inception.

TABLE 6.12: Profit position of APCCADB

(*Rs. in lakhs*)

Year	Amount	Year	Amount
1961-62	10.66	1974-75	134.31
1962-63	11.33	1975-76	175.80
1963-64	13.16	1976-77	181.56
1964-65	15.90	1977-78	176.25
1965-66	21.29	1978-79	209.78
1966-67	31.16	1979-80	355.13
1967-68	39.60	1980-81	Loss
1968-69	45.45	1981-82	255.64
1969-70	75.39	1982-83	145.14
1970-71	111.69	1983-84	318.45
1971-72	126.90	1984-85	Loss (505.39)
1972-73	102.67	1985-86	Loss (156.47)
1973-74	140.68		

Source: Annual Reports of APCCADB.

7

FINDINGS AND CONCLUSIONS

Co-operation has failed but Co-operation must succeed.

— All India Rural Credit Survey Committee

The study of co-operative agricultural development banks in rural finance has been with reference to Rayalaseema Region, one of the three economic regions of Andhra Pradesh. The coverage is restricted to only this region of co-operative agricultural development banks registered under the Andhra Pradesh Co-operative Societies Act, 1964. The main aspects examined in the present study have been the way in which they have been formed, their sources of funds, utilisation of funds and performance of financial operations. The major findings are in respect of proportion of members capital, extent of Government share capital participation, owned funds, working capital, borrowed funds, credit recoveries, outstanding, instalment demand, overdues, foreclosed loans and other operations of these banks in the co-operative sector. It was found that the agriculturists, both of small farmers, marginal farmers and agricultural labourers, who constitute the members owners of the banks hail from varied economic education and social background.

The role of Co-operative Agricultural Development Banks in drought prone areas such as Rayalaseema has special significance. The region covers the tract of ceded or deccan districts. This region, a historical part of this state, long suffered untold sufferings. The cyclical trend of drought has been closely associating with this region. Accordingly out of 42 taluks in this region, 38 taluks have been declared as chronically drought affected and 25 taluks fall in the hare-care category. It is because of the lowest average annual rainfall the Rayalaseema region has been long called as stalking ground of famines. The climate is hot for major portion of the year and it is quite severe in some parts. As against total main workers a large number of workers engaged as cultivators or agricultural labourers. Table 2.7

discloses the particulars of agricultural labourer. We have observed in Chapter two that holding size between 5.0 — 7.0 hectares, the number of holdings were 0.71 lakhs while the area was 4.65 lakhs.

In this region a number of financial institutions both of organised and unorganised have been operating to extend necessary financial assistance and other services. Thus the rural credit structure is essentially a multi agency system. The region has a distinct feature in co-operative movement. The movement in the region had originated under varying set of circumstances, because it was for long included in the composite Madras State. Thus the region obtained the movement partly from Madras state. The co-operative knowledge in the neighbouring states is also calculated to have its impact on the progress of credit movement in this region. Thus the co-operative credit developed in the state in general and in the region in particular developed under peculiar political, social and economic background. But the region did not possess unique in having had the original impetus as was prevailing in the state in particular and the country in general.

The co-operative rural credit movement developed and expanded, though slowly and steadily, covering the entire region. During the Five Year Plans due importance has been given to the co-operative sector. The Government of Andhra Pradesh accorded priority to co-operation through Five Year Plan schemes formulated and a separate head of development has been created for co-operation in the Five Year Plans. The most distinguishing feature of co-operative movement in the country is that the Government of Andhra Pradesh introduced "Single window Rural Credit Delivery Scheme". In order to facilitate it the entire rural co-operative credit structure has been re-organised.

The need for separate long-term co-operative credit institutions can not be over emphasised and its importance needs no elucidation, in relation to this region. The type of credit that the farmers in drought areas needed is that of long-term credit for creation of durable and productive assets. The short-term credit structure composed of PACS, DCCBs and APCOB extend only short-term credit to finance seasonal agricultural operations. Hence in drought regions long-term credit institutions are more necessary to finance for long period so as to enable the farmers to bring about permanent improvement on land, construction of wells, tanks, repayment of old debts, purchase of land, tractors, installation of irrigation machinery and land reclamation. In other words the PCADBs have a distinct and important role to play and the need for such organisations arises on several practical counts. Accordingly, the co-operative movement has become farmers' movement and co-operatives have been increasingly used as instruments for development of agriculture and other allied activities in backward regions.

To say the agricultural development bank means a co-operative society registered under the Co-operative Societies Act extending loan for productive purposes discussed in chapter three. In so far as the structure of co-operative agricultural development banks in the state is essentially a federal one. At grass root level there exist primary co-operative Agricultural Development Banks (PCADBs) and at the state level there exist an Apex Bank by name Andhra Pradesh Co-operative Central Agricultural Development Bank (APCCADB). The primaries are affiliated to the apex bank which is the only bank extending credit to the primaries to lend in turn to the farmers.

It is seen from the discussion in Chapter four the membership coverage and resource mobilisation capacity of the co-operative banks. The compound growth rate for the region was 2.53, in Chittoor district it was 4.60, 0.29 in Cuddapah district, 1.06 in Kurnool district and 4.71 in Anantapur district. The growth rate had been considerably lower in Cuddapah and Kurnool districts, much less than regions' average. However, membership expansion by itself is no index of effective coverage. The proportion of beneficiaries or borrowers to total members on rolls continue to be low as indicated in Chapter four. To find out the average rate of change in membership of the co-operative banks in the district to that of beneficiaries in the district, the elasticity of co-efficient is studied. The elasticity co-efficient explains the rate of change. The elasticity co-efficient of membership and beneficiaries has been positive in respect of some districts and negative in respect of some other districts. The elasticity co-efficient of membership and beneficiaries alongwith rank figures are arranged in a statement under elasticity co-efficient paragraph in Chapter Four.

It may be mentioned that it is the primary object of rural co-operative credit institutions to promote thrift and mutual aid among their members. However, this primary objective has, by and large remain unachieved and these banks have come to be perceived as mere lending institution borrowing heavily from the central financing agencies, apex bank. Consequently, the financing structure of these banks in this region dependent on the feeble capacity of resource mobilisation on the part of the members, whose capacity is inherently weak. The amount of share capital collected from the members has been very small and inadequate in relation to outstanding, overdues etc. The non-availability of adequate funds internally is a main factor responsible for high dependence on state level apex bank which is in turn mobilising funds by issue of debentures which are again in turn subscribed by the Government, financial institutions, sister co-operative institutions, commercial banks etc. The sources of funds are share capital, borrowings from apex bank. A small proportion from other sources.

Though there has been a considerable increase in the mobilisation of share capital but not corresponding in view of the magnitude of demand for loans. In general it is observed that the percentage of Government's paid up share capital over the total paid up share capital has been very small proportion as indicated in Table 4.4. The internal funds constitute important component of working capital. But the ploughing back of profits represents a very small proportion in working capital available for loan operation. Because the banks have been running on losses they could not maintain sufficient reserve fund.

As discussed in Chapter IV under paragraph borrowings, even though the lending operations of these banks have over the years increased considerably in absolute terms, the progress can not be considered encouraging when compared with the extent of borrowed funds and the achievements in the owned funds which are relatively low. The mean percentage of borrowings over working capital in the region was more than 50 per cent. In some years the proportion was more than that i.e., 58.12 per cent in 1979-80, 63.76 per cent in 1980-81, 58.49 per cent in 1982-83, and 52.66 per cent over the period as indicated in table 4.8.

The analysis of debt-equity ratios revealed 195 per cent in 1977-78; 212 per cent in 1978-79; 188 per cent in 1979-80; 200 per cent in 1980-81; 118 per cent in 1981-82; 168 per cent in 1982-83; 125 per cent in 1983-84 and 119 per cent in 1986-87 as indicated in Table 4.10, bank-wise; and district-wise and for the region the calçulated debt-equity ratio results are discussed in Chapter Four.

Table 4.14 discloses the ratios of borrowings to owned funds during the years from 1977-78 to 1986-87. The mean ratio of borrowing to owned funds was 1.50:1 in 1977-78; 1.94:1 in 1978-79; 1.73:1 in 1979-80; 1.92:1 in 1980-81; 2.32:1 in 1981-82; 1.52:1 in 1982-83; 1.51:1 in 1983-84; 0.86:1 in 1984-85; 1.25:1 in 1985-86 and 0.93:1 in 1986-87.

The working capital represents aggregate of funds available for loan operations. Raising funds by issue of equity shares play as the most significant element in providing working capital finance. Acceptance of deposits both from members and non-members, though an important source of working capital, but constitutes a very small proportion. Funds from loaning operations, borrowings from the sister co-operative institutions, issue of additional equity on admission of members, admission fee, gifts, donations, subsidy are the important sources of working capital. Among the various sources of working capital a substantial part of the working capital has been coming from apex bank.

The ultimate goal of these banks is to provide long-term credit to the members out of their owned funds and borrowing funds pool. This aspect has been examined and analysed in chapter five. The figures shown in Table 5.1 indicate bank-wise and year-wise beneficiaries of these banks. In general in the first five years of the period the number of beneficiaries were not only more comparing to the later part of the period but also show an increasing trend except in 1981-82. The scientific measure of dispersion is co-efficient of variation which was 47.02 for the region. It may be pointed out that the percentage of beneficiaries to membership for the region was highest of 14.54 per cent in 1980-81 and lowest percentage of beneficiaries to membership was 3.16 per cent only in 1984-85. The calculated figures, bank-wise particulars are displayed in Table 5.2.

It can not be over looked in the matters of credit disbursement, that these banks made a remarkable progress over the years. The apex bank and the NABARD have been formulating schematic pattern of advance and accordingly the primary banks have been disbursing the loans. Purpose-wise classification of loans advanced cover wells; development of wells; pumpsets; tractors; power tillers and other types of agricultural machinery; Land development under irrigation projects including CAD; Horticulture; Diversified purposes (Dairy, sheep rearing, poultry, pisciculture, Bullocks and Bullock carts); Sericulture; Gobar Gas Plants; Advances to cyclone affected areas; Advances to Andhra Pradesh State Electricity Board; other Development purposes (Tobacco barns, pipelines, shares in sugar factories, lift irrigation schemes and Land Development schemes etc).

There has been a phenomenal increase in the lending operations and the quantum of loans issued which have gone up substantially. It is evident from the figures given in Table 5.3 relating to credit disbursement. There is a perfect positive correlation between working capital and credit. The interesting feature in the loan operations has been the proportion of loans advanced to owned funds. These banks have been now providing credit over and above the amount of owned funds. Table 5.4 shows that these banks suffer from inadequacy of funds and the bulk of loans advanced consists of borrowed funds. This is the only reason to depend more on borrowed funds. For the region as a whole the percentage of credit to working capital was 54.79 in 1977-78 and 50.37 per cent in 1986-87. The minimum average loan per beneficiary in the region was Rs. 5200 and maximum was Rs. 8000 during the period under study. However, there are cases where some co-operative banks recorded average loan per beneficiary to the extent of nearly Rs. 10,000.

The results of location quotient of credit and elasticity co-efficient of credit are arranged in Table 5.07 which reflects that these banks well responded in the distribution of credit to borrowers. The calculated ratios of beneficiaries outstanding to beneficiaries depicted in Table 5.09 reveals ratios of beneficiaries outstanding to beneficiaries showing relationship between the number of beneficiaries outstanding to the beneficiaries. The mean of loan amount outstanding for the region was Rs. 1763.713. During the period of 10 years there has been a steady increase in the amount of outstanding. The aggregate of outstanding amount represents both of owned funds and debt funds. Among these two funds the proportion of borrowed funds has been more than owned funds. Indices of owned funds and borrowings to outstanding can be seen from Table 5.11.

The amount of borrowing outstanding due to by the primary banks to the apex bank and the amount of loan outstanding due by the beneficiaries to the primary banks are analysed to know the inter-relationship between due to and due by. In the year 1977-78 for every one rupee of outstanding due by the outstanding due to was 97 paise. In 1980-81 the outstanding ratio was nearly equal to unit. In the year 1986-87 the outstanding ratio was 1.05:1. The total instalment amount demand recoverable from member borrowers during the year 1977-78 aggregated to Rs. 311.75 lakhs which represents 25.15 per cent to outstanding and 34.20 per cent in 1986-87. The mean percentage of instalment demand to outstanding 38.38 in 1981-82; 43.05 per cent in 1983-84; and 40.36 per cent in 1985-86, while it decreased by 3.55 per cent in 1986-87. The study of experience of these banks in recovery front reveals the recovery potential performance of these banks. In Chapter five, we have pointed out the recovery has not been effective. The figures indicated in Table 5.14 support this conclusion.

The major problem confronting the co-operative long term banks in respect of many banks has been mounting overdues. The magnitude of overdues in these banks over period is indicated in Table 5.16 in Chapter five. In overdue size below 25 per cent there were 10 banks in 1977-78, a banks in 1978-79 and 7 banks in 1979-80 and in rest of years one bank in each year from 1980-81 to 1986-87. Gradually the distribution of banks in the overdue size of 41 per cent and above constituted a major proportion. The percentage of overdues to outstanding, bank-wise and year-wise figures are arranged in appendix VII. It is evident from the appendix that there has been a significant increase in the percentage of overdues to outstanding. The proportion of overdues to outstanding has gone up from 3.93 per cent in 1977-78 to 20.95 per cent in 1982-83 and subsequently decreased to 17.43 per cent in 1986-87.

The impact of agro-economic factors on overdues is studied. The phenomenon is explained by fitting in the Regression co-efficient Analysis ($Y = a + b^x$). The overdues were explained by independent variables at 97.57 per cent, 81.49 per cent, 91.00 per cent and 83.60 per cent respectively for the four districts. The contribution of individual characteristics to total overdues are calculated and are given in appendix VIII.

The problem of foreclose has serious implication. The co-operative banks have experienced with the problem of poor recovery and mounting overdues, consequently, therefore, the loans have been closed, either on account of arrears of instalments or on account of alienation. The analysis of financial results of co-operative banks in terms of profits earned and losses incurred enabled us to know the operational efficiency and availability of these banks. As indicated in chapter five most of the banks have been running on loss and in respect of many banks they have been on loss continuously for many years. Even the banks which have been earning profit the amount of profit has been insignificant. The observation of profit and loss figures as indicated in Table 5.25 and Table 5.26 reveals that no bank had earned profit of one lakh except Proddatur PCADB.

As already pointed out in Chapter II the structure of long-term co-operative credit is federal in character having two-tier structure. There is state level apex Central Co-operative agricultural development bank. Before formation of Central bank there were two regional apex banks known as, as referred in Chapter Six, the Andhra Co-operative Central Mortgage Bank covering Andhra part of the State and the Hyderabad Co-operative Central Land Mortgage Bank for the Telangana region. Though an integrated state of Andhra Pradesh was constituted in 1956, but the formation of APCCADB took place in the year 1961 through a scheme of amalgamation. It is a co-ordinating bank and all the PCADBs are affiliated to the apex bank. It established regional offices in all 22 districts of the state. One of the important functions of the apex bank is to raise funds and lend to the member banks so as to enable them in turn to lend to the members.

The ARDC/NABARD has been extending re-finance to increase agricultural production on approved schemes. It has been raising funds by issue of debentures of various types like rural debentures, ordinary debentures and special development debentures and the figures relating to debentures issued and in circulation are indicated in Table 6.8. To support the schemes, the Government of Andhra Pradesh has been extending guarantee to the debentures issued by the APCCADB since its inception and to date. The Government of India, Government of Andhra Pradesh, Reserve bank of India, Sister Land Development Banks, ARDC, LIC, Commercial Banks SBI, Co-operative Institutions, Local Bodies, trusts, Individuals and other have been investing in the ordinary debentures floating by the APCCADB as indicated in Table 6.6 in Chapter Six.

As discussed earlier that there are three economic regions in the state. In order to provide investment credit for balanced regional development the bank fixed ratios of advances in the ratio of 40:20:40. The most disquieting feature in this regard is that the advances could not confirm to ratio set for Rayalaseema region. The advances made by the primary banks in Rayalaseema could not reach the level of 20 per cent investment ratio as evidenced by Table 6.11, appended to Chapter VI. In all, the working results of the bank has been satisfactory in terms of profit earned. Except for the years 1984-85, and 1985-86, the bank earned profit since its inception. This is supported by Table 6.12.

Suggestions

In the context of the increase in the number of primary co-operative agricultural development banks and increasing trend of need for more long term credit, a specialised co-operative financial institution on the lines of corporation is conspicuous by its obsense in the state. So it is more desirable to establish a specialised Andhra Pradesh Co-operation Development Corporation like one National Co-operation Development Corporation. In the State there exist a wide and large co-operative base today, and more may come in the future. It is urgently necessary to established a separate and specialised financial body.

The ploughing back of earning is very poor in these banks. The retention of profits in the bank is a neglected area of financial management. In order to increase the self financing capacity of the co-operative banks, they should appropriate more and more of their profits to build up more reserve fund. Accordingly, it may also necessary to amend the Co-operative Societies Act and Bye-laws to provide that a society should transfer out of its profit to reserve fund not less than 40 to 50 per cent of profit, while at present the rate is only not less than 25 per cent.

One of the basic aims of the movement is to encourage the habit of thrift and savings among the members. It has been observed that long term Co-operative banks have not succeeded to achieve this object. These banks could not achieve fundamental virtues of mutual help and self reliance. There is a lack of drive on the part of these banks to mobilise local savings. This results is the excessive dependence on external source. Each co-operative bank should launch a special deposit mobilisation schemes locally suitable to collect the savings of local people both from member and non-members. It is also desirable to explore sources like Government departments, local authorities, educational institutions, clubs and other local organisations to get their funds or balance to be deposited in these societies. A relatively high rate of interest could attract the savings of earning conscious people.

The need for strengthening of owned funds in working capital should be greatly emphasised. The primary co-operative banks in this region suffer from inadequacy of funds. Though share capital contribution of members is a principal source of working capital but the aggregate of such funds are disproportionately not sufficient in view of demand for long-term credit. In case of many banks the borrowed funds constitute bulk of the working capital. The members should be educated to take additional shares out of their incremental income. Reserve funds out of loan business, deposits from members and non-members, more Government share capital contribution as state partnership in co-operative movement etc., are the important components which should be strengthened.

The borrowing owner members are mostly illiterates and ignorants. The documents used and procedure followed to get the loans should be simple, easy and not time consuming. The legal documents, applications etc., should be simple, lucid, unambiguous in language and procedure to be followed should be shorter. All these must reflect the spirit of co-operative principles and aspirations of members whose interest the banks seeks to sub-serve rather than emphasis on strict procedures and rules. The All India Rural Credit Review Committee found that loans sanction procedure has been cumbersome and time consuming, hence undue delay in sanction of loans. It recommended for simplification of procedure.

The loan policies adopted should be sound and purpose oriented. The practice today is still security oriented rather than productive oriented. The loan eligibility of a farmers should be based on credit needs for productive purposes. Loans partly in kind is more desirable. The policy followed should be uniform for assessing the repaying capacity of the borrower and the property to be mortgaged as security. It may be stated that the period for the repayment of loan should be determined on the basis of repaying capacity of the member borrower. Following the guidelines contained in the Reserve Bank's Manual on Production Oriented System of Lending for Agriculture would help in a great way in this direction.

Under the Co-operative Societies Act the State Government is empowered to nominate persons on the managing Committee of the banks which received aid from the Government. This amounts to interference of the officials of the Government in co-operative management. They should be made self governing institutions and the appearance of the nominee of the Government distroys the co-oprative principles of exclusive organisation and the management by the members. The process of decision making and managing affairs should be exclusively vested in the hands of the members. Alternatively to this end the necessary provisions of the Co-operative Societies Act should be amended suitably in such a way as to delete the powers of the Government to nominate a person on the committee. Alternatively, the Government can extend financial assistance on the security of the society's property without a Government's nominee on the committee.

Co-operative agricultural development banks often becoming weak. The Reserve Bank of India has been identifying the weak banks based on their financial results. Rehabilitation of weak banks has become a regular feature. It is more desirable to make them viable on time by taking effective steps. So as to enable them eligible for higher loaning special schemes to be formulated and efforts to be undertaken to secure better recovery in areas where these banks have been identified as weak. More Government share capital contribution helps in a great way to strengthen the financial base. Besides, the improvement in recovery is the best solution which makes them eligible for unrestricted loaning.

The existence of inter-regional disparities in their loaning operations have been well noticed. So the long-term co-operative credit movement has not developed on a uniform basis in the state. There is glaring regional disparity and un-evenness in its financial operations. This would be evident from the fact that ratios fixed for credit disbursement for three economic regions is not achieved. Further that ratios of credit for removal of regional imbalances should be on the basis of credit needs than the population and geographical area. In drought region like Rayalaseema where these banks play an effective role in rural development. These are only banks providing long term credit. Drought areas are the only areas where more long term investment is necessary to create durable and productive assets. In order to solve the problems of drought the credit ratios should be fixed in such a way more in favour of this region say 30:40:30 for coastal Andhra, Rayalaseema and Telangana regions respectively. It may be mentioned that just fixing ratios is not sufficient but the apex bank or regional offices must see that the advances made by these banks must reach the level of 40% ratio fixed.

The most unsatisfactory situation in the working of these banks has been increasing overdues. Serious steps should be taken to arrest the growing trend of overdues. Coersive action should be taken against the defaulters. Effective follow up action and utmost continuous vigilance should be there. There are number of causes for mounting overdues particular and peculiar to this region, namely failure of crops, and rains, lack of incremental income due to low output and yield. The study team on overdues had recommended to the State Governments to amend the State Co-operative Societies Act for automatic disqualification of the members of the managing committee of societies if the amount, number of defaulters exceed 70 per cent of the total demand total number of indebted membership for a continuous period of two years and also for denial of credit to sureties of defaulters. The Committee to Review Arrangements for Institutional

Credit for Agriculture and Rural Development in its report 1981 suggested that no State Government should, as a rule, interfere with the recovery endeavours of co-operatives and it further suggested : The tempo of recovery drive should be maintained by the societies throughout the year instead of initiating it towards the close of the year.

It may be further suggested that the co-operative banks should introduce a novel scheme known as COOP. CARD (Co-operative Card) like bank Card, credit card etc, as introduced by the commercial banks. Similarly, since single window rural credit delivery scheme has been introduced in the state to render multi-credit services to the members, it is more desirable to introduce passbook system. In this book all debit and credit or loan taken and repayment amount particulars of short-term, medium-term and long-term details can be recorded. From this it is very easy to know the total credit life of the farmer in relation to co-operative credit. As a step towards encouragement incentive facility to the farmers may be adopted by way of higher rebate of specified percentage who repay their loans in time. This acts as an encouragement for prompt payment. The NABARD is expected to play an effective role in this direction.

A Co-operative Vikas Volunteer Vahini (CVVV) an innovative approach in co-operative rural banking should be formulated and implemented on the lines of Vikas Volunteer Vahini (VVV) as conceived by NABARD for rural banking. The CVVV is a body of co-operators, non-officials, farmers, financial agencies etc. The Vahini should undertake campaign to propagate the philosophy and principles of co-operative credit institutions. The vahini should educate the beneficiaries the importance of long-term credit, prompt repayment of loan instalments in time and regularly so as to re-cycle the co-operative credit. In recent years the organisation of "loan melas" to distribute loans easily and liberally have become common feature in respect of Indian rural credit system by rural banks, commercial banks. On a similar line it is more appropriate to recommend strongly to organise "Co-operative recovery melas", drafting participants from different concerned fields like co-operators, NABARD, apex banks, farmers, Government nominees political people etc.

Conclusions

To sum up that the suggestions offered above in relation to problems in the working of Primary Co-operative Agricultural Development Banks bearing on policy implications. These banks in this region occupy a crucial position in the multi-agency frame work of rural credit particularly long-term credit. Efforts are therefore, to be diverted for strengthening co-operative credit structure than often going for reorganisation of structure. The single window rural credit delivery scheme as introduced in the state is expected to play an effective role in extending multi-credit in an integrated manner. In view of the ineffective role in the present credit structure the co-operative credit structure has been reorganised, under single window. The single window which is now providing multi-credit and rendering multi-functional services the window should not neglect, the operations of long-term activities in view of diversified activities. The future prospects of co-operative long-term credit structure occupies pre-eminent position in view of suitability of this sector in rural credit as an effective instrument to provide long-term finance.

APPENDICES

If Co-operation Fails, there will fail the best hopes of Rural India.

— Royal Commission on Agriculture.

APPENDIX I

SINGLE-WINDOW RURAL CREDIT DELIVERY (SWRCD)

Existing Structure

In Andhra Pradesh, Co-operative Credit hither to is made available to the farmers through two separate and distinct lines — one for short term and the other for long term. Both these channels also extend medium term credit to the farmers. The short term credit is made available through a three tier structure with the primary agricultural credit societies (PACS) at the village level, the co-operative central Banks at the district level (DCCBs) and the State Co-operative Banks (APCOB) at the Apex level. Within their jurisdictions the DCCBs also have branches at taluk/sub-taluk head quarters or other important centres. The long term credit is made available to the farmer through a two tier structure with the Primary Agricultural Development Banks (PADBS) as the taluk/sub-taluk level and the Andhra Pradesh Co-operative Central Agricultural Development Bank as the Apex institutions at the State level. The Apex Bank does not have an intermediary tier as in the short term structure though it has 22 Regional Offices spread over the state. At present there are 6,500 primary societies, 27 district Co-operative Central Banks with one short-term State Apex Bank, 218 primary Agricultural Development Banks with one State level long-term apex bank. The marketing structure consists of one State level marketing federation, 22 district Co-operative Marketing Societies. Of 396 societies 297 are territorially organised at the taluk' sub-taluk/Mandal level as general purpose and 99 are special single commodity co-operative marketing societies.

Hazari Committee

The Government of India appointed a committee under the Chairmanship of Dr. R.H. Hazari in the year 1975. The committee in its report 1976 recommended for the integration of co-operative credit structure for the convenience of the farmers to enable them to avail of various types of credit. The National Development Council while adopting the approach paper on the Seventh Five Year Plan recommended integration of two co-operative credit structures (short term and long term) as a general policy. The approach paper states that the effective steps should be taken to bring about the integration of two parallel credits.

The Concept

Developing a strong integrated co-operative credit structure at all levels in place of the existing two parallel organisations in the underlying theme of reorganisation of co-operative credit delivery system. The schemes of reorganisation and consequent result is the single-window service scheme or single-window rural credit delivery system. The single society rendering multi credit and multi functional services. The society rendering multi-services is called single-window service unit. Under this scheme at village level at one place the economic requirements of the farmer are supplied. A one parallel organisation or from one source the farmer can obtain credit for production, investment, for agriculture and allied activities. Single roof and multi-services is the principle. Andhra Pradesh State is first in the country to undertake re-organisation and integration of credit and marketing structure under single-window rural credit delivery scheme from 1987.

Features *

The salient features of the scheme are :

1. Re-organisation of the existing 6,500 Primary Agricultural Co-operative Societies on fresh viability criteria such that there is one society for every 5-10 villages covering a population between 10,000 — 20,000 with a cropped area of about 4,000 hectares and a potential business of Rs. 30 to 40 lakhs. However, as far as possible, Primary Agricultural Co-operative Societies which have been working well and which have been making profits consecutively for 3 years would remain

* *Seventh Five Year Plan*, Andhra Pradesh, 1985-90, p. 104.

undisturbed, except that 2 or 3 villages might be added if necessary as a part of the proposed re-organisation. The Headquarters of Primary Agricultural Co-operative Societies should be within a distance of 5 to 10 km from the peripheral villages.

2. The re-organised Primary Agricultural Co-operative Societies will be disbursing all types of credit i.e., short-term, medium-term, long-term and also undertake distribution of agricultural inputs and essential commodities, besides undertaking agro-processing and marketing.
3. Establishment of new integrated co-operative credit institution at the District level which would undertake sanction and disbursement of all types of credit including long-term credit. The 27 Co-operative Central Banks will be re-organised as 22 Co-operative Central Banks to be coterminus with Revenue District. The Branches of Co-operative Central Banks and Primary Agricultural Development Banks will be merged and could operate under one roof.
4. Establishment of Apex Integrated Co-operative Credit Institutions at State level which would be handling all types of credit including long-term credit. The Andhra Pradesh Co-operative Central Agricultural Development Bank will be integrated with Andhra Pradesh State Co-operative Bank.
5. Reorganisation of the Co-operative marketing structure is such that the Primary Agricultural Co-operative Societies is organically linked to the District Co-operative Marketing Societies. No changes are contemplated at Apex and District level tiers which would be retained. The sub-district tier at the taluk level would be merged with the new integrated institution.

Objectives

The following are the objectives of single-window service scheme :

1. To provide at one place multi-term credit and to render multi-functional services to the farmers.
2. To eliminate deficiencies in the existing co-operative credit and marketing structure.
3. To improve the viability of the PACs by fixing new criteria to identify the viable societies to make them economically viable, vibrant and responsive to all the economic needs of farmers.

4. To make rural credit and other services convenient to the farmers to avail them at a single contact point.
5. To make Co-operative Central Banks coterminous with the revenue jurisdiction of the districts concern.
6. To achieve sizeable results under rural deposit mobilisation.
7. To make general financial position of credit and marketing institutions extremely sound.

Re-organisation

The introduction of Single Window Co-operative Rural Credit delivery structure and marketing system involved re-organisation of existing co-operative credit structure of two levels. Andhra Pradesh State is the first state in the country to undertake a structural re-organisation of rural co-operative credit. The re-organisation is in relation to two parallel organisations of short-term and long-term. The state formulated the scheme of re-organisation based on the recommendations of the Hazari Committee which recommended integration of both the co-operative credit structure and strengthening the base level primary societies on the criteria of viability. The scheme is for the purpose of convenience of the farmers. The single window enables them to avail multi-term credit i.e., short-term, medium-term and long-term and multi functional services viz. input supply, storage, distribution of essential commodities through the primary Agricultural Credit Societies at village level at the point. The implementation of the re-organization of Co-operative Credit Delivery and Marketing Schemes now under implementation in the first phase envisages:

1. Re-organisation of Primary Agricultural Co-operative Societies.
2. Re-organisation of Central Co-operative Banks on the criteria of one Bank for one district.
3. Abolition of Primary Agricultural Development Banks transferring their assets and liabilities to Co-operative Central Banks, as also enabling Primary Agricultural Co-operative Societies to deal with long-term credit in future.
4. Re-organisation of Co-operative Marketing structure from three tier to two tier by eliminating co-operative Marketing Societies.

Central Concurrence

The Central Government's Concurrence is also necessary for re-organisation of societies under single-window scheme. It is necessary because the financing agencies at all India level are under the Agencies of the Government of India, like National Bank for Agriculture and Rural Development, Reserve Bank of India, National Co-operative Development Corporation etc. A proper under-standing of the scheme by the Central Government and central agencies is desirable. The State Government sent a scheme Report to the Government of India. In turn Government of India constituted a committee under the Chairmanship of Sri Ardhanareeswara, along with representative of RBI, NABARD and the State Government, to examine the scheme. The Committee also appointed, a State level Task Force. Finally the Government of India has given a green signal for the implementation of the scheme, subject to certain conditions. The conditions are such as the criteria for deciding on viability of societies, financial assistance from State Government to strengthen the long-term structure in particular, that the eligibility criteria by NABARD will not be relaxed, and suggesting elections, to be held for co-operatives immediately, as these had been delayed.

Multi-term Credit

The re-organisation of co-operative credit institutions under single window Rural Credit Delivery system involves channelling of all types of rural credit through the primary agricultural credit societies at village level at one place. Multi-term credit includes short-term, medium-term and long-term credits. The formers can approach single-window society for three types of loans. This system is not only convenience to the farmers but also to make the existing societies economically viable, vibrant and responsing to all the economic needs of the farmers.

Multi-Functional Services

Single window system not only involves the re-organisation of two parallel organisations but also re-organisation of co-operative marketing structure from three tier to two tier by eliminating co-operative marketing societies. At village level a single point is to render multi-functional services also along with multi-term credit. The multi-functional services are input supply, storage, distribution of essential commodities, agroprocessing and marketing. The Primary marketing co-operative societies will get merged with the district co-operative marketing societies. It means in a re-organisation of co-operative marketing structure under single window scheme that the primary agricultural societies is organically linked to the district co-operative marketing societies. The apex marketing society and district level marketing societies would remain unchanged. The taluk level marketing institutions would be merged with the single window society.

New Viability criteria

The single window rural credit delivery scheme involving re-organisation of credit structure and marketing structure is intended to make them economically viable, vibrant and responsive to all the economic needs of farmers by enlarging their territorial jurisdiction wherever necessary, by transfer of areas of new societies and by merge of non-viable societies. The re-organisation of primary agricultural co-operative societies will be undertaken broadly on the basis of new viability criteria fixed by State level task force. The 9 point new viability criteria to identify viable society cover various aspects like loans outstanding (short-term), agricultural loans (medium-term), agricultural loans (medium-term), medium term conversion cropped area distance, loan recovery, infrastructure facilities, irrigation and population, non-credit activities, deposits etc.

Abolition of Long-term credit Banks

With the effect on and from the data of April 1987 the Primary Co-operative Agricultural Development Banks registered under the Principal Andhra Pradesh Co-operative Societies Act, 1964 stood abolished. On such abolition of Primary Agricultural Development Banks under Andhra Pradesh co-operative Laws (Amendment) Act., 1987:

(a) All rights and assets vesting in the said banks and all liabilities against it shall devolve on the co-operative Central Bank of the district concerned;

(b) all contracts made by or on behalf of the said Bank prior to its abolition and subsisting on the date of such abolition shall be deemed to have been transferred to the Co-operative Central Bank of the district concerned;

(c) persons who were members of the said Bank prior to its abolition shall, not with-standing anything in section 19 or the rules or bye-laws, be deemed to be nominal members of the Co-operative Central Bank of the district concerned without the right to vote till their loans are discharged;

(d) the Registrar may transfer the officers and other employees who immediately before such abolition were in the service of the said Bank (including those belong to a centralised service) to the service of the Financing Bank or to a Primary Agricultural Co-operative Society in the manner prescribed: Provided that;

(i) the terms and conditions applicable to such officers and other employees, consequent on their absorption in the service of the Co-operative Central Bank or the Primary Agricultural Co-operative Society shall not be less favourable than those applicable to such employees immediately before such abolition as respects pay and allowances, leave, gratuity, provident fund and age of superannuation; and

(ii) the service rendered by any such officer or other employee under the said Bank up to its abolition shall be deemed to be service under the Co-operative Central Bank or, as the case may be the Primary Agricultural Co-operative Society and he shall be entitled to count that service for purpose of increment, leave or provident fund and gratuity.

Legal Views and Queries

To implement the scheme, necessary amendments have been made to Andhra Pradesh Co-operative Societies Act, 1964, called the Principal Act. The Act has been duly amended by the Legislative Assembly of the State of Andhra Pradesh and the Act is called as the Andhra Pradesh Co-operative Laws (Amendment) Act, 1987. The amendment empowers the Registrar that if the Registrar is of the opinion that it is necessary to amalgamate or merge any society with any other such society or to divide and restrict or transfer the area of operation of a society or to liquidate a society for any of the following purposes, namely :

(a) for ensuring economic viability of any or all the societies concerned; or
(b) for avoiding overlapping or conflict of jurisdictions of societies in any area; or
(c) for securing proper management or any society; or
(d) in the interest of the co-operative movement in general and of co-operative credit structure in particular in the state taken as a whole; or
(e) for any other reason in the public interest, he may identify the viable and non-viable societies which may be retained or divided with consequential restriction of the area of operation or the transfer of such area or amalgamated or liquidated, as the case may be, and may by a notification to be published in the prescribed manner, specify the area of operation of each such society or societies to be retained divided or amalgamated with any other society indicated in the said notification and invite objection or suggestions from the societies or any members, depositors, creditors, employees or other persons concerned with the affairs of each such society to be received within twenty one days from the date of publication of the notification.

Consequences

The Registrar on making such an order for re-organisation :

(i) the societies affected by the amalgamation shall be deemed to have been amalgamated with the society or societies with which each one is amalgamated;
(ii) the registration of every amalgamated or divided society shall stand cancelled where upon such society shall cease to exist as a corporate body;
(iii) the area added to the area of operation of the society shall be deemed to have been transferred to such society to which it is added;
(iv) the assets of such amalgamated or divided society shall stand transferred to and it liabilities shall devolve on, the society with which it is amalgamated and all immovable properties located in the area transferred shall be deemed to be transferred to the

society to which the area is transferred;

(v) every member of such amalgamated or divided society and residing in the area so transferred shall be deemed to have been transferred together with his loans, share capital, deposits to the society with which it is amalgamated or to which the area is transferred and he shall have the same rights, privileges and liabilities which he has had in the amalgamated or divided society;

(vi) the Committee of the amalgamated or divided society shall stand dissolved and thereupon, the Registrar shall nominate a committee or appoint a person or persons, wherever necessary to manage the affairs of such society for a period not exceeding six months and arrange for the conduct of elections before the expiry of the term;

(vii) it shall be competent for the Registrar to allot, by order, employees of such societies which are amalgamated or divided to any society or societies; and

(viii) not withstanding anything in this Act or in any other law, or in any contract, award or any other instrument for the time being in force, the provisions of the order of the Registrar under sub-sections (2) and (3) shall be binding on all societies and their members, depositors, creditors, employees and other persons having any rights, assets or liabilities in relation to all or any o the concerned societies.

Resultant structure

The new integrated resultant credit structure would be three tier set up. They are re-organised (1) Primary Credit Societies at the base level (PACS) at present there are 6,500 of such societies (2) The District Co-operative Banks for Agriculture and Rural Development (DISCOBARD) at the district level with 22 co-operative central banks and with about 330 branches at taluk level (3) The Andhra Pradesh State Co-operative Bank for Agriculture and Rural Development (APSCOBARD) at the state level. The Primary Co-operative Agricultural Development Banks stand abolished. At the State level both the existing organisations viz., APCOB and APCCADB are transferred to the newly created Bank APSCOBARD. There is no change at the Apex level of marketing structure. The primary credit societies is organically linked to the District Co-operative Marketing Societies. The result is the integration of short-term and long-term credit along with marketing and allied services at primary agricultural co-operative societies level. The service of old long-term loans will be rendered by the Central Co-operative Banks. Hereafter Primary Agricultural Co-operative Societies will issue fresh long-term loans. All the existing 218 primary co-operative agricultural development banks have been merged with the 22 District Co-operative Central Banks. All the reorganised PACS in the districts are the members of the District Co-operative Marketing Societies which achieves marketing linkage.

Existing and Resultant Structure

DIAGRAM I

MARKETING STRUCTURE

Before Reorganisation			*After Reorganisation*
Village Level			
Taluq Level	:	396 societies *	
District Level	:	22 DCMS	32 DCMS
Apex Level	:	MARKFED	MARKFED

* Include 297 taluq societies and 99 single commodities

DIAGRAM II

PACS STRUCTURE

Before Reorganisation			*After Reorganisation*
Village Level	:	6500 PACS Short term	PACS Viable Societies
Taluq Level	:	218 PADBs Long term	22 CCBs with nearly 330 branches at taluq level
District Level	:	27 CCBs short term	DISCOBARD
Apex Level	:	APCOB short term APCCADB Long term	APSCOBARD

DISCOBARD : District Co-operative Central Bank for Agriculture and Rural Development

APSCOBARD : Andhra Pradesh State Co-operative Bank for Agriculture and Rural Development.

APSCOBARD is created by merging short term state apex body APCOB and State long term apex body APCCADB.

APPENDIX II

STATEMENT SHOWING THE TALUK-WISE PERCENTAGE DISTRIBUTION OF AREAS UNDER DIFFERENT SOILS (CULTIVABLE LAND) IN KURNOOL DISTRICT

Taluk	Black clay	Black loams	Black sandy	Red clay	Red loams	Red sandy	Total
1	2	3	4	5	6	7	8
1. Adoni	54	11	-	2	33	-	100
2. Aluru	85	5	-	-	10	-	100
3. Allagadda	6	15	6	23	25	25	100
4. Atmakur	50	-	-	-	50	-	100
5. Banaganapalli	50	-	-	50	-	-	100
6. Dhone	12	-	-	-	38	50	-
7. Giddalur	4	-	-	96	-	-	100
8. Kurnool	85	-	-	-	15	-	100
9. Koilkuntla	33	40	10	7	8	2	100
10. Markapur	25	-	-	75	-	-	100
11. Nandyal	20	20	20	10	25	5	100
12. Nandikotkur	80	5	5	-	10	-	100
13. Pathikonda	-	-	25	-	-	75	100

CHITTOOR DISTRICT

Taluk	Black clay	Black loams	Black sandy	Red clay	Red loams	Red sandy	Total
1. Madanapalli	-	2	3	-	50	45	100
2. Vayalpad	-	-	-	-	-	10	100
3. Chandragiri	-	11	-	11	67	11	100
4. Chittoor	-	-	-	35	35	30	100
5. Palamaner	-	-	-	-	67	33	100
6. Punganur	-	6	-	-	41	53	100
7. Kalahasti	-	-	-	-	53	47	100
8. Puttur	-	-	-	-	80	20	100
9. Kuppam	57	-	-	-	14	29	100
10. Satyavedu	-	-	-	-	20	80	100
11. Bangarupalem	-	-	-	6	81	13	100

1	2	3	4	5	6	7	8	
ANANTAPUR DISTRICT								
1.	Anantapur	-	5	-	-	90	5	100
2.	Tadpatri	-	45	-	-	50	5	100
3.	Gooty	-	5	-	-	50	-	100
4.	Uravakonda	-	70	-	-	30	-	100
5.	Dharmavaram	-	5	-	-	80	15	100
6.	Kalyandurg	-	15	-	-	75	10	100
7.	Rayadurg	-	60	-	-	37	3	100
8.	Penukonda	-	10	-	-	85	5	100
9.	Kadiri	-	-	-	-	75	25	100
10.	Hindupur	-	15	-	-	80	5	100
11.	Madakasira	-	2	-	-	88	10	100
CUDDAPAH DISTRICT								
1.	Cuddapah	12	9	-	23	33	23	100
2.	Rayachoty	-	7	-	7	64	22	100
3.	Kamalapuram	62	-	10	-	12	16	100
4.	Rajampet	18	-	5	9	55	13	100
5.	Sidhout	-	5	7	23	19	46	100
6.	Badvel	41	14	-	3	42	-	100
7.	Jammala-madugu	66	6	11	11	6	-	100
8.	Proddatur	58	3	3	-	33	3	100
9.	Pulivendla	33	33	-	-	28	6	100

Source : Planning and Development of Backward Regions, A Case study of Rayalaseema, Planning and Co-operation Department, Govt. of Andhra Pradesh, 1971, pp. 116-118.

APPENDIX III

BANK WISE PERCENTAGE OF OWNED FUNDS TO LOAN OUTSTANDING

Sl. No.	Name of the Bank	1977-78	78-79	79-80	80-81	81-82	82-83	83-84	84-85	85-86	86-87
1.	Chittoor	15.87	16.73	17.63	15.18	14.40	13.14	13.45	12.37	12.71	12.82
2.	Chandragiri	13.63	13.78	12.89	12.27	12.32	13.98	14.97	15.07	6.78	12.37
3.	Madanapalli	19.71	10.91	9.60	9.16	9.59	9.63	10.49	10.80	18.86	12.45
4.	Rajampet	25.92	9.73	11.44	11.36	11.61	11.60	12.87	13.38	14.51	13.53
5.	Cuddapah	10.57	11.05	11.27	10.93	11.64	11.91	12.07	11.78	11.34	11.71
6.	Proddatur	9.47	10.67	10.74	10.40	11.16	11.16	11.28	4.91	10.85	7.82
7.	Banaganapalli	13.70	14.73	15.84	14.06	14.07	13.72	13.61	11.69	12.74	12.63
8.	Kurnool	15.18	16.31	16.47	15.74	16.57	15.02	14.04	14.32	13.48	13.94
9.	Nandyal	13.49	12.88	12.87	12.32	11.74	11.64	11.76	11.87	11.68	11.77
10.	Dharmavaram	13.97	14.66	14.48	12.71	13.48	13.23	13.55	13.20	13.16	13.29
11.	Hindupur	11.00	11.36	11.28	11.09	11.52	11.10	11.80	11.66	11.52	11.65
12.	Tadpatri	12.64	11.81	11.89	11.05	10.97	10.81	11.28	11.49	11.44	11.40
	Mean	14.60	12.89	13.03	12.19	12.42	12.25	12.60	11.88	12.42	12.12

Source: Table 4.15 and Table 5.10.

APPENDIX IV

INDICES PERCENTAGE OF BORROWED FUNDS TO LOAN OUTSTANDING

Sl. No.	Name of the Bank	1977-78	78-79	79-80	80-81	81-82	82-83	83-84	84-85	85-86	86-87
1.	Chittoor	12.47	18.15	16.07	35.90	23.70	34.53	31.48	19.01	26.39	25.48
2.	Chandragiri	23.98	34.68	35.27	26.07	12.59	20.40	4.30	6.18	12.93	7.71
3.	Madanapalli	36.60	47.13	32.98	21.47	4.75	12.85	4.12	3.88	11.84	5.72
4.	Rajampet	31.95	26.70	21.76	26.15	7.80	7.66	15.43	0.59	4.69	7.19
5.	Cuddapah	20.33	20.83	19.60	16.89	9.22	11.33	13.88	13.27	18.11	15.19
6.	Proddatur	23.76	24.99	22.51	22.02	10.30	17.92	20.61	6.40	15.71	11.92
7.	Banagarapalli	4.67	14.05	14.85	18.55	17.67	31.05	20.32	14.27	20.44	18.20
8.	Kurnool	4.47	7.61	14.00	14.97	15.88	19.86	15.11	17.50	13.00	15.17
9.	Nandyal	12.25	23.03	13.90	24.40	16.20	18.71	11.91	9.31	16.16	12.55
10.	Dharmavaram	20.75	12.57	21.06	22.60	13.85	19.15	12.81	12.76	13.68	13.10
11.	Hindupur	28.74	19.00	17.73	16.57	8.10	13.62	9.11	8.71	13.17	10.40
12.	Tadpatri	29.35	31.54	24.99	30.54	24.08	19.16	14.73	7.24	10.51	10.83
	Mean	20.78	23.36	21.23	23.01	13.68	18.85	14.48	9.93	14.72	12.79

Source : Table 4.07 and Table 5.10

APPENDIX V

PERCENTAGE OF INSTALMENT DEMAND TO OUTSTANDING

Sl. No.	Name of the Bank	1977-78	78-79	79-80	80-81	81-82	82-83	83-84	84-85	85-86	86-87
1.	Chittoor	29.28	31.16	32.60	25.00	28.10	25.64	24.73	25.24	33.89	28.17
2.	Chandragiri	27.09	25.31	22.84	22.58	35.30	32.35	39.11	26.82	43.87	36.51
3.	Madanapalli	19.00	15.75	17.53	18.23	35.54	36.55	47.37	26.90	60.95	42.45
4.	Rajampet	16.92	18.19	22.46	18.37	18.71	13.11	40.78	32.05	37.12	36.71
5.	Cuddapah	24.42	28.20	34.16	31.20	51.60	52.71	61.17	38.34	40.15	46.07
6.	Proddatur	19.33	23.54	28.98	25.77	46.05	43.09	40.39	11.56	33.36	23.47
7.	Banaganapalli	36.44	33.86	43.98	35.96	51.41	48.63	50.43	31.92	42.82	41.21
8.	Kurnool	43.81	55.09	57.50	38.90	50.26	45.95	52.53	41.99	50.44	48.23
9.	Nandyal	33.80	34.68	42.93	29.36	38.85	41.78	47.19	46.01	54.57	49.38
10.	Dharmavaram	31.52	35.30	36.14	26.53	42.16	39.35	51.08	31.67	37.45	39.80
11.	Hindupur	23.49	21.39	25.39	24.08	38.06	38.02	35.16	18.89	25.70	26.46
12.	Tadpatri	23.07	21.39	24.25	18.46	25.10	26.12	26.69	18.98	23.97	23.23
	Mean	27.35	28.66	32.40	26.20	38.38	36.94	43.05	29.20	40.36	36.81
	Region	25.15	25.46	28.55	23.95	36.29	34.86	41.93	24.47	38.14	34.20

Source: Table 5.10 and Table 5.13

APPENDIX VI

PERCENTAGE OF RECOVERY OF OUTSTANDING

(in Percentage)

Sl. No.	Name of the Bank	1977-78	78-79	79-80	80-81	81-82	82-83	83-84	84-85	85-86	86-87
1.	Chittoor	28.51	29.65	31.65	20.88	24.42	20.43	20.57	16.69	28.94	22.26
2.	Chandragiri	23.19	19.80	16.69	10.92	20.18	9.24	20.35	10.87	27.09	19.32
3.	Madanapalli	-	-	37.12	11.23	39.68	15.95	55.82	18.81	47.02	40.54
4.	Rajampet	-	14.94	17.49	7.90	12.19	4.81	20.82	9.61	25.93	18.49
5.	Cuddapah	19.03	18.41	22.22	10.54	26.07	19.79	25.90	10.26	14.34	16.57
6.	Proddatur	18.70	19.20	22.67	9.41	28.32	22.96	24.65	5.49	15.65	12.33
7.	Banaganapalli	29.65	23.83	33.72	15.63	31.75	26.06	27.66	14.70	18.82	20.00
8.	Kurnool	21.30	24.41	26.63	11.88	22.60	13.91	23.46	6.33	21.26	16.84
9.	Nandyal	26.69	22.35	30.09	14.93	19.43	16.76	23.05	12.30	17.69	17.68
10.	Dharmavaram	21.49	20.12	20.66	7.61	21.21	11.45	24.60	8.14	14.06	15.39
11.	Hindupur	22.06	16.11	17.26	7.94	21.18	13.92	20.99	6.47	9.55	12.18
12.	Tadpatri	18.92	16.11	19.90	9.44	16.96	15.87	19.41	12.54	14.68	15.55
	Mean	19.13	18.74	24.68	11.53	23.67	15.93	25.61	11.02	21.25	15.93
	Region	21.22	18.80	21.00	9.49	20.67	13.91	23.12	9.30	19.39	16.77

APPENDIX VII

PERCENTAGE OF OVERDUES TO OUTSTANDINGS

(percentage)

Sl. No.	Name of the Bank	1977-78	78-79	79-80	80-81	81-82	82-83	83-84	84-85	85-86	86-87
1.	Chittoor	0.77	1.51	0.95	4.12	3.68	5.21	4.16	8.55	4.95	5.91
2.	Chandragiri	3.90	5.51	6.14	11.66	15.13	23.11	18.76	15.96	16.78	17.18
3.	Madanapalli	-	-	1.66	13.57	18.30	29.24	21.53	18.19	24.45	20.88
4.	Rajampet	-	3.25	4.97	10.47	5.98	8.30	19.96	22.44	11.19	18.22
5.	Cuddapah	5.39	9.80	11.94	20.65	25.53	33.04	35.27	28.08	25.81	29.50
6.	Proddatur	0.62	4.34	6.30	16.36	17.73	20.13	15.74	6.07	17.72	11.14
7.	Banaganapalli	6.80	10.04	10.25	20.34	19.66	22.57	22.76	17.22	24.01	21.21
8.	Kurnool	22.51	30.68	30.87	27.02	27.66	32.04	29.28	35.66	29.18	31.39
9.	Nandyal	7.11	12.34	12.84	14.43	19.42	25.02	24.14	33.69	36.88	31.70
10.	Dharmavaram	10.02	15.18	15.49	18.92	20.96	27.90	26.48	23.53	23.40	24.41
11.	Hindupur	1.44	5.28	8.13	16.14	16.88	24.10	14.16	12.42	16.14	14.28
12.	Tadpatri	4.15	5.28	4.35	9.02	8.14	10.25	7.28	6.44	9.30	7.68
	Mean	5.23	8.60	9.49	15.23	16.59	21.74	19.96	19.02	19.98	19.46
	Region	3.93	6.66	7.55	14.46	15.62	20.95	18.82	15.17	18.75	17.43

Source : Table 5.10 and Table 5.16.

APPENDIX VIII

PERCENTAGE CONTRIBUTION OF VARIABLE TO OVERDUES

District	Working capital (X_1)	Rainfall (X_2)	Cropping Intensity (X_3)	Irrigated area to net area sown (X_4)	Commercial crops area to net area sown (X_5)
1	2	3	4	5	6
ANANTAPUR					
Mean (Mi)	231.66	46.33	111.00	13.44	40.66
Coefficients (Ci)	0.5034	(-)1.8369	(-)2.1130	(-)14.9840	(-)10.5197
Mi x Ci	123.7064	(-)85.1036	(-)234.5430	(-)201.3840	427.7310
% to total	14.99	(-)10.31	(-)28.43	(-)24.41	51.84
CHITTOOR					
Mean (Mi)	254.09	63.33	111.11	21.33	39.88
Coefficients (Ci)	0.1402	(-)4.6453	(-)24.2823	(-)11.0631	(-)17.2681
Mi x Ci	35.6234	(-)294.1863	(-)2698.0063	(-)235.9759	(-)688.6518
% to total	0.92	(-)7.58	(-)69.51	(-)6.08	(-)17.75

APPENDIX VIII *(Contd.)*

1	2	3	4	5	6
CUDDAPAH					
Mean (Mi)	242.68	57.80	111.66	24.44	39.88
Coefficients (Ci)	0.3974	(-)0.9933	(-)9.1396	(-)16.4032	(-)9.8815
Mi x Ci	96.4410	(-)57.6079	(-)1020.5277	(-)400.8942	(-)394.0742
% to total	5.42	(-)3.24	(-)57.44	(-)22.56	(-)22.18
KURNOOL					
Mean (Mi)	172.13	62.00	114.33	18.77	51.44
Coefficients (Ci)	1.1466	(-)3.9407	(-)0.1031	(-)7.7396	(-)17.1955
Mi x Ci	197.3642	(-)244.3234	(-)11.7874	(-)145.2723	(-)884.5365
% to total	18.13	(-)22.14	(-)1.08	(-)13.35	(-)81.26
REGION					
Mean (Mi)	214.78	57.16	112.13	20.19	42.97
Coefficients (Ci)	0.2461	(-)0.3766	(-)0.0348	(-)1.1974	(-)1.5034
Mi x Ci	52.8573	(-)21.5264	(-)3.9021	(-)24.1755	(-)64.6011
% to total	86.16	(-)35.09	(-)6.36	(-)39.41	(-)105.30

APPENDIX IX

RESULT OF STATISTICAL ANALYSIS

District	Overdue				Fore closed loans outstanding (No)				Fore closed loans [outstanding (Amount)]			
	Mean	CGR	CV	LGR	Mean	CGR	CV	LGR	Mean	CGR	CV	LGR
1. Chittoor	60.91	42.96	69.33	16.40	322.9	3.56	22.01	3.79	8.33	11.56	53.20	12.50
2. Cuddapah	85.19	24.30	48.06	12.82	320.5	14.12	54.55	13.55	14.51	26.23	66.67	19.53
3. Kurnool	45.94	14.65	38.87	12.38	191.2	-6.23	21.49	-6.52	6.16	-2.78	24.16	-2.53
4. Anantapur	65.94	17.35	43.77	11.60	310.8	12.72	40.09	11.25	14.02	20.82	59.08	17.30
5. Region	258.18	21.73	48.42	13.31	1145.4	6.75	24.67	6.82	43.02	15.68	46.62	14.28

BIBLIOGRAPHY

Books

Aaron G. Nelson and William G. Murray : *Agricultural Finance*, USA, IOWS State University Press, 1975.

Andhra Pradesh Central Co-operative Agricultural Development Bank : *A Study on Overdues in Telangana Regions, (Memio)* Hyderabad, 1974.

Andhra Pradesh State Co-operative Bank : *A Note on the Short-term Co-operative Credit Structure in Andhra Pradesh, 1956-57 to 1968-69.*

Anwar Iqbal Qureshi : *Co-operative Movement in Hyderabad State*, (1947).

Bakken Henry, H. : *Basic Concepts, Principles and Practices of Co-opeation, Winconsin;* 1963.

Balshaw, H. : *Provision of Credit with Special Reference to Agriculture*, Cambridge; Heffer and Sons Limited, 1931.

Bedi, R.D. : *Theory, History and Practice of Co-operation*, International Publishing House, Meerut, 1981.

Bhattacharya, P.C. : *Central Banking in Developing Economy*, Bombay; Vora & Company, 1971.

Bogardus Erory, S. : *Principles of Co-operation.*

Calvert, H. : *Co-operation in Colonies*, London, 1945.

Calvert, H. : *The Law and Principles of Co-operation*, 1959.

Cherrian, K.C. : *"Loaning Policies in India" Agricultural Credit in South East Asia*, Bombay, Asia Publishing House, 1967.

Chowbey, B.N. : *Agricultural Banking in India*, New Delhi; National Publishing House, 1953.

Dadhichi, C.L. : *Overdues in Farm Co-operatives Credit: A Study in Rajasthan*, Bombay, Popular Prakasam, 1977.

Derashi : *Co-operative Financing for Agricultural Development — some Essentials for its success: Role of Co-operative Credit in Agricultural Development*, Jodhpur.

Deshpande, V.D. : *Crop Loan System — A Case Study*, Poona; Gokhale Institute of Politics and Economics, 1971.

Dey, S.K. : *Co-operative Commonwealth, Sehakari Samaj*, Bombay; Asia Publishing House.

Dubhashi, P.R. : *Principles and Philosophy of Co-operation*, Vaikunth Mehta National Institute of Co-operative Management, Pune, 1972.

Elavia, B.M. : *The Study of Co-operative Development Banks in Gujarat*, Baroda; M.S. University of Baroda, 1977.

FAO. : *Agricultural Credit Through Co-operatives and Other Institutions*, Rome, 1965.

FAO. : *Efficient Use of Fertilisers.*

FAO. : *Inter-Relationship Between Agrarian Reforms and Agricultural Development*, 1953.

Food and Agriculture Organisation : *"Credit Through Co-operatives and other Institutions". Agricultural Studies no. 68*, 1966.

Gadgil, D.R. : *Writing and Speeches on Co-operation, Gokhale Institute Studies No. 64*, Pune; Gokhale Institute of Politics and Economics.

Ghosal, S.N. : *Agrcultural Finance in India with Special Reference to Land Mortgage Banks*, Bombay; Asia Publishing House, 1968.

Goel, S.L. and Goel, B.B. : *Administration of Personnel in Co-operatives*, Sterling Publishers Pvt. Ltd., New Delhi, 1979.

Goel, S.L. and Goel, B.B. : *Principles, Problems and Prospects of Co-operative Administration*, Sterling Publishers, Delhi, 1979.

Gosh, B.B. : *Problems of Rural Credit in India*, Calcutta, 1948.

Government of Andhra Pradesh : *Planning and Development of Backward Regions — A Case of Rayalaseema*, Vol. I , Government of Andhra Pradesh, Central Press, Hyderabad, 1970.

Government of India : *Studies in the Economics of Farm Management*, Ministry of Food and Agriculture, New Delhi.

Government of India : *Rural Man Power and Occupational Structure*, 1954.

Government of India : *Studies in Agricultural Economics*, 1956-60.

Government of India : *Economic Survey of Indian Agriculture*, 1961, 1970.

Government of India : *Memorandum on the Development Agriculture and Animal Husbandary in Indiaa*, 1944.

Government of India : *Co-operation Today and Tommorrow*, 1960.

Government of India : *Co-operation in India*, 1965.

Government of India : *Co-operation at a Glance*, 1960.

Government of India : *Co-operation for Rural Development*, 1958.

Hajela, T.N. : *Principles, Problems and Practice of Co-operation*, Shivalal Agarwala Co., Delhi, 1982.

Hough, E.M. : *Co-operative Movement in India*, Oxford University Press, Bombay, 1958.

ICAR. : *Hand Book of Indian Agriculture*, 1967.

ICAR. : *Soils in India*, 1963.

Iyengar, A.S.K. : *A Study of Co-operative Movement in India*, Bombay, 1961.

Jain, S.C. : *Management in Agricultural Finance*, S. Chand & Co., Delhi, 1970.

Jha, D.N. : *Planning and Agricultural Development*, Vikas Publications, Delhi, 1974.

Hohl, S.S., and Moore C.V. : *Essentials of Farm Management*, New Delhi, 1970.

Kadam, D.B. : *A Study of Well Finance* (Unpublished Thesis), Gokhale Institute of Politics and Economics, Pune, 1968.

Kalyankar, S.P. : *Crop Loan Overdues of Co-operative Finance*, Rainbow Publications, Coimbatore, 1983.

Kamat, G.S. : *New Dimensions of Co-operative Management*, Himalaya Publishing House, Bombay, 1978.

Karnataka State Co-operative Land Development Bank : *A Study of Overdues* (Memo.), Bangalore, 1976.

Khanna, P.N., Sinha, S.L.N., and Raman, A., (Eds.) : *Credit Planning and Policy*, Vora & Co., Bombay, 1974.

Krishnaswami, O.R. : *Co-operative Democracy in Action*, Delhi, 1978.

Kulkarni, K.R. : *Theory and Practice of Co-operation in India and Abroad*, Co-operators Book Depot, Bombay, 1958.

Kurulkar, R.P. : *Agricultural Finance in Backward Region*, Himalaya Publishing House, Bombay, 1983.

Laud, G.M. : *Co-operative Banking*, Himalaya Publishing House, Bombay, 1956.

Mamoria, C.B. : *Rural Credit and Agricultural Co-operation in India*, KItab Mahal, Allahabad, 1983.

Mathur, B.S. : *Co-operation in India*, Sahithya Bhawan, Agra, 1973.

Mathur, B.S. : *Land Development Banking in India*, National Publishing House, Delhi, 1974.

Ministry of Community Development : *Shahakari Samaj, A Symposium of Co-operative Movement in India*, Delhi, 1963.

Mishra, S.D. : *"Bank Credit and Farm Income", Economic and Business Review*, January-March, 1985.

Naidu, V.T. : *Farm Credit and Co-operatives in India*, Vora and Company, Bombay, 1968.

Narayana, B.K. : *A Survey of Industries in Telangana*, Keshav Publishers, Secunderabad.

Narayana N.V. : *Financing of Small Farmers*, (Unpublished Thesis), S.K. University, Anantapur, 1985.

National Co-operative Land Development Banks Federation : *A Study on Overdues and Impact of the Discipline Governing Regulation of Advances in Maharashtra*, 1979.

National Co-operative Land Development Banks Federation : *Proceedings and Collections*, (Seminar on Procedure of Recoveries and Problems on Overdues of Land Development Banks held at Pune, on 31st January – 2nd February, 1980).

National Co-operative Land Development Banks Federation : *Proceedings and Collections*, (Seminar on qualitative Aspects of Loans and Repayment in Land Development Banks held at Bangalore, on 15th March, 1983).

National Co-operative Union of India : *Anthology of Co-operative Thought*, Vol. I, New Delhi, 1975.

National Planning Committee : *Crop Planning and Production*, 1948.

National Planning Committee : *Soil Conservation and Afforestation*, 1948.

National Planning Committee : *Land Policy, Agricultural Labour and Insurance*, 1948.

N.C.A.E.R. : *Techno-Economic Survey of Andhra Pradesh*, 1961.

N.C.U.I. : *Proceedings of the Sixth Co-operative Congress*, 1971.

Nicholson, F.D. : *Report Regarding Possibility of Introducing Land and Agricultural Bank in Madras Presidency*, Vol. I, Madras, 1895, (Reprint 1960).

Parthasarathy, G. *Green Revolution and Weaker Sections*, Thacker & Co. Ltd., Bombay, 1971.

Planning Commission : *Study in Waste Lands and their Reclamation Measures*, 1963.

Radhakrishnan, S. : *Nidhis — An Indigeous Financial Institution*, 1980.

Rahman, M. : *Genesis of Agricultural Co-operative Credit Societies*, S. Chand & Co., Delhi.

Rao. C.H.H. : *Technological Change and Distribution of Gains in Indian Agriculture*, Mac Graw Hill Book Company Ltd., New Delhi, 1975.

Rao, L.R. : *Rural Ço-operatives*, S. Chand and Sons, Delhi, 1974.

Rayudu, C.S. : *Economics of Textile Co-operatives*, Discovery Publishing House, Delhi, 1988.

Rayudu, C.S. : *Rural Credit in India*, Mittal Publications, Delhi, 1988.

Rayudu, C.S. : *Management of Rural Development*, Discovery Publishing House, Delhi, 1989.

Reddy, C.R. : *Farm Credit by Co-operative Agricultural Development Banks*, S.K. University, Anantapur, 1978.

Reddy, C.R. : *Co-operative Long Term Finance — A Regional Study*, Mittal Publications, Delhi, 1987.

Reddy, C.R. : *Rural Banking in India*, Rainbow Publications, Coimbatore, 1987.

Reserve Bank of India : *Studies in Agricultural Credit*, 1970.

Reserve Bank of India : *Land Mortgage Banks*, 1951.

Reserve Bank of India : *Agricutural Finance by Commercial Banks*, 1968.

Sammuddin and Mahafoozur Rahman : *Co-operative Sector in India*, S. Chand and Sons Ltd., New Delhi, 1983.

Saxena, K.K. : *Evolution of Co-operation Thought*, Somaiya Publications, Bombay, 1974.

Schumpter, J.A. : *The Theory of Economic Development*, Harward University, Press, Cambridge, 1934 (Reprint (1983).

Sengupta and Galina S. Dasyuk : "Economic Regionalisation of India Problems and Approaches", *Monograph No. 8*, Census of India.

Sharma, R.D. : *Farm Financing by Commercial Banks — A Regional Study*, Bharat Book Depot, Bhagalpur, 1979.

Shukla, Tara : *Capital Formation in Indian Agriculture*, Vora and Company Publishers Private Ltd., Bombay, 1965.

Sinha, S.L.N. : *Credit Management*, Institute for Financial Management and Research, Madras, 1978.

Srivastava, G.P. : Traditional Forms of Co-operation in India, New Delhi, 1962, pp. 1-5. quoted in Rural Credit and Agricultural Co-operation in India, Dr. C.B. Mamoria, Part 2, Page 11.

Srivastava, R.M. : *Management of Banks*, Pragathi Prakasan, Meerut.

State Co-operative Union, Andhra Pradesh : *Co-operative Movement in Andhra Pradesh*, Andhra Pradesh State Co-operative Union Limited, Hyderabad.

Taimni, K.K. : *Co-operative Organisation and Management*, Delhi, WAFM, Farmers Welfare Trust Society, 1976.

Tyagi, R.B. : *Recent Trends in Co-operation in India*, Asia Publishing House, Bombay, 1968.

U.N.O. : Rural Progress Through Co-operative, 1954.

U.N.O. : Land Reforms — Defects in Agrarian Structure as Obstacles to Economic Development, 1951.

Reports

Reserve Bank of India : *Report of the All India Rural Credit Survey Committee*, 1954.

Government of India : *Report of the Committee on Co-operative Credit*, 1960.

Government of India : *Report of the Committee on Co-operative Law*, 1957.

Government of India : *Report of the Working Group on Co-operative Farming*, 1959.

Government of India : *Report of the working Group on Panchayats and Co-operatives*, 1961.

Agricultural Refinance and Development Corporation : *Report of the Committee on Integration of Co-operative Credit Institutions*, 1974.

Government of Andhra Pradesh : *Report of the Irrigation Commission*, Hyderabad, Central Press, 1973.

Government of India : *Report of the Royal Commission on Agriculture*, 1929.

Reserve Bank of India : *Report of the Committee on Co-operation in India*, 1912.

Government of India : *Report of the Study Team on Co-operative Training*, 1961.

Ministry of Community Development and Co-operation : *Report of the Committee on Tacava Loans*, 1962.

Reserve Bank of India : *Report of the Expert Group on State Enactment Having a Bearing on Commercial Banks Landing to Agriculture*, 1971.

Reserve Bank of India : *Report of the All India Rural Credit Review Committee*, 1969.

Reserve Bank of India : *Manual on Production Oriented System of Loaning for Agriculture*, 1972.

Reserve Bank of India : *Report of the Study Team on Overdues in Co-operative Credit Structure*, 1974.

Reserve Bank of India : *Report on the Role of the Co-operative Credit in Farm Production — A Survey Report*, 1974.

Reserve Bank of India : *Report of the Expert Group on Agricultural Credit Schemes of Commercial Banks*, 1978.

Reserve Bank of India : *Reports of the Committee on Regional Rural Banks*, 1977.

Reserve Bank of India : *Report of the Committee on Co-operative Land Development Banks*, 1975.

Reserve Bank of India : *Report of the Committee on Consumption Credit.*

Reserve Bank of India : *Report of the Committee on Overdues.*

Reserve Bank of India : *Report of the Working Group on Multi-Agency Approach to Agricultural Credit*, 1977.

Government of India : *Report of the Committee on Co-operation*, 1914.

Reserve Bank of India : *Report of the Committee on Regulation of Rural Banks*, 1977.

Reserve Bank of India : *Financing of Primary Agricultural Credit Societies by Commercial Banks.*

Reserve Bank of India : *Loan Policies and Procedural Agreements in Relation to Institutional Credit System in India.*

Reserve Bank of India : *Report of the Co-operative Planning Committee*, 1946.

Reserve Bank of India : *Report of the Rural Banking Enquiry Committee*, 1953.

Reserve Bank of India : *Evaluation of the Co-operative Movement*, 1957.

Reserve Bank of India : *Report of the Working Group on Co-operative Policy*, 1958.

Reserve Bank of India : *Report of the Working Group on Co-ordination of short, Medium and Long Term Loans*, 1964.

Reserve Bank of India : *Report of the Information Group on Institutional Arrangements for Agricultural Credit*, 1964.

Reserve Bank of India : *Report of the Committee to Review Arrangements for Institutional Credit for Agriculture and Rural Development*, 1981.

Government of Andhra Pradesh : *Planning and Development of Backward Regions — A Case Study of Rayalaseema*, Vol. I, 1970.

Government of Andhra Pradesh : *Draft Report on Socio-economic Survey of Rayalaseema*, 1970.

NCAER : *Techno-economic Survey of Andhr Pradesh*, 1961.

NCAER : *Survey of Back-ward Districts of Andhra Pradesh.*

Government of Andhra Pradesh : *Report of the Development Commissioner of the Rayalaseema Development Board*, 1954.

A.P.C.C. Land Mortgage Bank : *Long Term Co-operative Credit in Andhra Pradesh.*

Government of Madras : *Possibility of Introducing Land and Agricultural Banks into the Madras Presidency*, 1895.

Government of Andhra Pradesh : *State Administrative Reports.*

Reserve Bank of India : *Reviews of Co-operative Movements in India.*

Government of Andhra Pradesh : *Report on the Working of Co-operative Societies in Andhra Pradesh* — Annual.

Government of Andhra Pradesh : *Rayalaseema Co-operative Enquiry Committee*, 1946.

Government of Madras : *Vijaya Raghava Charya Committee on Co-operation*, 1940.

Government of Madras : *Report of the Famine Code Revision Committee*, 1938.

Government of India : *Report of the Famine Enquiry Commission*, 1946.

Government of India : *Report of the Indian Delegation to China on Agrarian Co-operatives*, 1957.

ILO : *Joint Farming Co-operatives — A Priliminary Survey.*

Planning Commission : *Report of the Committee of the Panel on Land Reforms.*

Reserve Bank of India : *Report of the Committee on Direction : All India Rural Credit Fallowup Survey*, 1960.

Government of India : *Report of the Central Banking Enquiry Committee*, 1931.

Stastistical Reports

1. Statistical Atlas of Andhra State, 1950-51., Bureau of Economics and Statistics, Government of Andhra Pradesh.
2. Statistical Atlas of Madras State, 1951, Govt. of Madras.
3. Statistical Statements Relating to Co-operative Movement in India, RBI, Annual.

4. Hand Books of Statistics, A.P., Bureau of Economics and Statistics, A.P.
5. Census of India, 1981.
6. Handbooks of Statistics on Co-operative Movement in Andhra Pradesh, Registrar of Co-operative Societies, A.P.
7. Andhra Pradesh Darshini, Data News Features, Hyderabad.
8. Data, Andhra Pradesh, Data News Features, Hyderabad.
9. Statistical Abstract, A.P.
10. Comparative Statistics of Andhra Pradesh and other States of India, Bureau of Economics and Statistics, A.P.
11. Seasonal Crop Reports of Andhra Pradesh, Bureau of Economics and Statistics, Government of A.P.
12. Annual Reports of the Andhra Pradesh Co-operative Central Agricultural Development Bank and Primary Banks.
13. Hand Book of Statistics on Co-operative Movement in A.P. – Annual.

Five Year Plans

Planning Department, Government of Andhra Pradesh:
First Five Year Plan.
Second Five Year Plan.
Third Five Year Plan.
Annual Plans.
Fourth Five Year Plan.
Fifth Five Year Plan.
Sixth Five Year Plan.
Seventh Five Year Plan.
Review of Progress of Five Year Plans and Annual Plans.
Review of Economic Trend and State Plan – Annual.

Acts and Laws

Andhra Pradesh Co-operative Societies Act, 1964.
Andhra Pradesh Co-operative Societies Rules, 1964.
Andhra Pradesh Co-operative Societies Act, 1964, E.L. Bhagirath Rao, 1980, Asia Law House, Hyderabad.
The Hyderabad Co-operative Societies Act, 1952.
Multi-Unit Co-operative Societies Act, 1942.
Madras Co-operative Societies Act, 1952.

Co-operative Credit Societies Act, 1904 (Central Act of X of 1904).
Co-operative Societies (Amendment) Act, 1912.
Madras Co-operative Land Mortgage Banks Act, 1934.
Hyderabad Co-operative Central Land Mortgage Banks Act, 1953.
Bye-laws.

Journals

1. *Indian Co-operative Review* – quarterly.
2. *Co-operator* – Fortnightly.
3. *Co-operative Perspective* – quarterly.
4. *Yojana* – Fortnightly.
5. *Changing Villages* – Bi-monthly.
6. *Co-operative News Digest* – Monthly.
7. *Sahakara Samacharam* – Monthly.
8. *Khadi and Gramodyog* – Monthly.
9. *Kurukshetra* – Monthly.
10. *Land Development Bank Journal* – Quarterly.
11. *Rural India* – Monthly.
12. *Maharashtra Co-operative Journal* – Quarterly.
13. *Tamilnadu Journal of Co-operation* – Monthly.
14. *Indian Journal of Agricultural Society* – Monthly.
15. *NAFED Marketing Review* – Monthly.
16. *Kisan World* – Monthly.
17. *Southern Economist* – Fortnightly.
18. *Social Welfare* – Monthly.

INDEX